M000198715

(B)ordering Britain

Manchester University Press

(B)ordering Britain

Law, race and empire

Nadine El-Enany

Manchester University Press

The right of Nadine El-Enany to be identified as the author of this work has been asserted by her in accordance with the Copyright, Designs and Patents Act 1988.

Published by Manchester University Press
Altrincham Street, Manchester M1 7JA
www.manchesteruniversitypress.co.uk

British Library Cataloguing-in-Publication Data
A catalogue record for this book is available from the British Library

ISBN 978 1 5261 4542 0 hardback

First published 2020

Typeset by
Servis Filmsetting, Stockport, Cheshire
Printed in Great Britain by
Bell & Bain Ltd, Glasgow

For Mum, Dad and Bridget

Contents

Preface

In England's green and pleasant Land[1]

My mother and father travelled from Egypt to Britain in 1977, moving from London to Exeter, a city in the south-west of England, in 1978. My father tells me that when they arrived in Exeter they were struck by its natural beauty combined with the peace and quiet of this rural city. For my parents, Exeter was a place they felt fortunate to have found, an idyll that could not have been further from the noisy, crowded streets of Cairo. Immediately behind their house farmland stretches out as far as the eye can see. They made Exeter their home. When my father retired, a neighbour asked him when he would be going back to Egypt. My parents have lived in the same suburb for forty years. Still, this neighbour has been quietly waiting for my parents to one day pack up and go back to where they came from.

(B)ordering Britain is not only the centuries-long legal and political process that this book traces, it is also a mindset. Hanging over my parents will always be the assumption that their life in Britain is contingent and temporary. This comes of their identity as Egyptians, as non-white immigrants, as racialised people living in a predominantly white

British space. Their British citizenship is by the by. It might give them the legal right to be in Britain, but it conveys no veneer of entitlement. When my mother did jury service, a neighbour asked her what she thought of 'our legal system'. Legal status does not alter the way in which racialised people are cast in white spaces as guests, outsiders or intruders, as here today, but always potentially gone tomorrow.

Yet my parents are the lucky ones. They have British passports. They came to Britain on an aeroplane, study visas in hand. They did not have to travel by boat, or in the back of a lorry, in secret, risking their lives. Law's lesson is that some people are entitled to space, presence, resources and opportunities and others are not. Immigration law in particular teaches white British people that Britain and everything within it is rightfully theirs. 'Others' are here as their guests. Yet Britain would not be the wealthy, plentiful place that it is without its colonial history. We should not wait for the law to rule on our entitlement to colonial spoils. Even when we are granted access, we are not seen as belonging in Britain. And yet a Britain understood as the spoils of empire already belongs to us.

For the reader who wonders why I refer to Britain rather than the United Kingdom, it is because I am allowing myself, as I ask you to do as you read this book, to imagine Britain, if you possibly can, as it appears on the cover of this book, without its colonies.

Introduction:
Britain as the spoils of empire

In answer to a question about why annual net immigration was above the Conservative Party's tens of thousands target in 2012, the Home Secretary Theresa May stated that her aim was to 'create, here in Britain, a really hostile environment for illegal immigrants'.[1] 'What we don't want', she said, 'is a situation where people think that they can come here and overstay because they're able to access everything they need.'[2] The notion of the <u>unjustly enriched migrant</u> has long been at the heart of British immigration policy. It is spurred on by a widespread and concerted refusal to understand contemporary British politics in the context of Britain's colonial history. The failure to connect the presence of many racialised[3] people in Britain to the destruction and dispossession of British colonialism is as profound as it is pervasive. Absent from mainstream political discourse is any acknowledgement that the making of Britain's modern state infrastructure, including its welfare state, was dependent on resources acquired through colonial conquest. At the same time, people with personal, ancestral or geographical histories of colonisation cannot escape their condition of coloniality. There is a direct causal link between colonialism and

*✝ CRAZY

*TERM

ongoing global wealth disparity and inequality in income and land distribution in former colonies.[4] Poverty, dispossession and exponentially high mortality rates are lasting legacies for populations in Britain's former colonies.

Meanwhile, for the racialised poor living in the heart of the imperial metropole, insecurity and a disproportionate vulnerability to premature death is a long-standing and everyday experience.[5] The 2017 Grenfell Tower fire and the 2018 Windrush scandal are illustrative of Britain as a domestic space of colonialism in which the racialised poor find themselves segregated and controlled, vulnerable to deprivation, exile and death. The abstraction of day-to-day life in Britain from its colonial history means that immigration law and policy, whether in the form of the hostile environment, visa requirements or other external border controls, are not seen as ongoing expressions of empire. Yet this is what they are; part of an attempt to control access to the spoils of empire which are located in Britain. British colonialism is thus an ongoing project, sustained via the structure of law. It is Britain that has been unjustly enriched through centuries of colonialism, and immigration law is the tool that ensures that dispossessed peoples have no claim over what was stolen from them.

Britain is a place produced by colonialism and slavery, which were key to its industrialisation and the growth of its capitalist economy.[6] In 1833 Britain abolished slavery and raised the modern-day equivalent of £17 billion through taxation and loans to pay compensation to British slave-owners for the loss of their 'property'. The compensation scheme was the largest state-sponsored pay-out in British history until it was superseded by the bank bailouts of 2008.[7] The funds paid out built and infused Britain's commercial, cultural, imperial and political institutions.[8] The scheme is just

one example of a direct financial link between slavery and ✗
imperialism and the place that is Britain today. The rein-
vestment of profits from slavery and post-abolition compensation are demonstrative of place-making in a most material
sense. On the eve of the abolition of slavery in Britain, over
a third of investors in the West India and London docks
were active in the slave trade, whether by owning slaves or
in shipping, trading, financing or insuring slave produce.[9]
The redeployment of profits from slavery and compensation
in commercial and industrial activities and physical infrastructure occurred over the nineteenth century and into
the twentieth and even twenty-first.[10] Wealth derived from
British slave-ownership has by no means been evenly dis-
tributed in Britain. It has helped to enrich and sustain elite
institutions, individuals and families and has sewn inequality deep into the fabric of British society, helping to make it
the most unequal place in Europe.[11] Yet Britain's healthcare
system, welfare state, transport infrastructure, cultural and
educational institutions, battered and unequally accessible
as they are in the wake of privatisation and austerity policies, are colonially derived, along with the private wealth
amassed over the course of the British Empire and retained
after its defeat via systems of inheritance.

CAPITALISM

Britain is a young nation-state, but an old imperial power.
The task of bordering Britain is an ongoing and centuries-old
process. Britain's borders, articulated and policed via immigration laws, maintain the global racial order established by
colonialism, whereby colonised peoples are dispossessed of
land and resources. They also maintain Britain as a racially
and colonially configured space in which the racialised poor
are subject to the operation of internal borders and are disproportionately vulnerable to street and state racial terror.
Britain is thus not only bordered, but also racially and

CLAIM

colonially ordered, through the operation of immigration control – hence the title of this book: *(B)ordering Britain.*

The 1960s, 1970s and 1980s are particularly important decades in the story of immigration law and the making of modern Britain. Over the course of these decades immigration law played a crucial role in Britain's transition from an empire to a sovereign, bordered nation-state. As colonial populations drove the British from their territories, winning their independence, British politicians were forced to come to terms with the defeat of the British Empire. The myth of imperial unity and equality was fast abandoned by British lawmakers as they moved to introduce controls targeted at racialised subjects and Commonwealth citizens. This legislation culminated in the 1981 British Nationality Act, which raised for the first time the spectre of a post-imperial, territorially defined and circumscribed Britain. It severed a notionally white, geographically distinct Britain from the remainder of its colonies and Commonwealth.

The move was both materially and symbolically significant. A territorially distinct Britain and a concept of citizenship that made Britishness commensurate with whiteness made it clear that Britain, the landmass and everything within it, belongs to Britons, conceived intrinsically as white. According to the 1971 Immigration Act, only patrials, those born in Britain or with a parent born in Britain, had a right of abode, and therefore a right of entry and stay in Britain. In 1971 a person born in Britain was most likely (98%) to be white. The 1981 Act continued this process of racial exclusion by constructing British citizenship on the foundation of the 1971 Act's concept of patriality, tying citizenship to the right of entry and abode. The effect of the 1981 Act along with changes to immigration legislation in the course of the 1960s and 1970s was to put the wealth of Britain, gained via colonial conquest, out of reach for the vast majority of people racialised through colonial processes, most of whom had geographical or ancestral histories of British colonialism. The 1981 Act did not signify an end to British colonialism but was itself a significant colonial manoeuvre. It was an act of appropriation, a final seizure of the wealth and infrastructure secured through centuries of colonial conquest. British immigration law, in serving to legitimise ongoing theft of colonial wealth, must therefore be understood as being on a <u>continuum</u> of colonialism. It is through immigration law's policing of access to colonial spoils that the racial project of capitalist accumulation is maintained, a project which I argue is legitimised through judicial rulings in immigration and asylum cases.

Immigration law is also the prop used to teach white British citizens that what Britain plundered from its colonies is theirs and theirs alone. Racial place-making projects like that of bordering Britain, and before it the expansion of the British Empire, rely on the institution of racial terror.[12] State racial terror, as Sherene Razack has argued, 'evicts from the circle of law and humanity those persons deemed unable to progress into civilisation'.[13] Once the enactment of racial terror is initiated by the state it is a task assumed by citizens. They are taught, in part through immigration law, that the parameters of the imperial, and national, project of ensuring white entitlement to wealth gained in the course of colonial conquest are theirs to enforce. Immigration law is not therefore the seemingly harsh but fair mode through which the deserving are separated from the undeserving. Instead, it is a crucial mechanism for ensuring that colonial wealth remains out of the hands of those from whom it was stolen. A case which powerfully demonstrates the way in which access to colonial spoils is withheld from

Margin annotations: ✶ MECHANISM · CLAIM · SINGH · 1984 VIBES ·

people with geographical or ancestral histories of colonisation is that of *N*, which I discuss in Chapter 4.[14] N's life depended on access to medical treatment in Britain and she sought to challenge a removal decision to Uganda on the basis of Article 3 of the European Convention on Human Rights (ECHR), which protects people from being sent to places where they would be at risk of torture or inhuman or degrading treatment or punishment. In ruling that Article 3 does not 'oblige' states to grant migrants access to their healthcare systems, the Supreme Court effectively handed N a death sentence. The court adopted the rationale that a decision in favour of N would have risked more people seeking to travel to Britain to access vital healthcare to which they are not entitled. The judges employed a depoliticising logic, arguing that wealth inequalities between nations and illnesses are natural or chance occurrences. The effect is to obscure colonial powers' role in producing global wealth and health disparities and their reparative obligations towards colonised populations.

Racialised people thus remain the foremost target in Britain's ongoing imperial project, their lands and their bodies ongoing sites of colonial extraction and expulsion. Although we are more familiar with how such extractive processes occur in formally colonial regimes, I argue for the urgency of tracing how colonialism shapes the metropole's space over time. Britain cannot be understood as a legitimately bounded nation space. Since colonialism it has been a space shaped by its colonies. As such, it achieves its coherence as a nation by maintaining its inner space, the island(s) of Britain, as one of order, privilege and entitlement, and its outer space, its former colonies, as one in which insecurity, poverty, illness and violence are the norm. Yet inside Britain's borders, the racialised poor are differentially

6

yet systematically vulnerable to being marginalised, controlled, policed, deported and killed. For instance, embodied in the amendments introduced in the 2014 Immigration Act, which rolled out the hostile environment, is both the reification of secure status in the form of citizenship, and the precaritisation of racialised life whereby people who do not have a secure status live under the threat of expulsion. In Chapter 4 I discuss the Supreme Court's ruling in the 2018 case of *Rhuppiah*, in which the meaning of a 'precarious' status, as per amendments made by the 2014 Immigration Act, was held to include all temporary statuses.[15] The judgment means that courts will attach 'little weight' to the private life established by people on a status other than indefinite leave to remain in cases where they challenge a removal decision on the basis of Article 8 of the ECHR, which protects the right to a private and family life. The effect of legislative changes along with the decision in *Rhuppiah* is that familial and close personal relationships cannot be safely created by those with a temporary status. ✱ I show how even racialised people who attain the status of indefinite leave to remain or British citizenship remain disproportionately vulnerable to being deprived of what might appear to be a secure legal status.

Law's violence in the context of immigration is dual. It serves as the means of obstruction of the vast majority of racialised people from accessing wealth accumulated via colonial dispossession, as well as being the primary means of recognition for those seeking a legal status. Regimes of legal status recognition whereby British authorities determine entitlement to statuses such as citizenship, settlement or indefinite leave to remain or refugee status serve to legitimise the claim that colonial wealth, as it manifests in Britain, belongs behind its borders, only to be accessed

7

with permission. The result is that people with histories of colonisation have found themselves trapped in regimes of recognition. Invited to petition for inclusion, whether by applying for citizenship, refugee or another legal status, they find themselves legally rebuffed again and again, even as their efforts enable the racial state to characterise itself as post-colonial. The bestowal or extension of British subject-hood, or citizenship in its current guise, can never be any-thing other than a colonial act. In the colonial era British subjecthood was held up as a superior category from which the civilising benefits of British rule flowed. Yet British colonialism was genocide, mass murder, slavery, dispossession of land, exploitation of labour and theft of resources, all predicated on white British supremacy. Even so-called 'free' British subjects seeking to move to different parts of the British Empire were met with racist immigration laws in places such as Canada and Australia, which, as I discuss in Chapter 1, heavily influenced Britain's first immigration law, passed in 1905. British subjecthood did not, therefore, protect racialised subjects from the violence of white British supremacy. Its very existence as a legal category was a manifestation of that violence.

Whenever it has suited the British government, it has treated its subjects as aliens for legal purposes, evicting them from the scope of legal status and protection with devastating consequences. The effect of the hostile environment policy, for instance, was to deny long-settled former colonial subjects and their descendants access to healthcare, housing, employment and other vital services, and to detain and expel them. The 2018 Windrush scandal illustrates well the challenges posed by recognition-based arguments for migrant solidarity and the inclusion of racialised people within the colonial state, for example the assertion that the Windrush generation were British citizens and should be recognised as such by the government.[16] This argument raises important legal, ethical and strategic questions in a context in which changes to British immigration law and policy have had the effect of disproportionately stripping racialised people of their rights. Although insisting on the immediate reinstatement of legal entitlements denied to the Windrush generation is crucial, it is equally important not to elide the <u>colonial context</u> in which legal status is bestowed. Citizenship, as the primary contemporary legal status signalling belonging to the British polity, is a legal structure that maintains a racially and colonially ordered Britain. The same can be argued for other legal status recognition regimes which carve out entitlement to access resources in Britain for select groups of people according to narrow criteria, such as refugee law. *(B)ordering Britain* thus offers a critique of law and the politics of recognition in the context of immigration. By tracing the colonial origins of processes of legal categorisation I show how decisions to include and exclude certain people from legal status, whether in the form of recognition as a refugee or through the bestowal or revocation of citizenship, are intricately tied to processes whereby colonial power is legitimised. The recognition trap obscures and legitimises the colonial structures underlying British immigration, asylum and citizenship law. It also hinders the articulation of more radical, empowering and redistributive claims to stolen colonial wealth and resources, material and temporal.

Handwritten margin note: CITIZENSHIP AS A PRIVILEGE

Handwritten margin note: THE WORK THE BOOK IS DOING

Method and structure of the book

If British immigration law is the colonial state at work, any analysis of it must take into consideration Britain's colonial

9

history and identity. Yet the bearing of the colonial on the emergence of Britain's administrative and legal immigration regime is rarely acknowledged in legal scholarship in the field of migration. Although there are works that consider the relationship between the British Empire and aspects of its citizenship and immigration law regimes,[17] this book departs from them in significant ways both conceptually and empirically. *(B)ordering Britain* centres race in the analysis, the relevance of which, along with the colonial history that produced it, has long been neglected in legal literature on migration.[18] The method of legal analysis I adopt is informed by critical race and postcolonial theories. While in other disciplines the use of theories of race and racialisation as core analytical tools is established, this is less so for law, which has tended to rely on narrower analytical frameworks that make race implicit or peripheral rather than central and explicit. Racism tends to be left out of legal discourse and replaced instead with soft signifiers such as discrimination, which is to be addressed within the frameworks of human rights and anti-discrimination law. These fields construct racism as being an aberration from legal norms and as perpetuated by individuals, rather than being structurally produced and sustained in part through law. Yet ideas about racial superiority continue to carry purchase in all corners of the world. Legacies of colonialism have meant that the majority of racialised people have neither inherited 'the reachability'[19] of crucial resources, nor the power to determine their management and material distribution.

Due in part to the way in which asylum, immigration and border control are governed, legal research on migration has tended to treat them as distinct, albeit related, fields. While immigration and border control are generally considered to lie within the discretionary purview of the state, the refugee

WHERE THERE IS RACE,
THERE IS RELIGION

NO CHOICE

is protected by various international and human rights law instruments. While the link between refugee protection norms and immigration and border control measures has been acknowledged,[20] legal scholars have tended not to consider the former in the context of the latter,[21] focusing instead on either immigration or asylum law.[22] However, in spite of the distinctive features and seeming separateness of the two fields, they are inextricably intertwined. It is not only migrant experiences that defy arbitrarily drawn legal categories; the histories of these fields are connected and must be studied together.

In the decades immediately preceding and following the 1981 British Nationality Act, Britain was establishing itself as a post-imperial nation-state. Legislative developments made in this period laid the groundwork for contemporary immigration and asylum law. In *(B)ordering Britain*, I take ✳ legal categories by turn and subject them to race-critical analysis, drawing on a range of primary and secondary material, tracing the connections between colonial processes of categorisation and the emergence of contemporary immigration law practices. The objective is to challenge mainstream acceptance of these categories both in and outside academia. The traditional acceptance of legal categories as defined in international and domestic law has the effect of concealing the law's role in producing racialised subjects and racial violence. It further impedes an understanding of law *as* racial violence. Take, for example, the category of the refugee, relatively valorised as compared with the irregularised migrant.[23] Individuals falling outside the legal definition of a refugee are often described as 'illegal', 'irregular' or 'economic migrants', and are at risk of removal and denied access to healthcare, housing and work. A decision to deny legal status carries serious, sometimes fatal,

AGENCY

consequences, and can be a politically expedient move on the part of a government seeking to apportion degrees of belonging, entitlement and exclusion among populations under its control. Addressing the historical contingency and artificiality of legal categories, the violence in their production and their ongoing material effects allows us to understand how Britain remains colonially and racially configured. Understanding how legal categorisation is central to processes of colonisation and racialisation also helps to militate against the appeal of demands for state recognition and opens the way for the development of emancipatory and reparative discourses and strategies for migrant solidarity and racial justice.

The categories that form the springboard for my analysis are aliens, subjects, citizens, migrants, asylum seekers, refugees, European Union (EU) citizens and third country nationals. Although I take them in turn, the book is offered holistically. In order to meaningfully understand the content and effects of one category, each must be considered in terms of its relationship to the others. What becomes apparent is not only the interconnectedness of legal categories, but their violent histories and effects. Immigration law emerges as being on a continuum of colonial violence and an important means through which Britain continues to assert colonial power.

I begin the book by setting out the racial infrastructure of Britain's immigration law regime in Chapter 1, explaining the relationship between colonialism, migration and law. British imperial administrations depended on the exploitation of hierarchies based on supposed differences between categories of people. The use of race as an ordering principle played an important part in enabling and justifying colonialism. I trace the line between the honing of processes of categorisation in the colonial era and immigration law as a practice of racial ordering in modern Britain. I argue that British immigration law is a continuation of British colonial power as enacted in the former British Empire. The categorisation of people into those with and without rights of entry and stay sustains and reproduces colonial racial hierarchies. Contemporary immigration law thus maintains the global racial order established by colonialism, whereby racialised populations are disproportionately deprived of access to resources, healthcare, safety and opportunity and are systematically and disproportionately made vulnerable to harm and premature death.[24] In this context recognition and refusal decisions in relation to claims for immigration status in Britain are the everyday work of the colonial state.

In Chapter 2 I provide an account of the emergence of the legal category of alien and question the idea that there is a clear distinction between the categories of subject and alien in colonial contexts. The legal category of alien contributed to the institutionalisation of a hierarchy of people in a context of British colonial expansion. Immigration laws passed in the colonies which targeted racialised subjects were at times clumsily disguised through the use of apparently race-neutral provisions. Such concealment of racism was in the service of maintaining the lie of the unity of the British Empire. In 1905, mirroring immigration legislation in the colonies, the Aliens Act was passed in Britain with the purpose of preventing the entry of poor Jewish people fleeing persecution in Russia and Eastern Europe. Although British subjects in the colonies were not the Act's targets, it was a product of the British Empire and legislators did not forget its mechanisms when it came to the task of drafting future immigration legislation targeted at racialised colony and Commonwealth citizens.

Chapter 3 tracks the years between 1948 and 1981, during which the rights of British subjects expanded and retracted drastically. Over the course of these decades legal statuses associated with the British imperial polity proliferated, their content and meaning shifting according to fluctuating imperial ambitions. The year 1948 marked the rolling out of the colonial status of Citizenship of the United Kingdom and Colonies, part of an effort to hold together what remained of the British Empire and the Commonwealth. In casting the nationality net wide, Britain's priority was the maintenance of global white British supremacy in the form of its imperial relationships with the white settler colonies. An unintended consequence of the 1948 Act was the facilitation of the movement of racialised colony and Commonwealth citizens to Britain, which British governments sought to quell. In the face of the defeat of the British Empire, as colonial populations ousted British rule and won their independence, British authorities quickly cast off the myth of imperial unity and equality, passing a series of immigration laws in the 1960s and 1970s which specifically targeted racialised colony and Commonwealth citizens for control. Racialised subjects were treated as aliens for legal purposes in the traditional manner of expedient imperial rule. These legislative moves culminated in the 1981 British Nationality Act, which drew a border around the British mainland, physically marking out for the first time a Britain distinct from the remainder of the colonies and the Commonwealth. The effect of these statutory changes was to create Britain as a domestic space of colonialism in which colonial wealth is principally an entitlement of Britons, conjured as white, and in which poor racialised people are disproportionately policed, marginalised, expelled and killed.

In Chapter 4 I examine the categories of refugee, migrant

and asylum seeker in the context of the post-1981 newly conceptually and geographically configured Britain. People who were previously legally associated to the British polity with rights to enter Britain were now categorised as refugees, migrants and asylum seekers. Much of the migration studies literature refers to people seeking asylum in Britain following the 1981 British Nationality Act as spontaneous arrivals.[25] Yet these arrivals were entirely predictable. The descriptor 'spontaneous' feeds an ahistorical understanding of contemporary migratory movements, erasing the connection between migration to Britain and its colonial history. The refugees and asylum seekers of today were the British subjects of yesterday, colonised, alienated and barred from access to wealth stolen from them. I show how courts function within a framework of state sovereignty within which they cannot challenge the legitimacy of Britain's post-colonial articulation of its borders and their dispossessory effects for colonised populations. I demonstrate this point through an analysis of Supreme Court case law including the 1987 case of *Bugdaycay*[26] in which the Supreme Court recognised that the 'life or death' situation that refugees find themselves in requires careful scrutiny of the decisions of immigration officials, but nevertheless rubber-stamped the closure of Britain's borders to racialised subjects and their alienation via immigration law processes.

Chapter 5 explores Britain's turn towards the European Economic Community (EEC), now the European Union, in the 1960s, which coincided with the introduction of immigration controls against racialised colony and Commonwealth citizens. In the face of the defeat of the British Empire, the British government began to look elsewhere for power and riches. Britain's economic and political prospects were argued by some to lie in European cooperation. Britain first applied to join the EEC in 1961, and ultimately became a member on 1 January 1973. Britain's EEC membership did not amount to a rupture with its colonial past. The EEC was accommodating of Britain's and other Member States' colonial ambitions in so far as these were compatible with its own. The result was that Britain avoided a process of reflection and accountability in respect of its history. The transition from empire to European integration has allowed imperial nostalgia and amnesia to fester in Britain. Decades later, in the course of the 2016 referendum on Britain's EU membership, the argument was made that leaving the EU would allow Britain to regain the global influence ostensibly diminished as a consequence of EU membership. Yet this was the very same rationale that drove Britain to apply to join the EU decades earlier.

APPLICATION

I conclude by considering the way in which immigration law and its violent enforcement is both authorised and reinforced by street racial terror. State and street racism is in part propelled by the idea that Britain is a place divorced from its colonial history. Immigration law casts the British Empire into shadow, obscuring its role in making Britain and driving people to move in its direction. I offer a counter-pedagogy to that of law, one that rejects immigration law's lesson of exclusive white entitlement to colonial spoils and instead understands 'host states' as colonial spaces and irregularised movement as anti-colonial resistance. This reframing troubles white supremacist structures, challenges mythological narratives about British colonial history, rejects a liberal politics of recognition, and paves the way for a more empowering and radical politics of racial justice and migrant solidarity.

Chapter 1

Bordering and ordering

Acknowledgement of the relevance of race to immigration control is a frequent omission in legal literature on migration. Even the formal exclusion of immigration control from the purview of discrimination law tends to be unblinkingly accepted by legal scholars and advocates. Side-stepping the racism in immigration law may be a practical necessity for those working as legal practitioners, but is not so easily forgiven in scholarship, particularly that which is geared towards advocacy.[1] In *(B)ordering Britain*, I take race and its colonial roots seriously in analysing law. I argue that British immigration law is a continuation of British colonial power as enacted in the former British Empire, an explicitly white supremacist project.[2] The categorisation of people into those with and without rights of entry and stay sustains and reproduces colonial practices of racial ordering. People without a right of entry to Britain, predominantly the racialised poor, are barred from accessing colonial wealth as it manifests in Britain today. Whether or not those whose movement is hindered have ancestral or geographical histories of colonial dispossession (the majority do), they nonetheless live under the weight of race and racism, products of colonialism. Contemporary immigration law thus maintains the global racial order established by colonialism, whereby colonised peoples are disproportionately dispossessed of land and resources within and outside Britain's borders. Britain must therefore be understood as a contemporary colonial space. In such a context, a critique of processes of legal status recognition becomes particularly salient. Recognition-based approaches to migrant solidarity that centre the inclusion of racialised people within the colonial state have the effect of obscuring and legitimising the colonial structures underlying British immigration, asylum and nationality laws.

Racial ordering

The bringing of order is, according to Edward Said, commonly found as one among many official justifications for colonial projects: '[e]very single empire ... has said it is not like all the others, that its circumstances are special, that it has a mission to enlighten, civilise, bring order and democracy, and that it uses force only as a last resort'.[3] Ordering was a crucial technique employed by the British authorities in the running of the British Empire and in the assertion of its power. Bernard Cohn has observed:

> From the eighteenth century onward, European states increasingly made their power visible not only through ritual performance and dramatic display, but through the gradual extension of 'officializing' procedures that established and extended their capacity in many areas. They took control by defining and classifying space, making separations between public and private spheres; by recording transactions such as the sale of property; by counting and classifying their populations, replacing religious institutions as the registrar of births, marriages, and deaths; and by standardizing languages and scripts. The state licensed some activities as legitimate and suppressed others as immoral or unlawful.[4]

Processes of categorisation, and in particular legal categorisation, thus enabled colonial control over vast numbers of people and resources. The law was frequently deployed and advocated as the means through which to establish a global white British supremacist order in and beyond British colonies. Colonisation, as Tendayi Achiume has argued, established the coloniser's 'advantage that now accrues to a set of beneficiaries broader than just the former European colonial powers'.[5] In what Lauren Benton and Lisa Ford have described as the 'British rage for order', British colonists 'embarked on a frenetic and polycentric effort to use legal change to order people, places and transactions stretching from the banks of the Rio de la Plata to the Persian Gulf to a vast Pacific archipelago'.[6]

In order for colonists to conquer entire civilisations, they needed to be known and filed under terms familiar to the coloniser.[7] Anglo-European scholars of the 1800s and 1900s provided the impetus for colonisation in their repeated intellectual reduction of entire non-Anglo-European civilisations as readable, translatable and ultimately understandable as inferior to 'Western civilisation' and therefore eminently conquerable. By contrast, 'non-Western' scholarship to this day remains posited as an inferior generator of culture and knowledge. Prime among the criteria for knowing and ordering civilisations in the colonial era was race, which was invoked as an organisational category.[8] The production and signification of the racial in post-Enlightenment era writing depended on the use of tools from science and history.[9] It is therefore important to ask how racial subjects are created in order to avoid the reproduction of 'racial others as already differentially constituted historical beings' prior to their 'entrance into the modern political spaces where they become subaltern subjects'.[10] Race became an 'ordering principle' at a time when imperial formations were competing with nation-states for dominance.[11] There was a fixation in the Enlightenment period with 'categorization and classification', on 'establishing what is inside and what is outside'.[12] On the question of 'who constitutes humanity', this could only be ascertained by determining 'what lies outside of the human'.[13] To this end the context of European colonialism meant that understandings of humanity were based on a distinction between white Europeans and non-Europeans. The justification of European colonisation on the basis of white supremacy was thus not 'pre-determined', but the result of theorisations of fixed racial difference along with the honing of Enlightenment methodologies of categorisation and differentiation.[14]

The violence of colonialism is, needless to say, not purely semantic. An extreme level of physical threat, force and brutality was administered to maintain the British Empire.[15] Colonisers have always been aware that despite their 'claim to have founded a durable order, that that order rested on a reversible relation of forces'.[16] The possibility of the reversal of colonialism through the actions of resistance movements required extreme violence, and its constant threat, against subjugated populations. At the same time, dismissals and brutal crackdowns on struggles for self-determination in the colonies necessitated justifications that rested on constructions of difference and their accentuation in official discourse.[17] The tendency in Enlightenment thought to categorise 'nature and man into types', the exaggeration of what were assumed to be 'general features', the reduction of innumerable objects to 'orderable and describable *types*'[18] was applied, with devastating consequences, in a colonial context to people. Ideas about racial superiority and inferiority underpinned the division of cultures into civilised and uncivilised and served as normative justifications for colonial conquest. For instance, British colonisers subjugated Aboriginal Australians and Native Americans, constructing them as having failed to socially progress, partly on account of their different relationship to land, and thereby justified colonial intervention, land dispossession and rule.[19] Within an Anglo-European understanding of linear time, indigenous people were seen as being primitive and contemptible, inhabiting a bygone era, one that Europeans had transcended. Edward Said thus describes sovereign orders as a 'monstrous chain of command' based on divisions of humanity and progress,[20] captured in the words of that devotee of the British Empire, Rudyard Kipling:

> Mule, horse, elephant, or bullock, he obeys his driver, and the driver his sergeant, and the sergeant his lieutenant, and the lieutenant his captain, and the captain his major, and the major his colonel, and the colonel his brigadier commanding three regiments, and the brigadier his general, who obeys the Viceroy, who is the servant of the Empress.[21]

The institution of this order is premised on a view that 'divides the world into large general divisions, entities, that coexist in a state of tension produced by what is believed to be radical difference'.[22] Thus, the theory and practice of ordering depends on assumptions and constructions of difference. For Said, the consequences of dividing humanity into 'clearly different cultures, histories, traditions, societies, even races' cannot be survived.[23]

There is a specificity to the version of white supremacy that underpinned British colonialism. Colonists operating at the height of the expansion of the British Empire propagated the idea that white British people were supreme over all other people, including other white Europeans, who were engaged in their own colonial projects. In 1877, for instance,

[handwritten margin notes: "FAILURE OF PROGRESSION; INFERIORISM", "GOOD", "SOCIAL CONSTRUCTS"]

in *Confessions of Faith*, Cecil Rhodes wrote, '[i]t is our duty to seize every opportunity of acquiring more territory and we should keep this one idea steadily before our eyes that more territory simply means more of the Anglo-Saxon race, more of the best, the most human, most honourable race the world possesses'.[24] Considering that Britain invaded 90 per cent (171) of the current 193 members of the United Nations,[25] it is not difficult to imagine the depth of arrogance and political investment of British colonists in the idea of white British supremacy.

Racial categories are not static, but fluid and malleable. Racialising processes and practices as well as the object to which race attaches 'may change across time or be articulated variously across space'.[26] As Stuart Hall observed, 'there is nothing solid or permanent' to the meaning of race.[27] Like language, race assumes its meaning 'in the shifting relations of difference'.[28] It is 'constantly re-signified, made to mean something different in different cultures, in different historical formations, at different moments of time'.[29] However, we must not lose sight of what Du Bois called 'the badge of colour'.[30] In spite of the fluidity and malleability of race, within the white supremacist context of Britain at this contemporary moment, with its particular colonial history, race materialises on particular persons. Racialised people are therefore those who are not white. As Lentin writes,

> [t]he most unavoidable dimension of race is its attachment to particular bodies ... the reason Black and non-white (brown) people are coded as racially inferior has everything to do with the fact that Black and Brown people were to be found in the territories invaded by Europe from which slaves were also taken.[31]

Race thus also attaches differently to people, producing racial hierarchies within racialised populations who have historically distinctive relationships to the colonial project. The intersections between race, class and gender ⭐ mean that the material effects of racialisation vary in their degree of severity within and across differentially racialised populations.

Racial categorisation was the basis for the control of movement within, into and out of colonised territories throughout the British Empire. As Bridget Anderson has noted, measures were taken 'to assert orderly movement within territories, ordering people through systematic ethnographies, and controlling them accordingly'.[32] People 'were classified, placed in a hierarchy, placed in their territories, differentiated by culture and race, personality and intelligence, declared "indigenous", "tribal", and "urban", with ethnicities tied to territories'.[33] Radhika Mongia has shown how the migration of Indians under British colonial rule to Canada in the late 1800s and 1900s brought about an explosion in the use of systems for 'generating, obtaining, and collating knowledge on every aspect of [this] movement'.[34]

Gargi Bhattacharyya has argued that 'techniques of racialised exclusion, division and differentiation continue to play a central role in the practices of capitalist exploitation'.[35] She describes the obstacles placed in the way of many migrants as being a core 'technique of racial capitalism'.[36] Administrative processes of stemming and regulating migration as well as processes of categorising people as irregular and undocumented all operate as means of 'differentiating populations and their entry into economic activity'.[37] Bhattacharyya shows how capital serves to 'divide and differentiate populations and that this differentiation has been a central feature of the history of capitalism'.[38] Certain groups become 'marked' as they are shunted into precarious labour market conditions or excluded from the

RACISM DEFINED IN RELATION TO CAPITAL

(handwritten margin note: WHAT WORK DOES "DESERVING" DO HERE? IS IT RELIGIOUS? HOW IS RACE RELATED TO BEING DESERVING?)

market entirely. This differentiated exclusion from the labour market is a racialising process. Exclusion for some becomes normalised via 'mythologies of race', including assumptions about productive abilities.[39] I argue that it is law, immigration law in particular, that is the structure that maintains the racialised apportionment of economic opportunity by deeming some people deserving of legal status and others not.

Migration law as a racial regime of power

Ideas and practices of racial ordering are constitutive of contemporary British immigration law. By allocating life and death on the basis of whether or not a person meets the criteria for a legal status, and by preventing those who do not from accessing Britain, law is central to ongoing processes of colonial dispossession. Law is thus the structure that underpins Britain's self-construction as an enclosed space within which resources and wealth obtained via colonial conquest belong to Britons, conceived in large part as white.

(handwritten margin note: LAW AS THE ENFORCER)

The law's categorisation of people into groups, those with and without rights of entry and stay, makes the latter disproportionately at risk of violence and premature death. Immigration law thus falls within Ruth Wilson Gilmore's definition of racism as 'the state-sanctioned and/or extra-legal production and exploitation of group-differentiated vulnerability to premature death'.[40] This description of racism as structurally produced is helpful for understanding the way in which 'systems of meaning and control', of which law is one, 'distribute chances at life and death'.[41] It allows us to move away from traditional discrimination law frameworks which concentrate on locating an individual who can be found to have intentionally discriminated,

(handwritten margin note: FATALISM, STAKES)

instead shifting the focus on to harmful conditions that are experienced across populations that the state targets for 'abandonment'.[42] The effect of law's division of people into groups with differentiated rights is to create hierarchies of people, some of whom have access to territory or to basic resources – a chance at survival – while others do not.

The particular population that immigration law targets for abandonment is the racialised poor, the vast majority of whom have personal, ancestral or geographical histories of colonisation. For racialised people <u>the border</u> is neither easily navigable, nor is it temporally and spatially limited. Whiteness as 'embodied racial power'[43] is apparent in the ease with which white people cross borders and move through white hegemonic spaces. White people tend not to be subject to (stringent) visa requirements and racial profiling, whereas the vast majority of racialised people are unable to purchase tickets for travel or to board planes due to visa rules and carrier sanctions and are disproportionately stopped and searched at airports.[44] This encounter with the border is a racialising process as a result of which people are made disproportionately vulnerable to harm. People who do not have a right of entry to Britain are forced to undertake treacherous, often fatal journeys.[45] The absence of a right of stay can mean homelessness, lack of access to healthcare, confinement to a camp or detention centre and deportation. People in these conditions are at risk of being subjected to physical and mental violence and death.[46] As the hostile environment policy demonstrates, racialised people also experience internal borders, which are invisible and permeable for most white people. Borders 'follow people and surround them as they try to access paid labour, welfare benefits, health, labour protections, education, civil associations, and justice'.[47] This process has been described as 'everyday "bordering and

"BORDERING" AS AN ACTIVE PROCESS

25

ordering"', which is productive of 'new social cultural boundaries'.[48] These boundaries are policed by 'anyone anywhere
– government agencies, private companies and individual citizens'.[49] Sarah Keenan has shown how borders' attachment to
racialised people means that they take with them the space
of the border, a space of disproportionate vulnerability to violence and premature death.[50] In her work on race, time and
title registration, Keenan shows how Gilmore's definition of
racism 'is useful in thinking about race as a temporal category
… in terms of how long racialised subjects are able to survive
in the world'.[51] The lives and futures of those without a right
of entry and stay are made precarious and contingent. People
without a legal status come to occupy, to borrow from Said, a
'time' that 'is over'.[52]

A spatial and temporal understanding of British immigration law enables us to see how it works to place land,
resources, healthcare, welfare, security and opportunities,
all of which can be understood as modern-day manifestations of stolen colonial possessions, out of reach of the vast
majority of those with ancestral or geographical histories
of colonisation. Sara Ahmed writes, '[w]hat is reachable
is determined precisely by orientations we have already
taken'.[53] A world that was 'made white' through colonialism is home only for bodies 'that can inhabit whiteness'.[54]
Bodies, Ahmed writes, 'remember' histories of colonialism,
'even when we forget them'. Histories of colonialism thus
'surface on the body'.[55] The result is that race becomes 'a
social as well as a bodily given'.[56] Colonialism has meant
that the vast majority of racialised people have 'inherit[ed]
the impossibility of extending the body's reach'.[57] They
must risk their lives for what the beneficiaries of colonialism take for granted, carrying with them the deadly weight
of colonial history, a burden they have inherited.[58]

[handwritten margin note: TAKING THE BORDER WITH THEM; BODIES AS BORDERS]

Drawing on Michel Foucault, Renisa Mawani understands race as 'a regime of power that cannot be reduced to ideology, corporeality, or exclusion alone' and that 'it is through the production of racial regimes of power that subjection and subjectification are made possible, occurring and unfolding as mutable and mobile forces, responding to various social relations and occurrences, and assuming different manifestations and meanings'.[59] Migration law is such a racial regime of power. While categorisation is important for the creation of meaning, it is the alignment of systems of categorisation and the assertion of power that makes racial subjugation possible.[60] It is therefore helpful to understand race, in Alana Lentin's words, as 'a series of logics and structures that mutually inform and constitute the other'.[61] Understanding migration law as a racial regime of power, as part of a colonial edifice, allows us to see the danger of accepting legal categories as givens. While legal categories may be articulated in terms that are race-neutral, their effect is to enable the colonial state to administer racial violence. Legal categories, such as 'refugee' and 'citizen', legitimise the incarceration, marginalisation, expulsion and death of those who are deemed not to fulfil the criteria required for the granting of these statuses. The widespread acceptance of legal categories of people moving as defined in international and domestic law thus normalises the racial violence in which the legal system is implicated.

Handwritten margin notes: RELIGION HOPE? ; LANGUAGE AS A RESOURCE

Britain as a contemporary colonial space

A bordered Britain, with its wealth and infrastructure secured via colonial conquest withheld from poor racialised people within and outside its borders, in defiance of claims for reparation and restitution, makes Britain a contemporary colonial space. Understanding Britain as such serves to partially collapse the distinction between settler and non-settler colonial contexts. The traditional distinction drawn between these colonial spaces is that '[u]nlike colonialism, which formally ended with independence, settler colonialism remains a continued project'.[62] In bringing legal histories of colonialism and settler colonial studies 'into conversation with each other', Renisa Mawani encourages a move towards methods that 'may reorient studies of law and settler colonialism by expanding the sites and surfaces of colonial legal power'.[63] In line with Mawani's approach, I argue that the traditional conceptual distinction between settler and non-settler colonial contexts obscures the ongoing colonial configuration of a non-settler colonial state such as Britain.

The border drawn around the spoils of British colonial conquest via immigration and nationality law introduced in the 1960s, 1970s and 1980s, discussed in Chapter 3, amounts to an unredressed act of colonial theft. Due to traditional understandings of property as being fixed and immovable in space and time, theft via the passing of immigration controls can be difficult to conceptualise.[64] Along with the resources and labour stolen in the course of colonialism, the social and cultural networks and relationships that were annihilated or radically reformulated as a result of colonial conquest were also material losses. Colonial dispossession not only determined the contemporary distribution of material wealth, but also radically altered subjectivity in the Fanonian sense of what people desire, consider themselves as entitled to and understand themselves to be.[65] Theft of intangibles such as economic growth and prospects, opportunities, life chances, psyches and futures occur in all colonial contexts, settler or otherwise. Yet such temporal losses are harder to discern in non-settler colonial contexts because they are traditionally understood as having come to an end.

Glen Coulthard has argued for the applicability of Fanon's analysis of the effects of colonisation in contemporary colonial contexts 'where colonial rule is not reproduced through force alone'.[66] Although Coulthard is writing about settler colonies, his argument is applicable to Britain as a contemporary colonial space. In such contexts, the perpetuation of colonial-state power 'requires the production of ... "colonized subjects": namely, the production of the specific modes of colonial thought, desire, and behaviour that implicitly or explicitly commit the colonized to the types of practices and subject positions that are required for their continued domination'.[67] In settler colonies such as Canada and Australia, indigenous people are forced to comply with the laws and evidentiary standards of those colonial legal systems in order to have their rights to land recognised. While there are important and complex historical differences between settler and non-settler colonial contexts, British immigration law is part of a colonial legal system. People with histories of British colonial dispossession are subject to its rules and criteria when they seek to access colonially derived wealth and opportunities in Britain. In this way a facade of racial inclusion has been built in the form of paths to legal status recognition that dole out immigration statuses to select racialised people who can fulfil certain criteria. Such recognition is always on the terms of the colonial state. Meanwhile, the vast majority of racialised people are prevented from accessing Britain and its wealth in part through the operation of internal and external borders, produced and enforced through law. These laws in turn convey a sense of entitlement to white British citizens, which can manifest in the form of street racism. Street and state racial terror are thus mutually reinforcing.

Migration and the politics of recognition

Appeals to legal status recognition as a strategy of migrant solidarity can be counterproductive in a context in which law is also the tool by which racialised people are denied access to vital resources. As Ahmed writes, recognition from the state is 'either precariously conditional ... or simply not given'.[68] I use the term 'recognition' to refer to the British state's piecemeal accommodation of the claims of racialised people seeking access to resources in Britain through legal status determination processes that leave its sovereignty intact and its colonial theft unredressed. While it is now an accepted argument in critical scholarship that settler colonialism is ongoing and structural,[69] the same critique has not been applied to non-settler forms of colonialism, which are considered to have ended. However, such a critique is relevant to Britain if we understand it as a contemporary colonial space. In view of the colonial configuration and dispossessing effects of British immigration law, scholars and migrant advocates should be wary of arguments for migrant solidarity that centre on legal status recognition, whether on the basis of human rights, refugee or other legal norms. Such recognition processes require applicants to fulfil various requirements, whether in the form of meeting the legal definition of a refugee or naturalisation eligibility criteria. Despite being built on colonial theft, the British state derives legitimacy in part through processes of recognition of legal status, whether in the form of recognition as a refugee or through the bestowal of citizenship. The creation of the status of Citizenship of the United Kingdom and

Colonies in the 1948 British Nationality Act for example, discussed in Chapter 3, was an instance of recognition of colonised people designed to hold together what remained of the British Empire. Through the creation of this status the British government was asserting its overarching power of recognition of its colonial subjects over that of the Canadian government after it defined its own citizenship concept.

The 2016 referendum on Britain's EU membership and the Windrush scandal of 2018 are illustrative of the challenges posed by recognition-based arguments for migrant solidarity that centre around the inclusion of racialised people in the colonial state. The hostile environment policy is both an instance of the withholding of access to colonially derived resources from people with geographical or ancestral histories of colonisation, and a reassertion of white British entitlement to them. Similarly, the EU referendum created a space for the accentuation of claims of white entitlement to colonially derived wealth. The Leave campaign constructed migrants, a category that operated as a catch-all for anyone not considered white and British, as unjustly enriched and undeserving of access to territory and resources. Britain was presented as belonging to white British people, illustrated by the rhetoric of 'taking back control'. In a context in which the Leave vote and the hostile environment policy are examples of ongoing and contested white nationalist claims to wealth accumulated via colonial dispossession, appeals to the law for inclusion of racialised people can operate to reinforce the idea that white British control over access to colonially acquired wealth is legitimate.

The hostile environment policy finds legal expression in the Immigration Acts of 2014 and 2016 and ensuing amendments. As a consequence of this legislation, people suspected of not having a legal status are denied access to housing, healthcare, education and financial services, and are at risk of detention and removal. For instance, landlords may be criminalised if they rent a property to those without valid visas. The result of the policy is that racialised people experience 'nation-state borders no matter their physical location'.[70] In 2018 it came to light that the heightened scrutiny of immigration status required by the 2014 and 2016 Acts led to thousands of people being detained, deported and denied access to housing, healthcare, education and financial services.[71] At least 11 of those wrongly expelled are known to have died.[72]

The ensuing outcry, which led to a government apology, the Conservative Home Secretary Amber Rudd's resignation and the establishment of a Windrush task force and compensation scheme for those affected, was frequently framed in terms that served to propagate a politics of recognition. The argument goes that the Windrush generation were British citizens when they arrived in Britain following the passing of the 1948 British Nationality Act. For instance, David Lammy MP, one of the most outspoken critics of the hostile environment policy, wrote in *The Guardian*:

> Last Thursday during the last of her statements to the House of Commons the home secretary said 'illegal' 23 times, but did not even once say the word 'citizen'. Last Wednesday the prime minister said: 'We owe it to them [the Windrush generation] and the British people.' This is the point the government still doesn't understand. The Windrush generation are the British people – their citizenship is, and always has been, theirs by right.[73]

The insistence on the Windrush generation being citizens, a claim also made by several scholars, while fulfilling an important immediate tactical purpose in individual legal cases, has the effect of legitimising the colonial British state's immigration regime by ceding to it the power of recognition. It further elides the reality that the 1948 Act's creation of the status of Citizenship of the United Kingdom and Colonies was done with the explicit purpose of reinforcing Britain's colonial power so that it could go on benefiting economically and politically from its empire. As I show in Chapter 3, racialised British subjects who travelled to Britain after the passing of the Act were not welcomed by the British government, but grudgingly accepted as an unfortunate by-product of Britain's ongoing colonial ambitions. Post-war labour gaps were filled primarily through the facilitation of white European labour. The arrival of the SS *Windrush* shocked the British government, which spent decades discouraging racialised colony and Commonwealth citizens from travelling to Britain, including by putting pressure on colony and Commonwealth governments to stop the movement at its source. Finally, racially targeted legislation was passed to end this migration in the 1960s and 1970s. British officials were facing victorious independence movements and quickly abandoned the lie of imperial unity and equality, which had been broadcast in the form of the 1948 Act in the interests of maintaining the stability of the Empire.

Recognition-based arguments for migrant solidarity also serve to buttress the official, mythological narrative of Britain's colonial history as an era symbolic of its global strength, generosity and inclusivity, rather than as one in which Britain violently enforced white British supremacy around the world. David Lammy thus spoke in Parliament of 'the remarkable greatness of Britain that allows me to be here'.[74] This discourse enables the hostile environment's effect on the Windrush generation and their descendants to be presented as an aberration rather than as part of a continuum of colonial violence, perceptible in the fabric of everyday life for the vast majority of racialised people in and outside Britain. Presenting the racist state violence they experienced as exceptional works to preclude the adoption of broader, connected, anti-colonial, anti-racist resistance strategies. Britain remains racially and colonially configured, a place where poor racialised descendants of colonised and enslaved people are made disproportionately vulnerable to premature death,[75] as we saw in the Grenfell Tower fire in June 2017,[76] in the wake of the hostile environment and in the course of Britain's imperialism masked in the language of humanitarian intervention, international trade and European cooperation.[77]

Glen Coulthard has argued that demands for recognition promise to 'reproduce the very configurations of colonial power' that those claims aim to overcome.[78] Recognition is merely seeming, its promise of freedom ultimately elusive. As Elizabeth Povinelli has argued, recognition by a colonial power is only possible insofar as it does not unsettle the structures of the colonial state.[79] The quest for legal status recognition has long framed scholarly and advocacy work in the field of migration. This is perceptible in the language of 'host states', 'asylum seekers', 'migrants' and 'refugees', and the demand that human rights be respected and that states fulfil their international legal obligations. The acceptance of legal categories as they are defined in domestic and international law elides the colonial dimension of processes of categorisation. The decision to include or exclude certain people from legal status is intricately tied to processes of legitimisation of sovereign and colonial power. Legal status recognition processes also confine the claims of racialised people to those of rights, whether in the form of asylum or citizenship, to the exclusion of more

empowering and radical claims of redistributive and reparative justice, which would entail the reinstatement of stolen
colonial resources and futures. As Coulthard has argued,
while a recognition-based approach 'may alter the intensity
of some of the effects of colonial-capitalist exploitation and
domination, it does little to address their generative structures, in this case a racially stratified capitalist economy
and the colonial state'.[80]

Drawing on Fanon's *Black Skin, White Masks*, Coulthard
has argued that empowerment and freedom from the colonial state requires turning away 'from the assimilative lure
of the statist politics of recognition', and 'toward our own
on-the-ground practices of freedom'.[81] In the Conclusion to
(B)ordering Britain, I develop a counter-pedagogy to that
of law, arguing for a reconceptualisation of irregularised
migration as anti-colonial resistance. Racialised people
deflected, policed and excluded by the colonial state must
both be understood, and understand themselves, as being
collectively entitled to the reclamation of wealth accumulated via colonial dispossession. Understanding that British
immigration law is an extension of colonialism enables us
to question Britain's claim to being a legitimately bordered,
sovereign nation-state. If we as critical scholars and activists can imbibe a counter-pedagogy to that of immigration
law, one which rejects the violence of legal categorisation
and embraces a more empowering, redistributive and radical politics of racial justice, we can begin to work our way
towards new strategies for organising collectively in the
service of anti-racism and migrant solidarity.

Chapter 2

Aliens: immigration law's racial architecture

The idea that there is a clear distinction between the status of British subject and that of alien performed a useful function for Britain as it sought to expand its territory and build the British Empire between the late sixteenth and early eighteenth centuries. The legal category of alien aided in the institutionalisation of a hierarchy of people and, accordingly, allowed for the differentiated apportionment of resources and entitlements. Aliens could be denied the rights that were granted to British subjects. British subjecthood was held up as a superior category from which the civilising benefits of British rule flowed. However, in the British Empire, where rule over populations entailed slavery, dispossession of land, exploitation of labour and theft of resources, all predicated on white British supremacy, the distinction drawn between alien and subject was both fragile and deceptive. Whenever it has suited the British government, it has treated its subjects as aliens for legal purposes, evicting them from the scope of legal status with devastating consequences. British subjecthood did not protect racialised subjects from the violence of white British supremacy. Indeed, its very existence as a legal category was a manifestation of that violence. The law is thus the weapon of, and the legitimising force behind, racial state violence. As I argue in what follows, even so-called 'free' British subjects seeking to move to different parts of the British Empire were met with racist immigration laws, which were the precursor to Britain's first immigration law. The 1905 Aliens Act, which primarily targeted poor Jewish people, categorised as 'aliens', who were seeking protection from persecution, imitated immigration legislation that had been passed in the colonies to control the movement of racialised colonial subjects. The Aliens Act set a legislative precedent for immigration control, which would later be primarily targeted at racialised British subjects and Commonwealth citizens. The Act had its origins in British colonialism, with many of its provisions having been modelled on controls in operation in settler colonies such as Canada and Australia. The Aliens Act had a racialising effect, making people categorised as aliens disproportionately vulnerable to harm and premature death, either because they were turned away at the border, or through exposure to violence and destitution in Britain.

I'd rather be an alien than a subject

Even if I really came from people who were living like monkeys in trees, it was better to be that than what happened to me, what I became after I met you.[1]

The legal category of alien first emerged in England, rather than in the conglomeration of islands and overseas territories now known as the United Kingdom of Great Britain and Northern Ireland. English law distinctions between aliens and subjects first manifested in the law of property and inheritance, rather than through rights of entry and stay.[2] Indeed, where physical expulsions were ordered,

37

these applied to aliens and subjects alike. For example, in 1290, following an increase in expressions of racial hatred against Jews, King Edward I ordered their expulsion from England. Those affected by the order would have included aliens and British subjects, despite the fact that Magna Carta granted subjects the right to remain in Britain and come and go freely.[3] 'Calvin's Case', decided in England in 1608, had determined that Scottish-born children were to be considered Crown subjects. For a person to be considered a Crown subject rather than an alien, she had to be born within the 'King's dominion' and her parents had to be 'under the actual obedience of the King'.[4] The property rights of Irish and Scots, as colonised peoples, indeed as English or Crown subjects, were limited by the English Parliament in the course of England's territorial expansion through colonial conquest. In 1652 the English Parliament decreed that Irish landlords forfeit their land. The Aliens Act 1705, passed to put pressure on Scotland to unite with England, prohibited the import of Scottish goods into England and committed to treating Scots as aliens rather than English subjects for legal purposes, meaning their property rights in England would be threatened. Scotland capitulated and in 1707 the Act of Union was passed. England, Scotland and Wales became the United Kingdom of Great Britain.[5] These examples make clear the dispossessing consequences that flow from British subject status, less surprising when understood not as a privilege, but as a consequence of colonisation by England.

Attention to the production and material effects of different forms of British subjecthood reveals the way in which 'racial power was fused to the very foundation of and architecture of imperial rule'.[6] Renisa Mawani notes that 'imperial territories were interconnected and interdependent', but 'were organized vertically in a hierarchy of racial worth and value'.[7] While English subject status permitted Scots under English colonial rule property rights, the Irish were denied them, as were Aboriginal Australians. This points to the fact that distinctions in rights attached to British subjecthood differed according to a multiplicity of factors, including how colonial territory was acquired.[8] The fragility of the distinction between subject and alien in the context of the British Empire can perhaps be seen most clearly and painfully with reference to Australia, a former British colony. Aboriginal people in Australia were British subjects, but this did little to protect their interests. In fact, the legal status served to legitimise the violence done to them, including through the theft of their land. There is no question as to the British subject status of Aboriginal people in Australia.[9] Every Aboriginal person 'born in Australia after 1829 (by which date the whole of the continent was part of the dominions of the Crown) became a British subject by birth'.[10] Yet, as Geoffrey Sawer has argued, '[b]eing a British subject is by itself worth little; it is the foundation on which further conditions of disqualification or qualification are built', such as racialisation.[11]

In the 1992 Australian High Court case of *Mabo*,[12] which considered the land rights of Aboriginal people in Australia, Brennan J stated that it 'would be a curious doctrine to propound today that, when the benefit of the common law was first extended to Her Majesty's indigenous subjects in the Antipodes, its first fruits were to strip them of their right to occupy their ancestral lands'.[13] Although Brennan J is dismissing the idea that a court would today (or in 1992) uphold the idea that the extension of the English common law to Australia legitimised stripping Aboriginal people of their land rights, his description of Aboriginal people in

Australia as 'indigenous subjects' belies the ambiguity of British subject status and what was deemed to flow from it. Australia exists as a settler colony today as a result of its settlement by white British subjects. Aboriginal people in Australia continue to suffer the consequences of this colonial settlement.[14] It is a painful irony, and indeed an insult, for a people with a history of genocide and land dispossession to be told in 1992 that the catastrophic effects of British colonialism occurred within the framework of the extension of 'the benefit' of anything, let alone the English common law. Even while the disastrous effects of British colonialism were being noted by Brennan J, euphemistically described as 'first fruits', the practical meaning of the English common law's extension of British subjecthood status to Aboriginal people is left unaddressed. Aboriginal people, having been cast as racially inferior and incapable of self-government, gleaned no protection from their status as British subjects. Indeed, their British subject status was symptomatic of their position of subjugation by the British Crown. It is thus a colonial fantasy to imagine that British subject status implied a lack of distinction between white British and racialised subjects.

Excepting colonial subjects

Britain experienced trans-migration throughout the twentieth century.[15] The overwhelming trend of movement of people across England's and later Britain's mainland borders was outwards. Indeed, until 1994 Britain was a place of net emigration.[16] In the eighteenth and nineteenth centuries Europe as a whole experienced far more emigration than immigration. Forced movement outwards from Europe was also a feature of this period. Following the 1718

Transportation Act and the criminalisation of vagrancy, which served to produce a significant convict population, Britain transported prisoners to work as labourers in the colonies.[17] Movement of white Britons out to the colonies was also facilitated through debt-financed emigration programmes.[18] Emigration was coterminous with colonial settlement. Although commentators have highlighted free-trade interests as being at the heart of the relatively free conditions of movement prior to the 1905 Aliens Act,[19] this elides the colonial context in which people migrated at this time and the catastrophic implications of white settlement for indigenous peoples in places such as North and South America and Australia.[20] The global movement of racialised people was and remains engineered in the interests of pre-dominantly white colonial powers. Anderson writes, '[a]s the British Empire consolidated and expanded, the rights of movement of people from England/Britain around the world to colonize, make war, explore, and conduct business were not at issue for the government in London'.[21] Between 1750 and 1960, the European continent sent 70 million people overseas to destinations such as North and South America, Australia and South Africa.[22] Patricia Tuitt writes that the 'age of discovery' was one 'in which mass migration (not classic war or conquest) was deployed to extend the territories of a power, or, crucially, to engineer "the destruction and/or transformation of other forms of social organisation and life" of communities assumed to be spent and useless'.[23]

Despite the decision in Calvin's Case on the Crown subject status of children born in Scotland, the extension of subjecthood was not automatic in overseas British colonies.[24] The British Empire entailed varied legal statuses and systems for their bestowal, though people in colonial jurisdictions were referred to as British subjects.[25] However, differential racialisation meant that there was little consistency across the Empire. The forced movement of racialised people was a major feature of Britain's colonial expansion. Britain had been trading in slaves since the 1500s. Slaves, and the children of slaves in British jurisdictions, were legally objects rather than subjects.[26] Trade in slaves was formally abolished in the British Empire in 1807. The Slavery Abolition Act 1833 led to the gradual abolition of slavery in the colonies and established a financial compensation scheme for slave owners.[27] Some slaves who gained their freedom as a quid pro quo for fighting for the British against American independence travelled to Britain at the end of the war. According to Vilna Bashi, '[j]obless and destitute, they were given assistance by the newly established Committee for the Relief of the Black Poor, but the programme evolved into a 1786 House of Commons-approved plan to expel the black poor and send them to a settlement in Sierra Leone'.[28] The horrific conditions on board a 1787 voyage to Sierra Leone have been likened to transport on slave ships. Many died, some driven to suicide by drowning,[29] demonstrative of the inescapability of the material effects of categorisation as 'negro', intrinsic to the operation of the system of chattel slavery, even after its abolition.[30] The production of black people as racialised not only rendered them enslavable, but continues to make them acutely and disproportionately vulnerable to state-sanctioned harm and premature death.[31]

Following the abolition of slavery, forced labour of racialised people continued in various forms, including through forced mass movement around the Empire of indentured labourers from India and China.[32] The systems created to regulate this movement varied across the colonies. Mongia has observed how in 1835 the Court of Directors of the

East India Company, responsible at the time for British administration in India, put in place centralised systems of regulation to record and control the movement of indentured Indian labourers who were being increasingly relied on across the British Empire to replace the labour of former slaves following the abolition of slavery.[33] In 1838 the British Parliament introduced the first formal regulation of 'free' British subjects. Colonial authorities treated overseas territories as exceptional places wherein the movement of 'free' subjects could be governed, even though this was not the case on the British mainland. This treatment was justified on the basis of the supposed inferiority of racialised colonial subjects. In the colonies, 'the elements of society' were said to be 'not the same therein as in Europe'.[34] Mongia thus writes that '[t]he peculiar situation of the colony ... justified the differential application of the law and made the term "British subject" itself "susceptible of important division and modification"'.[35]

Colonial governments' experimentation with immigration control was the forerunner of modern-day British immigration law, in particular the practice of legislating with the aim of racial exclusion but in apparently race-neutral terms. The exceptional space of the colonies can be seen in Britain's tolerance of the practices of the settler colonial governments in Canada and Australia, which sought to control the movement of 'free' racialised British subjects. Each passed immigration laws, using practices of information gathering, ordering and legal categorisation to control the movement of racialised populations.[36] Australia passed explicitly racist immigration law as part of the 'White Australia' policy. British colonial officials, keen to preserve the stability and longevity of the Empire, wanted to avoid being seen to blatantly discriminate against racialised British subjects in the

letter of the law. The difficulty for British colonial officials, according to Anderson, 'was that to limit mobility of
"Europeans" was unthinkable, yet any mention of "race"
could threaten to undermine assertions of equality and
benevolent rule'.[37] Colonial governments thus developed
means of restricting the movement of racialised labourers by
designing legislation that did not discriminate explicitly on
the basis of race but had this effect in practice. The government of the British colony of Natal, for instance, passed the
Immigration Restriction Act 1897, which required entrants
to be in possession of £25, about £3000 in today's currency,
and to have knowledge of a European language. Immigration
officers could choose the requisite European language in
which knowledge was expected, 'so an "Indian" English
speaker, for example, could be presented with a form in
German'.[38] In practice Europeans could meet the conditions
of entry, but racialised subjects, the non-indentured Indians
targeted for control, could not. The Prime Minister of Natal
explained to Parliament,

> [i]t never occurred to me for a single minute that [the bill]
> should ever be applied to English immigrants ... can you
> imagine anything more mad for a Government than that it
> should apply to English immigrants? The object of the bill is
> to deal with Asiatic immigrants.[39]

According to Mongia, in 1908 a growing 'deeply anticolo-
nial and nationalist' Indian public, combined with the emergence of outward migration as a major political issue, led
the British government of India to seek to minimise legislative measures that were explicitly discriminatory against
Indians.[40] Thus, it was suggested to the Canadians that they
adopt concealed means of discrimination, for example by
requiring 'certain qualifications such as physical fitness ...
and the possession of a certain amount of money'.[41] The

thinly disguised racial discrimination in these legislative measures was obvious to its targets, who made strategic arguments for legal change by appealing to their rights as British subjects. British Indian subjects in Canada thus wrote to the Colonial Office in London in 1910:

> The present Dominion Immigration Laws are quite inconsistent to the Imperial policy because they discriminate against the people of India who are British subjects; as they are forced to produce a sum of $200 before landing, whereas other British subjects are not ... The present Dominion Immigration Laws are humiliating to the people of India ... [since we] are not allowed to enjoy the birthright of travelling from one part of the British Empire to the other.[42]

Apparently race-neutral but in fact racist methods of restriction developed in the colonial context would be adopted to target the movement of 'undesirable' aliens to Britain and, later, racialised colony and Commonwealth citizens. To this day legislation that is race-neutral in its terms but that produces racialised effects is the modus operandi of immigration law. As Anderson has written, '[t]he laws governing the movement of subjects within the Empire were an important means of manufacturing the category' of race.[43] The colonies thus served as testing grounds for legal measures, paving the way for their adoption on the British mainland.

In tracing the emergence of the passport in the settler colony of Canada in the early 1900s, Mongia has argued that it surfaced as 'a state document that purport[ed] to assign a national identity rather than a racial identity – a mechanism that would conceal race and racist motivations for controlling mobility in the guise of a reciprocal arrangement between states described as national'.[44] It was thus 'through a recourse to the idea of states as securing sovereignty through an appeal to the "national"' that the principles of free movement for British subjects through-out the British Empire was discarded.[45] Yet Britain itself, at the helm of an empire, could hardly appeal to the national as the primary source of its power. It would be another sixty years before the British government was willing to countenance the introduction of immigration controls to prevent the entry of racialised British subjects to the British mainland. However, immigration law targeted primarily at poor Jewish refugees was passed in Britain as early as 1905 in the form of the Aliens Act. It borrowed in style from the apparently race-neutral immigration laws adopted in the colonies. As discussed in the remainder of this chapter, the 1905 Act contained provisions similar to those in the 1897 Natal Act, including the requirement that entrants be in possession of a minimum sum of money. The 1905 Act was thus both a product of and embodied the spirit of the white supremacist project of the British Empire.

The Aliens Act 1905: protecting white British supremacy at home

We are not a destitute-alien-importing people so much as we are a destitute-exporting people. There are far more Britons who go destitute into foreign countries, to earn their livelihood than destitute aliens who come here.[46]

By the time the 1905 Aliens Act was passed, the British Empire was well established and the transatlantic slave trade and slavery had been abolished. The wealth accumu-lated through slavery and colonial conquest infused Britain, and along with it, the idea that white Britons occupied a position of superiority in a global racial hierarchy. The passing of the 1905 Act, primarily to prevent the arrival in Britain of poor Jewish refugees, is an early instance of the use of immigration law on the British mainland as a means of preserving domestic white British supremacy. Although it was not targeted at racialised British subjects but at 'aliens', it mirrored in method and content aspects of racist immigration laws previously adopted in British colonies, and established the infrastructure for future iterations of immigration control in Britain.

Until 1905 Britain had been legislating the rights of entry and stay of aliens in an ad hoc manner. The Aliens Act 1793 was passed in response to the arrival of people from France following the French Revolution. The legislation was designed 'to protect the British state against French subversives who might stir up revolutionary fervour in the domestic population'.[47] The Act introduced an early version of carrier sanctions, with ships' captains being required to provide details of people categorised as aliens brought into the country on pain of a fine. The Act also authorised the removal of 'aliens' considered to be subversives.[48] The aim of the legislation was to ensure the maintenance of the rule and power of the British monarchy and aristocracy. The Removal of Aliens Act 1848 renewed powers of removal 'in readiness for another "alien menace" from continental revolutionaries'.[49] The Act empowered the Home Secretary and the Lord Lieutenant of Ireland to expel 'aliens' if they were deemed to threaten the 'preservation of the peace and tranquillity of the realm'.[50]

Britain and other European countries' colonial activity had long led to people seeking to enter the British mainland. In the late 1800s, for instance, Jewish refugees arrived in Britain fleeing the Boer War, a colonial war waged by Britain against Dutch colonists as each vied for control over the South African gold mines. In the 1900s some of those escaping antisemitism in the Russian Empire, Austria, Romania and other eastern European countries travelled to Britain. This movement led to the introduction of Britain's first immigration control legislation in 1905. The campaign in support of controls was run by the far right organisation, the British Brothers' League. Racism against Jews has a long history in Britain.[51] Those campaigning for controls blamed Jewish refugees for causing overcrowding in factories and housing, and for spreading disease. Intimately associated with the League was the Conservative MP for Stepney, William Evans-Gordon. After serving in the British Indian Army and the Foreign Department of the Indian government, Evans-Gordon built his domestic political career on pushing forward a racist, anti-'alien' agenda. In 1902 he stated that 'not a day passes but English families are ruthlessly turned out to make room for foreign invaders'.[52]

In the course of the introduction of the 1905 Act there was debate about whether immigration controls were a necessary or suitable solution to problems such as poor health and poor-quality housing and work conditions. People categorised as aliens were treated as a cheap source of labour. In the early 1900s welfare provision was limited in scope. The government did not consider welfare as one of its tasks. Seeking access to welfare could have a detrimental effect for people seeking a legal status in Britain. Deborah Hayes has noted the connections between the Poor Law and laws of settlement whereby the cost of the relief was made the responsibility of the claimant's parish of settlement.[53] This resulted in towns having the power of removal to the parish of origin in cases where sick, elderly and unemployed people claimed relief. People categorised as aliens were the most affected. They were deterred from applying for support and this exposed them to labour exploitation.[54]

The 1905 Aliens Act was a result of the work of the Royal Commission on Alien Immigration established by a Conservative government following increased pressure for control. The Royal Commission rejected in spirit the sensationalist anti-immigrant rhetoric which had led to its establishment, noting that people from eastern Europe had not caused a crime wave and that only 1 per cent of 'aliens' were receiving Poor Law payments. It nevertheless recommended the adoption of immigration legislation. Two of its members voiced their opposition in the form of a dissenters' memorandum attached to the Commission's report. In it Sir Kenelm Digby, permanent Under-Secretary at the Home Office, and Lord Nathaniel Rothschild, leader of a delegation from the Board of Deputies of British Jews,[55] argued that the Commission's recommendations were not substantiated by its findings.[56] Digby considered that the recommendations would be impossible to implement due to the absence of personnel tasked with immigration control. He also questioned the link between immigration and problems of overcrowding in East London, suggesting that rather than immigration legislation, the Public Health Act of 1891 might be a more appropriate tool for dealing with poor work and housing conditions.[57]

The Royal Commission also produced a report entitled *Measures Adopted for the Restriction and Control of Alien Immigration in Foreign Countries, and in British Colonies*.[58] The colonies examined were Canada, Natal, Cape Colony, Australia, New Zealand and Tasmania. In the colonies, 'people categorised as criminals, idiots, lunatics and "persons likely to become a charge on public funds" were prohibited from landing, and in some instances from leaving a home country'.[59] Similar categories of persons, along with the general category of 'undesirable aliens', also popular in colonial immigration laws, found their way into the 1904 Aliens Bill. Medical inspection of 'alien' arrivals, also common in the colonies, was adopted in the Bill. The notion of carrier sanctions whereby ship operators would pay a penalty for transporting people deemed undesirable was another colonial influence, a provision borrowed from Australian law. An important difference between colonial immigration controls and British legislation against 'aliens' is that the colonies, for the most part, did not differentiate between aliens and British subjects.[60] Indeed, as discussed above, racialised subjects from different parts of the Empire were often the primary targets of control in white settler colonies. For Britain, the introduction of controls against British subjects seeking to travel to the heart of the Empire was considered to go against the interests of imperial rule. How could the lie of imperial unity and equality be sustained if Britain treated its subjects differently as far as the motherland was concerned?

On introducing the 1904 Bill, the Conservative Home Secretary, Aretas Akers-Douglas, used dehumanising and incendiary rhetoric to describe the migration to Britain of poor Europeans. He stated, 'there is a certain class of undesirable aliens who are not so welcome, and whose repatriation is very desirable'.[61] He spoke of 'aliens' as having 'occupied a very large number of dwellings from which they have driven the bona fide inhabitants'.[62] People coming to Britain, he said, are those 'excluded by the United States, and therefore it is fair to say that we only get the refuse'.[63]

The Bill was opposed by some for its limitation of the movement of 'free white men', indicating the fluidity and lack of clarity around the racialisation of the targets of the 1905 Act. The Liberal Party MP Sir Charles Dilke stated that it was 'extraordinary' that Parliament 'should be called upon to consider a measure ... which, for the first time, was going to prevent European white men from coming, at their own cost, as free men to a free country'.[64] Dilke considered the legislation to be a hypocritical move by the government, which at the same moment was proposing to import indentured Chinese labourers into the Transvaal colony (in South Africa),[65] described by some as being tantamount to the reintroduction of slavery.[66]

Lord Alfred Milner, High Commissioner for Southern Africa and Governor of Cape Colony, was an enthusiastic proponent of the indentured labour scheme and encouraged those opposed to it on the basis that it would do injury to white labour in South Africa to 'turn their attention to the injury done to white labour in [Britain] by the dumping down of 80,000 foreign aliens, the riff-raff of Europe, many of them criminals, who compete at starvation wages, and in many cases take the bread out of the mouths of our struggling working men'.[67] Dilke emphasised in turn that many of those whose entry to Britain would be prevented by the Act were people in flight from persecution, 'people whom we shall afterwards be ashamed we have excluded'.[68] Quoting from the Royal Commission's report, he spoke of the 'persecution which sends these people to this country – "The Russian persecution stands in some degree apart from other forms of the Anti-Semitic movement on account of its unparalleled magnitude and ferocity"'.[69] Thus despite some acknowledgement of a moral obligation to extend protection to people experiencing antisemitism among the dehumanising talk of poor people as 'refuse', parliamentary debate on the Aliens Bill betrayed the scope and depth of racism as enacted daily across the British Empire and imbibed in the mindset and discourse of British politicians, whether levelled against subjects overseas or 'aliens' at Britain's shores.

The government's failure to take measures to counter overcrowding and ill-health in poverty-stricken urban areas allowed 'aliens' to be constructed as their cause. Rather than introducing and enforcing stringent public health standards in factories and housing and stemming the influence of the growing far right, the government sought to eliminate the presence of migrant populations from certain areas. The 1905 Aliens Act permitted the expulsion of 'aliens' unable to support themselves financially or living in overcrowded conditions. Under the Act, the Home Secretary could order the expulsion of an 'alien' who 'had been in receipt of any such parochial relief as disqualifies a person from the parliamentary franchise or been found wandering without ostensible means of subsistence or been living under insanitary conditions due to overcrowding'.[70]

The English courts had already ruled in 1891 that 'aliens' did not have a legal right to enter Britain.[71] Later, *Poll* v. *Lord Advocate* had established that 'the sovereign power – the supreme executive – of every state must be held to be absolute' and an 'alien' could not bring a legal action against the state.[72] In 1906 the Privy Council affirmed the existence of a Crown prerogative to expel 'aliens'.[73] The 1905 Act, despite being much less extensive than the originally proposed Bill due to the heavy opposition it encountered in the House of Commons, nevertheless established a statutory framework for immigration control. The Aliens Bill would have given the Home Secretary wide powers to restrict the presence of 'aliens' in Britain as well as to designate regions from which those categorised as aliens would be excluded.[74] The Act established a body of officers with the power to refuse entry into Britain to 'undesirable aliens', which included those with little financial means. Passengers exempt from control were 'cabin passengers', those permitted use of the ship's cabin, store rooms and saloons.[75] Controls applied only to 'steerage passengers', who were those with the cheapest tickets, and who arrived on a ship which carried more than twelve, and later twenty, such passengers. Shipping companies found a way around the controls by ensuring that they carried twenty or fewer such passengers.[76]

The Aliens Act provided that an 'alien' was to be considered 'undesirable' and could be refused entry:

a) if he cannot show that he has in his possession or is in a position to obtain the means to decently supporting himself and his dependants (if any); or
b) if he is a lunatic or an idiot, or owing to any disease or infirmity appears likely to be a charge upon the rates or otherwise of a detriment to the public; or
c) if he has been sentenced in a foreign country with which there is an extradition treaty for a crime.[77]

The colonial influence is apparent. The provision reads similarly to Section 38(c) of the Canadian Immigration Act of 1910, whereby those 'deemed unsuitable' or 'undesirable' or having a 'probable inability to become readily assimilated' could be denied entry.[78]

Persons considered to be fleeing certain forms of persecution could benefit from an exception to control.

In the case of an immigrant who proves that he is seeking admission to this country solely to avoid persecution or punishment on religious or political grounds or for an offence of a political character, or persecution, involving danger of imprisonment or danger to life or limb, on account of religious belief, leave to land shall not be refused on the ground merely of want of means or the probability of his becoming a charge on the rates.[79]

The clause is weak in the protection it offers. Protection is limited to entry and the burden of proof is placed on the entrant. It is lacking in nuance in its insistence that persons to be exempted from control show that they have travelled to Britain 'solely to avoid persecution', thus eliding the fact that people may have a variety of motivations in moving. Further, the provision states that denial of entry where the conditions set out in the clause are met is not to be merely for the reason that an entrant is poor. This suggests that there might be other reasons to deny entry to a person seeking safety from persecution. Despite the minimal protection it offers, having the clause inserted into the Act was not an easy task. The amendment was adopted as a result of the work of representatives of the Jewish community.[80] Local groups, on the advice of the Board of Deputies of British Jews, campaigned for a strengthening of religious protection in the Act, persuading the Liberals to lobby for the amendment.[81] The London Committee of the Board had raised concerns about individuals fleeing persecution and the problems they would face in proving their status through legal documentation.[82] Although the government might have been 'embarrassed by its own conscience' and thus included this exceptional clause, it was also faced with the threat of a withdrawal of contributions to campaign funds, and pressure from backbenchers.[83]

The clause allowing for the exemption from control of persecuted individuals in the 1905 Act was as close as Britain had come to legally defining a refugee. This restrictive, hesitant and limited articulation of legal protection for refugees, and its birth within the framework of immigration control, has since influenced the development of British refugee protection. The discretionary nature of refugee protection contributed to a lack of equivalence in its granting. Gina Clayton has noted that '[e]very history of immigration shows that in Britain each new group of arrivals has been regarded with suspicion and hostility'.[84]

However, the degree of hostility has differed markedly, increasing according to whether and how people are racialised. The Home Secretary defended the need for the 1905 legislation by differentiating 'the undesirable aliens' which the Act targeted from the more desirable Huguenots who had arrived in the seventeenth century.[85] Differential racialisation thus affects the degree to which racialised people find themselves vulnerable to abuse, harm and premature death. The British government's treatment of Jewish refugees who arrived in the early 1900s has been contrasted with that of the Roma, whose arrival also coincided with the passing of the Aliens Act. While limited concessions were secured for Jewish refugees, the Roma were deflected and expelled.[86]

Administering the Aliens Act 1905

Although the Aliens Act has been described as 'a weak measure with only limited state apparatus to implement it',[87] it nevertheless set a precedent for generalised immigration control. It also established the infrastructure and framework that was to facilitate the enactment of further immigration laws. The Conservative Party lost the general election of 1906 to the Liberals after passing the Act. The 'unwilling' Liberals were faced with the task of enforcing the legislation they had contested.[88] Due to the lack of an implementing structure, Board of Customs staff were given additional immigration duties and their numbers and pay increased to account for these extra tasks.[89] The Act required the specification of 'immigration ports' where people would be permitted to disembark. These were located on the east and south coasts and in London and Liverpool. The Home Office appointed medical officers to advise immigration officials stationed at ports on the health conditions of arrivals, many of whom were rejected on medical grounds.[90]

Passengers deemed 'undesirable' and rejected under the Act could appeal to an immigration board. The ship's captain was also permitted an appeal when a fine was levied for failure to provide details of persons brought to Britain. Interpreters were employed to enable communication with immigration officials and for people who appealed to an immigration board. People categorised as aliens faced expulsion on an order of the Home Secretary following conviction for a criminal offence where the sentencing court advised this outcome. The Home Office considered factors such as the nature of the offence, how long the individual had been residing in Britain as well as the hardship she or he was likely to face on expulsion.[91] Also subject to an expulsion order were people found to be in receipt of Poor Law payments within twelve months of having arrived in Britain.[92]

The Home Office had a wide discretion in determining the membership of immigration boards. Panellists had to be 'fit persons having magisterial, business, or administrative experience'.[93] The boards, whose composition was hotly disputed, comprised 'establishment figures in the towns concerned'.[94] Members of affected migrant communities in Britain argued that the boards were not sufficiently representative of them. Those in support of the controls pointed to a lack of representation of 'working men' on the boards. The Home Office immigration minister questioned the motivations behind concerns about the lack of 'working men' on immigration boards: 'It is difficult to guess the objective of this question. What is a workman wanted for? 1. To exclude the destitute alien, so as not to increase existing evils and diminish competition. 2. To admit him as being no worse than those already here. 3. To earn a guinea.'[95] The assumption, of course, was that the 'working man' was a white British subject. This mythological and racist construction of the working class as white to the exclusion of its racialised members, who are in fact disproportionately represented in this class both domestically and globally, persists to the present day.[96]

Legal protection for those facing immigration boards was limited. There was neither a judicial nor an administrative right of appeal against decisions. Questions regarding interpretation of the Act were to be referred to the Home Office, which monitored case outcomes in order to ensure uniformity in decision making, for example with regard to political and religious refugees.[97] The absence of a right of appeal to a court of law was a key concern of the Board of Deputies of British Jews. It questioned the legitimacy of immigration boards made up of 'nameless officials wielding ... arbitrary bureaucratic power'.[98] The Home Office's position was that allowing appeals to a court of law would lead to delays in the administration of the Act as well as requiring the introduction of new legislation, which the government considered politically undesirable.[99] After the adoption of the Act, it was eventually agreed that individuals should have the right to legal representation, though this was practically useless since there was no financial assistance provided.[100]

According to the Act an 'undesirable alien' was a person who could not 'show that he has in his possession or is in a position to obtain the means of decently supporting himself and his dependants'.[101] The Home Office's guidelines to immigration boards interpreted this as requiring an entrant to be in possession of at least five pounds (about £400 in today's currency) and two pounds for each dependent. Failing this, immigration board officials were to use their discretion in determining whether an entrant was in a position to achieve self-sufficiency. This necessitated the making of judgements about the work prospects of individual entrants according to their trade and the state of the labour market.[102] The Home Office guidelines began to be treated as rules by the immigration boards. The possession of five pounds became the determining factor in deciding the eligibility of a person to enter Britain. Relatives and migrant support groups worked to secure five pounds for those seeking entry to present to the boards.[103] It was common practice to circulate the same five pounds among entrants, prompting Permanent Under Secretary of State of the Home Office, Mackenzie Chalmers, to comment that '[w]e admit a pauper alien, who probably has to pay something for the temporary use of the necessary five pounds. He is not only without means, but also in debt into the bargain.'[104] The effect of the Aliens Act was thus to produce a category of people, 'aliens', who were marked as 'undesirable', and who were at disproportionate risk of destitution and exploitation as compared with white British subjects.

Conflict frequently arose between the Liberal Party politicians who had opposed the introduction of the Aliens Act and now wanted to see it loosely enforced, and the civil servants who were employed to administer it.[105] The Liberal government preferred to implement the Act loosely and avoid the debate that would ensue if it were brought before Parliament for repeal.[106] According to Jill Pellew, the compromise reached 'between administering the law as its legislators had intended and repealing it altogether' was to 'administer it badly'.[107] She concludes that '[n]o-one was satisfied about the way in which it worked: neither the Conservatives who enacted it; nor the Liberals who had to see to its execution'.[108] Despite the widespread dissatisfaction with the operation of the Act, along with the practical difficulties encountered in its implementation, it had the effect of preventing the arrival of thousands of individuals. In 1906, 38,527 non-transiting migrants arrived in Britain. By 1911, the number had fallen to 18,856. In total, between 1906 and 1913, 7,594 people categorised as aliens are known to have been refused permission to enter Britain.[109]

Exceptional and discretionary protection

In 1905, due in part to the persecution that Jews faced in Russia, more persons migrating and trans-migrating arrived in Britain than in any other year of the Act's operation.[110] Antisemitism was rife across Europe. There were pogroms in Russia and Romania and antisemitic ministers had entered government in Germany and Austria-Hungary.[111] It was clear that the British government had in mind a specific image of a refugee: a person of European origin in flight from religious or political persecution. It did not envisage its colonial activities overseas as productive of refugees. Home Office directions to immigration boards thus required their members to give the benefit of the doubt to all those persons coming from 'disturbed' parts of the European continent. The Liberal Home Office exercised leniency towards persons arriving from eastern Europe who had faced religious and political persecution. Although the Act's clause permitting exceptional admission of refugees was phrased in individualised terms, in practice the Home Office applied it in a collective manner, granting entry to persons on the basis of their country of origin. Mackenzie Chalmers explained to the Secretary of State that although this might seem to shift 'the onus of proof required by the Act itself', he considered that 'the present state of Russia may be taken to be so notorious that it is a matter of common sense that if a man proves that he comes from Russia and alleges that he is a refugee there is a presumption of fact that his statement is correct'.[112] In relation to the case of a 20-year-old Russian woman convicted of soliciting in Britain and facing expulsion, Chalmers wrote, '[s]he is a Russian. It would be very harsh to send her back to Russia. She has already been severely punished by being kept in prison after payment of her fine. Release and warn, but not expel.'[113]

Because the 1905 Act allowed for an individual seeking entry to Britain solely in flight from persecution to be granted entry even if poor, immigration board members had to distinguish between persons who were impoverished and fleeing persecution, and those who were only impoverished and thus to be turned away. The exemption clause was particularly vague, considering the circumstances in which people arrived. Very few carried documents proving their identity, and many had difficulty showing that their motivation for travelling lay 'solely' in flight from persecution. It became the practice among immigration boards to refer refugee cases to the Home Office, though it had not been intended to serve as an appeal court. The Home Office tended to admit the vast majority of these cases.[114] However, this practice came under threat as the government faced pressure from a growing right-wing lobby critical of an approach constructed as being soft towards 'criminal immigrants'.[115] In 1909 Judge Rentoul KC delivered a speech at the Bishopsgate Institute entitled, 'The British empire: its greatness, glory, and freedom', in which he told stories of his experience ruling in cases of 'criminal aliens', describing them as having been

> of the very worst type in their own country ... the Russian burglar, the Polish thief, the Italian stabber, and the German swindler ... people whom this country would be glad to rid

of and who had been practically kicked out of their own ...
[I]n the matter of alien immigration Empire should be placed
before party advantage.[116]

Contrary to Rentoul's narrative, the migrant prison population had been in decline since the passing of the Aliens Act,
and had fallen to 1.22 per cent of the total prison population
by 1910.[117] In spite of this, in 1911 the government introduced the Aliens (Prevention of Crime) Bill. This would
have required all 'aliens' to obtain licences if they wished
to carry firearms. Judges would have been forced to give reasons in cases where they did not recommend the expulsion
of an 'alien' found guilty of a criminal offence. Ultimately,
this legislation was not pursued. However, immigration
control quickly re-emerged as a legislative topic in a context of heightened national security concerns with the
growing tension on the international scene brought on by
approaching war.[118]

War and the maintenance of white British supremacy

War came to the British mainland in 1914, after nearly
half a century of relative peace among European powers at
home.[119] Britain and other European colonial powers had
been waging colonial wars against populations overseas for
centuries.[120] All the major colonial powers participated in
the First World War, including all the European states bar
Spain, the Netherlands, Switzerland and the Scandinavian
countries.[121] Colonised populations were sent to different
European imperial outposts to fight. The First World War
elicited the passing of immigration controls in Britain.
These affected European refugees seeking to enter Britain
as well as people resident in Britain who had been born
in other parts of Europe and had arrived previously, some

in flight from persecution. Britain went to war in order to ensure the maintenance of the British Empire in the face of threats, rivalry and colonial ambition on the part of other European colonial powers.[122] By the time the First World War began Britain was already an imagined white space, a spatial imaginary that colonialism both produced and sustained. Insofar as the war was about maintaining the global order of white British supremacy, this was also the structure that underpinned the immigration laws introduced to target the nationals of Britain's competitor states in the scramble for world domination.

An effect of the war was an increase in racist nationalism in Britain. Migrants were constructed as threats to national security. They were considered either 'good' or 'bad' depending on whether their country of birth or nationality was considered an enemy or ally. The exclusion of people deemed not to belong to the British polity was achieved in large part through the introduction of legal mechanisms as well as a deepening of centralised and discretionary control over people categorised as aliens. The Liberal Home Secretary, Reginald McKenna, stated that the Aliens Restriction Bill was intended 'to draw a distinction between alien friends and alien enemies'.[123] On 4 August 1914 Britain declared war on Germany and, on the following day, the Aliens Restriction Act, repealing the 1905 Aliens Act, was debated, passed and received royal assent. Unlike the 1905 Aliens Act, it was not preceded by hesitation and did not face great opposition. The Home Secretary was granted complete control over all foreign nationals in Britain. As is typical in times of national (or imperial) shifts and transformations, whether in times of war or, more recently, in the course of the 2016 referendum on Britain's EU membership, Britishness, the supremacy of which is at the core of the identity of the colonial state, becomes reified. This process leaves little space for other identities and forms of residency and legal status that should be equally secure, as we saw with the ratcheting up of the hostile environment policy following the EU referendum.[124]

Despite the Aliens Restriction Act having been introduced as an emergency measure, it was to be the foundation of permanent immigration control legislation.[125] The Act enabled broad restrictions to be placed on the entry of people categorised as aliens and required them 'to reside and remain within certain places'.[126] Registration requirements were imposed on all 'aliens', their internment and expulsion were permitted, and scope was provided for the introduction of measures 'for any other matters which appear necessary or expedient with a view to the safety of the realm'.[127] While the 1905 Aliens Act was primarily concerned with keeping 'undesirable' migrants out of Britain, the 1914 Aliens Restriction Act moved the border further inwards, constructing migrants resident in Britain as undesirable, dangerous and a threat to security.

People of German origin were particularly affected by the Aliens Restriction Act. They were forced to register their presence and prohibited from living in certain places without a permit. The Act demonstrated that 'popular and official hatred' were 'mutually reinforcing'.[128] The new legislation's categorisation of certain groups as a risk to 'the safety of the realm' ignited fears and served to legitimise hatred and violence. Migrants and those perceived as such suffered street attacks. Persons thought to be German were particularly at risk. One account tells of the shop of a naturalised Russian being damaged by a crowd who believed the owner to be of German origin.[129] The Act was used to expel or intern the majority of Germans in Britain: 70,000–75,000 Germans were classified as 'enemy aliens' and of these around 32,000 men were interned and 20,000 were expelled.[130] Some of those labelled as enemies of the state and interned had arrived in Britain as refugees. By the end of the First World War, the German communities of Britain had been drastically reduced. The 1911 census showed that there were 877 German-born residents in Hampshire. By 1921, the number was 228, the result of rigorous state efforts.[131]

The judiciary showed themselves unwilling to intervene to limit the highly discretionary executive powers introduced in the 1914 Act.[132] The case of *Sarno* concerned an expulsion order by the Home Secretary under the Act and Article 12 of the Aliens Restriction (Consolidation) Order 1914.[133] Sarno claimed to be a refugee from Russia. Lord Reading CJ described the issues raised as

> undoubtedly of supreme importance, in reference to the right or power of the Secretary of State to send back to the country where he was born a person who had sought asylum in this country by reason of his having, or being suspected of having, committed a political offense in his own country.[134]

He stated that,

> if we were of opinion that the powers were being misused, we should be able to deal with the matter. In other words, if it was clear that an act done by the Executive with the intention of misusing those powers, this Court would have jurisdiction to deal with the matter.[135]

However, Lord Reading was neither convinced that in making the expulsion order the Home Secretary had acted beyond his legal power, nor that Sarno was 'in the ordinary sense, a political refugee'.[136] In the case of *R* v. *Secretary of State for Home Affairs, ex parte Duke of Château Thierry*, the Court of Appeal was of the opinion that despite the absence of safeguards for refugees in the 1914 Act, 'the Executive had no intention whatever of taking advantage of their powers over aliens to deport political refugees'.[137] Dallal Stevens has observed that evident in the practice of the courts at this time was the 'continued legacy of Crown privilege', demonstrating their reluctance to 'peer behind the veil of absolute discretion'.[138]

In contrast to the demonisation of Germans, Belgians were considered deserving foreigners. Demands were made for the British government to come to the aid of the Belgian people. Stories of German atrocities in Belgium, some later discredited, were used by British politicians to justify the harsh measures imposed on German residents.[139] According to Tony Kushner and Katherine Knox, '[t]he construction of "Brave Little Belgium" could only be achieved with the parallel belief in the "evil Hun"'.[140] This was essentially an 'arbitrary construction of aliens/refugees in Britain as either devils or angels'.[141]

The War Refugees Board was established in August 1914 by a group of wealthy women to help facilitate the movement and resettlement in Britain of Belgians fleeing the war. Such initiatives followed 'tales of foreign persecution', which 'invited Britons to imagine themselves in the role of foreigners' rescuer',[142] a familiar colonial trope. The Board was largely publicly funded, a first for the British government.[143] However, it preferred the Board to appear as though it was privately sustained in order to dispel the idea that it might be directing funds towards 'aliens'. It also did not want to dissuade charitable organisations from setting up funds in aid of refugees, such as Manchester's Belgian Refugee Fund. The official position was that the task of providing humanitarian aid to refugees was to be assumed by voluntary organisations. In reality, the War Refugees Board was increasingly under the management of civil servants and reliant on state funding.[144]

Over a million people, almost one-sixth of the Belgian population, were forced to flee Belgium following attacks by the German forces. Half travelled to the Netherlands and the rest arrived in Britain and France. In January 1915 the British Local Government Board announced that around 4,000–5,000 Belgians were being given permission to enter Britain from the Netherlands on a weekly basis in order to relieve pressure on Dutch resources. Altogether a quarter of a million Belgians came to Britain during the First World War.[145] The Home Secretary stated that Belgian refugees were to be 'treated as friends, and no difficulty [would] be put in the way of their landing at any approved port, if they [could] satisfy the Aliens Officer that they [were] in fact Belgians and not Germans or Austrians'.[146] Belgians thus served as symbols of Britain's apparent righteousness in world affairs. Kushner and Knox interpret the move to protect the Belgians as a 'desperate' attempt to reinvigorate 'Britain's moral pride'.[147] The British 'delved into the past to place the Belgian refugees in context, and their search for a usable past took some as far back as the French Huguenots and other Protestant exiles'.[148] In reality, hostility towards anyone considered not to be British was high and calls for stronger immigration controls led the government to push for the rapid return of Belgian refugees as early as 1916.[149] There was a level of ambivalence in the official attitude towards the Belgians. They were considered to be an administrative and political challenge.[150] The regime established to protect them was characterised by elements of last resort and temporariness. Refugees were permitted entry on an exceptional basis and the length of stay was limited. Due to its intention to repatriate the Belgian refugees, the British government encouraged them to maintain their language and culture.[151] In November 1918 parliamentary debate centred around the timetable for the return of Belgians still in Britain. As early as 1914, in an exchange between the Foreign Office and the Home Office, the prospect of their becoming 'a considerable source of embarrassment' if 'their numbers should be large' was commented on.[152] The Home Secretary feared hostility from locals in settlement areas and a concerted effort was made to repatriate them as speedily as possible.[153]

The government's eagerness to repatriate extended not only to Belgian refugees, but also to black soldiers and seamen who had travelled to and fought for Britain in the First World War. As Vilna Bashi notes, 'these recruits were expected to return to their land of origin after their service'.[154] Despite their status as British subjects, the government sought to have them repatriated and subjected them to strict control, for example by confiscating their passports and limiting their access to work.[155] The Special Restriction (Coloured Alien Seamen) Order 1925 was, according to Kathleen Paul, 'ostensibly intended to prevent alien seamen from falsely claiming British nationality and thus rights of residence' in Britain.[156] Under the Order, '"coloured" seamen' who could not prove that they were British subjects were required to register as aliens. Paul has argued that '[t]he law was intentionally burdensome since, as the Home Office knew full well, the vast majority of black British seamen had no "proper" documentation and thus, by presumption became aliens, lost all privileges of citizenship, and became subject to deportation'.[157] The category of alien, despite seemingly existing in opposition to that of subject, nevertheless operated to disenfranchise racialised subjects on the British mainland as well as in overseas colonies. The

1925 Order was thus an example of British subjects being treated as aliens for legal purposes in the interests of the maintenance of white British supremacy, demonstrative of the fragility of the distinction between subject and alien. Its effect was to lead to the harassment of 'all "coloured seamen", "aliens and British subjects mixed", and to prevent as many as possible from settling' in Britain.[158]

The emergence of a protection regime for European refugees

The displacement of people following the First World War led to the emergence of new institutional contexts for the categorisation and management of people.[159] In the 1920s a number of European countries conducted bilateral negotiations in an attempt to arrange for the transfer of European refugees to other territories. These tended to fail on account of the refugees' lack of documents, which in the inter-state system were required to ensure admission and settlement on any territory.[160] As a result, states moved to deal with the presence of displaced persons through international cooperation. The largely voluntary organisations that had been assisting refugees found themselves overwhelmed at the end of the First World War.[161] According to one estimate, there were 9.5 million displaced people in Europe in the mid-1920s.[162] The mode of definition of a refugee first adopted at the international level was a collective one, with refugees recognised on the basis of group identity.[163]

By the 1930s European countries were becoming increasingly reluctant to fund relief efforts and receive European refugees, many of whom were Jews fleeing Nazi German rule and expansion. Calls were made for a comprehensive legal agreement for the protection of refugees and for creating an international refugee status.[164] The Convention Relating to the International Status of Refugees was agreed in 1933. With regard to the groups of European refugees protected under preceding Inter-Governmental Arrangements (of 1922, 1924, 1926 and 1928), the preamble to the Convention stipulated that 'refugees shall be ensured the enjoyment of civil rights, free and ready access to the courts, security and stability as regards establishment and work, facilities in the exercise of the professions of industry and commerce, and in regard to the movement of persons, admission to schools and universities'.[165]

This was the first time that European governments had collectively agreed to guarantee a number of socio-economic and civil and political rights to refugees. However, the legal arrangements were generally ineffective and failed to protect people fleeing persecution. They were neither universally accepted nor applied. The more legal obligations that were included in the agreements, the fewer ratifications followed. Fifty-six states had accepted the Arrangement with Regard to the Issue of Certificates of Identity to Russian Refugees of 5 July 1922, but a mere eight ratified the far more comprehensive 1933 Convention, and only three ratified the Convention Concerning the Status of Refugees Coming from Germany of 10 February 1938. The arrangements failed to ensure protection for refugees seeking to escape from Hitler's Germany.[166]

Welfare as entitlement to colonial spoils

The British welfare state has always embodied the assertion of white entitlement to the spoils of colonial conquest. The 1942 Beveridge Report perhaps captured this spirit best when it declared that 'housewives as Mothers have vital work to do in ensuring the adequate continuance of the

British Race and British ideals in the world'. Britain has
always been an internally bordered, hostile environment
for migrants, with access to welfare made contingent on
legal status. In 1908 the Liberal government introduced the
Old Age Pensions Act, and in 1911, the National Insurance
Act. State intervention through the provision of financial
assistance in general remained limited. The 1908 Act fixed
the pensionable age at 70 even though at the time of its
introduction the life expectancy for men was 48 years.[167]
The Act required all state pension beneficiaries to be British
subjects and to have been resident in Britain for twenty
years, a figure reduced to twelve in 1919. During debate on
the Pensions Bill, Arthur Fell MP stated, '[i]t might be that
crowds of foreigners of the age of forty-five or fifty might
come over here in the hope that, having resided in this
country for the required time, they might get a pension'.[168]
Those fleeing persecution were also excluded from the Act's
provisions.[169] Meanwhile the National Insurance Act 1911,
which covered healthcare and unemployment, attached eligibility for benefits to nationality and residence status.[170]
Steve Cohen has observed that

> legislation in the two decades following the Aliens Act 1905
> based welfare entitlements on immigration, residency or
> nationality status. This set the pattern for the rest of the
> 20th century and beyond, ensuring that British welfare and
> the British welfare state, far from being universalistic, are
> exclusive, narrow and nationalistic.[171]

Although people categorised as aliens residing in Britain
were eventually granted access to health insurance under
the National Health Insurance Act 1918, this was aimed
at reducing the administrative burden entailed in enforcing the discriminatory measures contained in the original
legislation. As Cohen notes, this legislative change 'was

not because of any principled revulsion against linking welfare with immigration status, rather it was because it was practically difficult to enforce such discrimination'.[172] Sir E. Cornwall, the minister who introduced the 1918 Act, stated,

> I dare say some people will be rather alarmed at our proposals that [aliens] should receive ordinary benefits but I can assure the House that it is not from any love of aliens. It is simply a business proposition. We find the arrangements in the original Act very complicated and it costs a great deal more than if we gave them ordinary benefits.[173]

As welfare began to be considered a more significant task for the government, the institutional context for its provision evolved. Rather than welfare provision being left to the 'friendly societies' of the early 1900s, there was increased centralisation in its administration.[174] This enabled a greater degree of ministerial discretion in the process, allowing immigration status to be given greater prominence in determining access to welfare. Whereas the 1911 National Insurance Act had not discriminated against migrants in terms of unemployment benefits, under the Unemployment Insurance, No. 2 Act 1921, the Minister of Labour could decide whether to extend unemployment benefits from 16 to 22 weeks.[175] In 1922 the Minister of Labour declared that 'benefit beyond 16 weeks should not be granted to aliens – other than British born wives or widows of aliens'.[176]

While lawmakers were working hard to write 'aliens' out of the emerging British welfare state, British rulers were raising revenue through exploitation and extraction in colonised countries.[177] The British had long been levying taxes on colonised subjects as a means of swelling government coffers. This was achieved through a tactic of British colonial administrations, which forged alliances with elites in colonised countries and used them 'to collect taxes and maintain political order'.[178] Revenues raised were used by Britain to pay for imports from colonised countries.[179] Thus racialised subjects were being forced to fund the British welfare state for white Britons. In time, colonised populations, on seeking access to Britain, would be constructed as burdens and a drain on public funds.

The following chapter shows how Britain's colonial exploits and fluctuating colonial ambitions meant that racialised subjects would not only be the primary objects of the law's violence in the colonies, but also in the metropole as they became the principal targets of immigration control. Although the 1905 Aliens Act was not written with racialised British subjects in mind, it nevertheless served as the legislative precursor for the control of their movements. The Aliens Act was in many ways a product of British colonialism, its legislative provisions lifted from the immigration laws of the colonies. British lawmakers did not forget its mechanisms when it came to the task of drafting future immigration legislation. Nor did they forget another important lesson learned from colonies keen to deflect racialised subjects: the art of writing race-neutral terms into legislation which would nevertheless produce racialised effects.

Chapter 3

Subjects and citizens: cordoning off colonial spoils

The historical account that follows is essential background to understanding how immigration law works not only to manage the movement of former colonial subjects, but also to ensure the maintenance of the racial project of a white Britain. British subjecthood and other legal statuses which have superseded it are products of Britain's colonial machinations and operate to legitimise its ongoing claim to white entitlement to wealth accumulated through colonial dispossession. The bestowal or extension of British subjecthood is necessarily a colonial act, one that is reproductive of a racial order. The 1948 British Nationality Act rolled out the colonial status of Citizenship of the United Kingdom and Colonies, which included a right of entry to Britain. The Act was a bid to hold together what remained of the British Empire and the Commonwealth. The principal reason for Britain's wide casting of the nationality net was the maintenance of white British supremacy through its migratory, political and economic relationship with the white settler colonies. An effect of the 1948 Act was to facilitate the arrival of racialised colony and Commonwealth citizens in Britain.

In the course of the 1960s, 1970s and 1980s, as the British Empire faced successive defeats, Britain transitioned from

[margin annotations: RACISM AS A PROJECT; LAW TO REINFORCE COLONIALISM]

TO ONLY WHITE PEOPLE IN BRITAIN?

OTHERING

RELATIONSHIP TO THE LAND; KIND OF SHIFTING ON AG, "PROPGERY" MAYX

empire to nation-state, effectively constituting itself as white. The imperial myth of unity and equality was jettisoned and the entitlement of racialised colony and Commonwealth citizens to enter and remain in Britain was ended. Through the concept of patriality the 1971 Immigration Act made whiteness intrinsic to British identity. Under the Act, only patrials, those born in Britain or with a parent born in Britain, had a right of abode, and therefore a right of entry and stay in Britain.[1] The concept allowed for the continued accommodation of white Commonwealth citizens' claims to Britishness, while the majority of racialised subjects and citizens were excluded. The 1981 British Nationality Act effectively announced Britain as post-colonial by drawing a geographical boundary around Britain as distinct from its colonies and the Commonwealth. This legislation, together with immigration laws targeted at racialised colony and Commonwealth citizens, was an act of colonial theft that remains unredressed. The spoils of colonialism are located within the borders of Britain and manifest in the form of infrastructure, health, wealth, security, opportunity and futures. Such losses as a result of colonialism can be more difficult to discern due to traditional understandings of property as being fixed and immobile.[2]

Immigration laws work to construct racialised people as not entitled to access vital resources. People without a legal right to enter Britain must make dangerous, often fatal, journeys.[3] Those inside Britain are denied access to crucial services as a result of internal borders implemented through policies such as the hostile environment.[4] Britain thus remains a colonial power, a place in which racialised people are disproportionately prevented from accessing colonially derived wealth and at risk of abuse, incarceration, deportation and death. In the course of tracing the making of immigration and nationality laws between 1948 and 1981, I discuss the 2018 Windrush scandal to illustrate how strategies for racial justice and migrant solidarity that rest on recognition of legal status by the British government serve to reinforce mythological narratives of the British Empire as a project of global strength and inclusivity and leave unchallenged law as the structure that underpins racial violence.

British nationality in the age of empire: casting the net wide

[G]ive me that map, blindfold me, spin me round three times and I, dizzy and dazed, would still place my finger squarely on the Mother Country.[5]

At a time when Britain was an established empire, the British Nationality and Status of Aliens Act 1914 set out a broad definition of who was to be considered a British subject. This definition existed in order to maximise the reach of British colonial rule. Under the 1914 Act British subjecthood flowed from allegiance to the Crown.[6] Subjecthood was acquired by birth within the Commonwealth, or by descent within one generation in the legitimate male line.[7] Although allegiance to the Crown determined subject status, the Act allowed for differential treatment of subjects by British dominions. According to the Act, colonial authorities were not precluded 'from treating differently different classes of British subjects'.[8] A 'natural-born British subject' encompassed any person 'born within His Majesty's dominions and allegiance' and anyone whose father was, at the time of birth, a British subject.[9] Persons born on board a British ship, the primary enabling tool of colonial conquest, whether in foreign territorial waters or not, were to be considered British subjects.[10] The 1914 Act, which replaced the Naturalisation Act 1870, required a prospective 'alien' applicant for nationality to have lived in Britain for at least one year immediately prior to making the application, and four years in total, either in Britain or in another part of the Empire.[11] Further requirements included good character, command of the English language and an intention to continue to reside in a dominion or to serve the Crown.[12] The cost of applying for nationality at five pounds per person, the equivalent of about £300 today, was prohibitively expensive, and once an application was made it often took years to process.[13]

Thus, despite the expansive reach of British subjecthood, the rights that came along with it were contingent on racialisation and gender, and naturalisation was at the 'absolute discretion' of the Home Secretary.[14] The Home Secretary could, 'with or without assigning any reason, give or withhold the certificate [of naturalisation] as he thinks most conducive to the public good, and no appeal shall lie from his decision'.[15] Although Britain did not formally pass anti-miscegenation laws, it sought to deter interracial marriages through nationality law. The 1914 Act stipulated that 'the wife of an alien shall be deemed to be an alien'.[16] Thus when British subject women married 'aliens' and acquired the nationality of their husbands, they would lose their British subject status.[17] In 1923 a report from the Select Committee on the Nationality of Married Women offered an anti-miscegenation rationale for retaining this rule: 'the loss of nationality was the only argument which the Foreign Office as a rule found to prevail with British women in such cases in deterring them'. To change this law would 'encourage mixed marriages of this particular kind, which are in the women's case nearly always most undesirable'.[18] Here we can see both the fragility of British subject

Handwritten margin notes: "GOOD CHARACTER WTF?" and "RELIGION "MISSING" FROM THIS LIST"

status in colonial contexts as well as how nationality law is deployed in the service of white British supremacy.

The British Nationality Act 1948

Mother thinks of you as her children.[19]

In the years between 1948 and 1981 the rights of British subjects expanded and retracted drastically. Over the course of this period legal statuses associated with the British Empire proliferated, their content and meaning shifting according to British colonial ambitions. The 1948 British Nationality Act passed by Clement Attlee's Labour government created the status of Citizenship of the United Kingdom and Colonies, of 'the United Kingdom and non-Independent countries', and 'of independent Commonwealth countries'. The Act therefore covered Britons together with all nationals of independent Commonwealth countries and those of British colonies. On 1 January 1949 a total of 48 territories, including the British mainland, were included in the description 'United Kingdom and Colonies'.[20] The statuses set out in the Act included 'an unqualified right to enter and remain in the United Kingdom'.[21] However, as Anderson has observed, the 1948 British Nationality Act is not to be regarded as part of immigration policy, but rather as 'a nationality policy with immigration consequences'.[22]

The Act was passed in response to Canada's introduction of the Canadian Citizenship Act 1946, which set out a definition of Canadian citizenship, stipulating that British subjecthood derived from it. Changes to Canadian nationality law were part of the settler colony's attempt to federate as a white nation, a process that continues to entail the destruction and dispossession of First Nations people.[23]

The British government's concern was that the effect of the
Canadian legislation was to have 'completely shattered', in
the words of the Labour Lord Chancellor, Sir William Jowitt,
the relationship between the Crown and British subjects
in Canada.[24] It was to be mediated through a concept of
Canadian citizenship rather than stemming from a direct
relationship between subjects and the king.[25] Pursuant to the
1946 Act, subject status could only be attained via Canadian
citizenship. British subjecthood was thus demoted. Those
with Canadian citizenship were to be entitled to British subject status.[26] The British government was faced with what
it saw as an unacceptable erosion of its status as arch-sov-
ereign with respect to Commonwealth nations. At the time
the Old Dominions were 'central to British foreign and economic policy, and the British political elite viewed them
with great affection'.[27] Introducing the Bill in the House of
Lords, Jowitt stated that, 'of all the remarkable contributions
which our race has made to the art of government, the conception of our Empire and Commonwealth is the greatest'.[28]

Alarmed by Australia's expressed intention to introduce legislation similar to that of Canada, and fearing that
South Africa would follow suit, the British government
concluded that unless British nationality and the principle of allegiance underlying subjecthood was restated anew,
there was a risk that the Old Dominions would abandon
their (subordinate) association with Britain and opt for an
entirely distinct national identity.[29] The 1948 Act's renewed
articulation of British subjecthood was, ironically, modelled on the Canadian legislation in making British subject status dependent on the status of Citizenship of the
United Kingdom and Colonies, rather than by evoking an
unbroken link between king and subject.[30] By creating a
further category of 'British subjects without citizenship' in

LOSS OF CONTROL

FREEDOM VS. LIBERTY

the 1948 Act, legislators demonstrated that the position of white British settlers was of the utmost importance. This was a category intended to ensure that white British settlers would retain British subject status in the event of changes to local citizenship laws in post-independence contexts that might leave them without the status of United Kingdom and Colonies citizenship or independent Commonwealth citizenship.[31]

PROBS PROTESTANT OR CHRISTIAN

The principal beneficiaries of the British Empire's system of subjecthood were white Britons, who could move and settle throughout the Commonwealth. Colonial settlement was sponsored and facilitated through agreements with Australia, South Africa, New Zealand and Canada.[32] The Old Dominions were considered 'Britain abroad', known 'in the jingoistic heyday of imperialism' as '"greater Britain"'.[33] Settlement of white Britons in Commonwealth countries (euphemistically termed emigration) worked in favour of the Dominion governments' immigration policies, which were seeking to cement whiteness as the basis of their nationhood. For Britain, the presence of white Britons in the Dominions was considered to 'orient their populations' sentiment and their leaders' policy' towards the further-ance of its interests.[34] The 1948 Act was intended to but-tress Britain's global identity as a colonial power and as 'first among equals' in the Commonwealth.[35] Equal rights to enter Britain for all British subjects was accepted in principle insofar as this was deemed necessary to main-tain the Empire. Introducing the 1948 Bill in the House of Commons, the Home Secretary, Chuter Ede, stated that '[t]he maintenance of the British Commonwealth of Nations ... is one of the duties that this generation owes to the world and to generations to come'.[36] He considered that 'the common citizenship of the United Kingdom and Colonies

JUST SEEING WHITENESS...?

is an essential part of the development of the relationship between this Mother Country and the Colonies'.[37]

That racialised colony and Commonwealth citizens would travel to and live in Britain was not contemplated in Parliament, though their theoretical right to do so was mentioned occasionally.[38] This omission, perhaps in part, allowed Jowitt to characterise the 'conception of the British Empire and Commonwealth' as being in the service of 'perfect freedom'.[39] He considered the Bill to be uncontroversial and went so far as to describe the principal advantage of the common status introduced as being 'mystical'. 'The conception of an all-pervading status or nationality is not primarily, not mainly, important because of its material advantage', he declared, '[i]t is, if you like, rather mystical. But none of us, I suggest, is any the worse for a little mysticism in our life. It is the mark of something which differentiates family from mere friends.'[40] The Act's introduction of the status of Citizenship of the United Kingdom and Colonies thus had nothing to do with encouraging or facilitating the immigration to Britain of racialised subjects. Lawmakers instead thought to be a magic trick of sorts, a legal sleight of hand that would conjure a British imperial polity anew and persuade the rest of the world that all was well in the British Empire. Indeed, fast forward to 1968, the year that saw the introduction of immigration controls targeted at racialised Commonwealth and colony citizens, and parliamentarians with living memory of the passing of the 1948 Act found themselves reflecting on their lack of foresight. Quintin Hogg, Shadow Home Secretary at the time, in the course of the House of Commons debate on the 1968 Commonwealth Immigrants Bill, reminisced about the state of mind he shared with former Prime Minister Clement Attlee, stating that 'neither he nor I had the smallest conception in 1948 of what we now call the immigration problem. How could we? We thought that there would be free trade in citizens, that people would come and go.'[41]

Despite legislators' lack of foresight, the 1948 Act's provisions facilitated the arrival of around 500,000 racialised people from British colonies and the Commonwealth between 1948 and 1962. These people were exercising their right to enter, work and reside in Britain under the 1948 Act. They included the 492 West Indians who boarded the *Empire Windrush*, a formerly German-owned ship seized as a war trophy by the British, following the operating company's advertisement of cheap tickets to fill places on its return from Australia to Britain.[42] They were not the first racialised British subjects to travel to Britain. In 1947, 108 people arrived on the *Ormonde*. Racialised subjects had been present in Britain for centuries, with the population standing at 20,000–30,000 in the late 1940s. However, following the passing of the British Nationality Act, colony and Commonwealth citizens increasingly travelled to Britain.

The headline of the *Evening Standard* on Monday 21 June 1948 read: 'WELCOME HOME! Evening Standard plane greets the 400 sons of Empire'. Despite the somewhat jovial tone of the article ('The airplane circled for 15 minutes, and gradually apprehension turned to joy as the passengers realised they were receiving their first welcome to England'),[43] the headline's infantilising portrayal of racialised British subjects as children arriving in the motherland betrayed the racist and possessive regard in which these subjects were held in the British psyche. The British authorities reluctantly permitted the *Windrush* passengers to disembark. One passenger, Sam King, who had served in the RAF in England during the Second World War, reportedly asked two ex-RAF wireless operators to

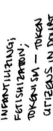

THIS SEEMS LIKE A BIG THING TO FORGET

INFANTILIZING; FETISHIZATION; TOKENISM - TOKEN CITIZENS IN DOUBT play dominoes innocently outside the ship's radio room and eavesdrop on incoming signals. They heard on the BBC that Arthur Creech Jones, then Colonial Secretary, had pointed out that: 'These people have British passports and they must be allowed to land.' He added that they would not last one winter in England anyway, so there was nothing to worry about.[44]

(handwritten margin note: HOW DO WE REVERSE THIS ON TO THE DESERT FROM SATIA? ALSO MYSTICISM QUOTE)

The assumption that people travelling to Britain from the colonies and Commonwealth were unsuited to a colder climate, or 'race-based environmental essentialism', was, as Ikuko Asaka has shown, at the heart of attempts across the British Empire to curtail the movement of colonial populations.[45] 'Tropicality' was thus a geographic concept which served as a 'transnationally operative tool of empire'.[46]

Contrary to popular mythological narratives, the *Windrush* arrivals did not receive a warm welcome.[47] This is reflected not only in government action and parliamentary debates, but also in public opinion polls,[48] and the racist street attacks faced by racialised subjects.[49] As the *Empire Windrush* was on its approach to Britain, Creech Jones issued a memorandum in which he stated that '[i]t will be appreciated that the men concerned are all British subjects. The government of Jamaica has no legal power to prevent their departure from Jamaica and the Government of the United Kingdom has no legal power to prevent their landing.' He insisted that its impending arrival 'was certainly not organised or encouraged by the Colonial Office or the Jamaican Government. On the contrary, every possible step has been taken ... to discourage these influxes.' He went on to say that however desirable legislation preventing the outward movement of Jamaicans might be, 'Jamaica has reached such an advanced stage on the road to self-government that it would be impossible to compel them to legislate in this sense by directions from London'.[50] The *Windrush* arrivals had taken the British government by surprise. The Colonial Office was so troubled by their arrival and the prospect of further such movements that it contemplated finding work for them in other parts of the empire, including British Guinea and British Honduras. Creech Jones even expressed the desire to send them to Africa, but for the 'psychological difficulties'[51] entailed in this prospect, presumably a clumsy reference to the slave origins of the Jamaicans now bound for Britain. Despite the racist hostility shown towards the arrivals, the introduction of controls was nevertheless initially resisted. There was a concern in some government quarters that the introduction of openly racist controls distinguishing between white and racialised subjects' rights to travel to Britain would jeopardise the stability of the Commonwealth as a whole.[52]

Despite Creech Jones's description of the movement of Jamaicans as a 'spontaneous [one] by [those] who have saved up enough money to pay for their passage to England',[53] their movement was entirely predictable when placed in the context of the economic and social conditions prevalent in colonial Jamaica. The *Empire Windrush* arrivals and those who followed were not only exercising rights granted to them under the 1948 Act, but were also escaping economic hardship and an absence of employment opportunities, along with other dispossessive effects of slavery and colonialism.[54] Jamaica was profoundly marked by both the transatlantic slave trade and colonialism. By the time the British colonised Jamaica in the seventeenth century, the country's 'indigenous peoples had already been wiped out by the Spanish, and [it] was populated mainly by enslaved Africans and white settlers'.[55] While the majority of those who travelled to Britain came unaided, some arrived on the basis of work schemes arranged by British employers, such as London Transport and the National Health Service, which saw the potential for migration to ameliorate post-war labour shortages. Although some recruitment schemes were targeted at racialised colony and Commonwealth citizens, the government did not encourage them.[56]

Post-war labour shortages were primarily addressed through the facilitation of white European and other white labour.[57] As Gurminder Bhambra writes:

> In the five years after the end of the second world war, close on 100,000 Eastern European refugee workers from displaced persons camps in Italy, Germany and Austria were recruited directly to work in Britain. Those who passed the medical examination, 'were transported to Britain and allocated three years' state-directed employment, accommodation, social welfare and education. They were then permitted to naturalise' (incidentally, European Jews were explicitly prohibited from the scheme). In addition, approximately 128,000 people of Polish origin (specifically, Polish armed forces in exile in Britain, along with their dependants) settled permanently in Britain under the terms of the Polish Resettlement Act, 1947.[58]

When governors in the West Indian colonies encouraged West Indian migration following the Colonial Office's call for migrant labour, British mainland government officials warned them that controls on black British subjects might be introduced.[59] The British government worked hurriedly to fill labour shortages in multiple sectors ranging from agriculture and mining to textiles, construction work and health by arranging for the arrival of 180,000 prisoners of war from the United States and Canada.[60] Women were also encouraged to take up employment. In October 1947 the government put in place a Control of Engagement Order, requiring people seeking work to apply through the Ministry of Labour, which could compel the unemployed to take up certain jobs. The British government introduced a labour voucher scheme, which the Home Secretary Rab Butler promoted for its race-neutral terms and racist effects. He stated that '[t]he great merit' of the labour voucher scheme 'is that it can be presented as making no distinction on grounds of race and colour'. While the scheme 'purports to relate solely to employment and to be non-discriminatory, its aim is primarily social and its restrictive effect is intended to and would operate on coloured people almost exclusively'.[61]

Civilian British subjects fell outside the jurisdiction of the Colonial Office, so their movement could not be controlled, as was the case with prior migration of military recruits.[62] A committee of ministers was established in 1950 to explore the means that might be adopted to limit migration to the British mainland of racialised colony and Commonwealth citizens.[63] Reporting to the committee were representatives from the Home Office, Labour and Housing ministries, who tended to be in favour of control. However, the committee, initially led by the Lord Chancellor and the Home Secretary, was influenced by its Colonial Office representatives, who cautioned against control.[64] In 1951 the committee recommended against introducing controls, stating that Britain 'has a special status as the mother country, and freedom to enter and remain in the United Kingdom at will is one of the main practical benefits enjoyed by British subjects'.[65] The committee considered that it was Britain's responsibility to preserve the content of British subject status, which was deemed 'the central issue at stake in controlling immigration'.[66] It reasoned that 'it would be difficult to justify restrictions on persons who are citizens of the United Kingdom and Colonies, if no comparable restrictions were imposed on persons who are citizens of other Commonwealth countries'.[67] Ultimately the committee decided to accept immigration of racialised colony and Commonwealth citizens because it did not want to limit entry rights of white subjects from the Old Dominions and thereby jeopardise the project of global white British supremacy.

The Colonial Office opted instead to instigate informal practices designed to make immigration of racialised people difficult. Prospective arrivals were cautioned about the challenges they would face in Britain in finding adequate housing and employment. The Commonwealth Office worked tirelessly to reach agreements with Asian Dominions to limit the number of people travelling to Britain.[68] Passports were withheld from who did not have the financial resources to make the journey or were deemed unsuited to work. Further, in September 1949 the Home Office instructed immigration officers not to give permission to land to people without evidence of British subjecthood or British Protected Person status.[69] The government also sought to limit the number of passports issued to racialised colony and Commonwealth citizens. Populations in the West Indies strongly resisted passport controls and lobbied their governments for relaxation.[70] Domestic resistance to such controls in India led the Indian Supreme Court to hold that it was illegal to withhold passports from Indian citizens.[71] In 1959 the Ministry of Labour projected negative trends in economic growth and unemployment due to the migration of workers from the Irish Republic (estimated at 60,000 per year). In spite of this, controls on Irish immigration to Britain were not contemplated.[72] Instead, the Ministry of Labour argued that 'there must be a limit to the extent to which the economy can go on absorbing unskilled labour' and insisted that administrative checks on West Indians as well as people from India and Pakistan remain vigilant.[73]

The pitfalls of reifying citizenship: an empire of unequals

Here we come up against the use of the word 'British' and the unfortunate ambiguity which attaches to that word.[74]

The question of whether post-1948 arrivals were British citizens and whether the imperial status rolled out by the 1948 Act could be considered equivalent to British citizenship as we understand it today came to the fore in 2018 with the breaking of the Windrush scandal.[75] The argument that the Windrush generation were British citizens and thus should be recognised as such by the British government raises important legal, ethical and strategic questions in a context in which changes to British immigration law and policy have had the effect of disproportionately stripping racialised people of their rights.[76] While insisting on the immediate reinstatement of legal entitlements denied to the Windrush generation is crucial, it is important not to elide the colonial context in which the 1948 Act was introduced. Although the Act facilitated the arrival in Britain of racialised colony and Commonwealth citizens, the status of Citizenship of the United Kingdom and Colonies could only emerge in a context in which Britain had an empire, founded on white supremacist ideals, and retained colonial ambitions.

Hansen, Anderson and Bhambra have each made the point that referring to people who arrived in Britain from colonies and Commonwealth countries following the 1948 British Nationality Act as 'migrants' is legally inaccurate because they were 'British citizens' according to the law.[77] This argument is premised on the assumption that Citizenship of the United Kingdom and Colonies, or British subject-hood, is equivalent to British citizenship. Yet British citizenship was not introduced as a discrete legal status until 1981. Indeed, in explaining the status rolled out by the 1948 Act in the House of Lords, the Lord Chancellor emphasised that 'the citizenship which for the first time we prescribe is not "citizenship of the United Kingdom," but citizenship "of the United Kingdom and Colonies." That is the species.'[78] It is clear that the catch-all status was not 'British citizenship' in its contemporary iteration. Lord Altrincham, calling the new status 'a sham' in view of racially discriminatory immigration laws in place in the Dominions, proposed in its place a more geographically limited concept of British citizenship, one that would be more akin to its contemporary form:

> Clearly, there must be established a United Kingdom citizenship. That I fully accept. But why should that not be called simply 'British citizenship'? That name covers, by ancient tradition, the peoples of England, Scotland, Wales and a large part of Northern Ireland. It is also a modern reality, for it denotes a great geographical, social and historic union which has made an exceptional mark on the history of the world.[79]

No such conception of British citizenship would emerge until 1981. How could it when Britain retained such fervent colonial ambitions? Indeed, the articulation of Citizenship of the United Kingdom and Colonies was done with the purpose of making clear the expansive geographical and jurisdictional reach of the British Empire. Chuter Ede thus stated that

> there has grown up a tendency to regard the term 'British subject' as meaning a person belonging to Great Britain, and to obscure its true meaning of a person belonging to any

country of the Commonwealth who is a subject of the King. We think it highly desirable that a definition should be discovered which will make it quite clear that that is a term which applies to every person in the British Commonwealth and Empire who owes allegiance to the King.[80]

Further, not all colony and Commonwealth citizens entering post-1948 were citizens of the United Kingdom and Colonies. They had varying legal statuses that permitted residence in Britain, ranging from British subjects to Commonwealth citizens.[81] Until the 1981 Act's creation of British citizenship, there were citizens of the United Kingdom and Colonies, British subjects without citizenship, and citizens of Commonwealth countries, known collectively as Commonwealth citizens.[82] Under the 1948 Act people could register as citizens of the United Kingdom and Colonies after twelve months' residence in Britain, but this was not automatic, and not all post-1948 arrivals in Britain chose to do this. Once colonies won independence, their citizens, including those residing in Britain, lost their status as citizens of the United Kingdom and Colonies and became Commonwealth citizens. Commonwealth citizens could still travel to Britain until changes to immigration laws introduced in the 1960s and 1970s, but had to register as citizens of the United Kingdom and Colonies once eligible to do so in order to attain this legal status.

The possibility of registering as a citizen of the United Kingdom and Colonies was ended with the 1981 British Nationality Act, which articulated for the first time a concept of British citizenship tied to a territorially defined Britain as distinct from its colonies and the Commonwealth. The 1981 Act, discussed below, was thus the final tool of alienation for all racialised British subjects associated with the British colonial project who had not already qualified for entry and settlement in Britain, and, as the Windrush scandal demonstrates, also for many of those long-settled, but who did not become citizens under the new regime. It is therefore legally inaccurate to argue that colony and Commonwealth citizens arriving in Britain following the 1948 Act were 'British citizens'. Indeed, there was such consternation in Parliament at the use of the word 'citizen' because of its 'republican flavour' and 'derogatory revolutionary' connotation, that Ede had to offer reassurances that the use of the term 'citizen' was merely a 'gateway' to British subjecthood.[83]

Even if Citizenship of the United Kingdom and Colonies was accepted as a citizenship of sorts, it is difficult to regard it as in any way equivalent to the status of British citizenship as articulated in the 1981 British Nationality Act. The fact that the 1948 Act's articulation of citizenship distinguished in name between the *United Kingdom* and *Colonies* demonstrates that legislators did not attribute the same meaning to these places and their citizens, regardless of the rhetoric of imperial unity and equality. Indeed, Ede spoke of the intention of finding a term to describe British subjects in another manner, because to Pakistan and Ceylon, then newly independent Commonwealth nations, 'the word "subject" unfortunately has the significance of being a member of a subject race'.[84] While denying that the government saw them thus, Ede's language demonstrated otherwise. He spoke patronisingly of these nations as having been 'trained' by Britain 'so that they are able to participate in this great self-governing group of nations', and accepted that 'we cannot admit all these backward peoples immediately into the full rights that British subjects in this country enjoy'.[85] Citizenship of the United Kingdom and Colonies was thus little more than a euphemism for British subjecthood.

It is also important to recall that not only did British sub-jecthood assume various forms that carried highly divergent material effects, but that a meaningful distinction between subject and citizen was contemplated by some legal minds at the time of the British Empire. As Renisa Mawani writes, S. L. Polak, a notable lawyer and honorary secretary of the Indians Overseas Association in South Africa, considered that

> the inhabitants of the empire were sharply divided into two classes, 'British citizens' and 'British subjects.' The latter ... were believed to be 'subordinate to the former [...]. "British citizens," merely by their being self-governing, in the political sense [...] are fitted to control the destinies of the subordinate class of "British subjects."' Indeed, 'it is their "supreme duty" to do [so], until the latter have achieved the sublime heights of self-government already gained by the more fortunate and superior – in fact, the Imperial – class.'[86]

The distinction between subject and citizen was thus a 'foundational dividing line in British colonial and impe-rial governance, a method of categorisation configured just as much by race as geography and territoriality'.[87] Indeed, Jowitt emphasised in the House of Lords that 'common nationality does not necessarily confer rights in other [Commonwealth] member States'. Citing Australia as an example, he made clear that the rolling out of the status of Citizenship of the United Kingdom and Colonies would not affect Australia's 'whites only' immigration policy, stating that Australia 'is perfectly entitled to legislate for herself as to whom she shall admit into her territory as settlers. She may insist upon certain qualifications with regard to char-acter, intelligence, creed or colour.'[88] Even the 'not incon-siderable advantages' attached to British subject status in comparison with alien status, which Jowitt could identify, he acknowledged as contingent:

> The British subject is free from those disabilities and restrictions which apply to aliens. He is entitled to enter or leave the country at any time, he qualifies for the franchise, he can become a member of the Privy Council or of Parliament, and, save in war-time, under certain limitations, he can become a member of the Civil Service, and he can own a British ship. As I say, there are various material advantages. It is for each particular territory, each particular country, to decide for itself, from time to time, what privileges are to be allowed and to what extent they are to be conditioned with regard to British subjects or anyone else.[89]

The 1948 Act was also configured according to gender. It amended the law so that 'alien' women who married a British subject would no longer automatically become British subjects.[90] The rationale behind this was set out by Jowitt, who told the Lords,

> previously, an alien woman, on marrying a British subject, automatically became British. I know of cases in the courts of women of very undesirable character who came over here and, when they got to Dover, married somebody whom they would never see again. They did that with the sole object of precluding their deportation from this country.[91]

The intersection between racialisation and/or the absence of legal status and class thus worked to disproportionately and more severely affect women.

The difficulty in determining the content, meaning and applicability of the various colonial legal statuses in part stems from the broader difficulty of defining what Britain is in view of its imperial identity. At the heart of colonial ideology is the idea that there are people who are uncivilised and that they should be civilised, by force where necessary. Colonial dictum required that uncivilised cultures be stamped out and replaced with that of the coloniser. The idea that certain people and cultures were uncivilised thus provided the normative justification for colonial conquest and exploitation. Certain cultures were presented as having failed to progress according to Western understandings of linear time and thus required colonial intervention. This developmental rationale justified the fatal violence that underpinned the colonial civilisational project. In such a context, citizenship was to remain 'a privilege of the civilised; the uncivilised would be subject to an all-round tutelage'.[92] Colonised peoples were violently forced into the category of British subject. As Mawani has written, '[t]he inauguration and imposition of British law in colonial contexts, no matter how negotiated or translated, was always already an act of racial and colonial violence'.[93]

Recognition-based arguments for the inclusion of racialised people in the colonial project that is 'Britain' thus have the effect of reifying British citizenship and can inadvertently reproduce colonial logics that justify differential treatment on the basis of a supposed absence of civilisation. As I discuss in Chapter 4, regimes of legal status recognition, such as citizenship laws, operate according to a colonial civilisational logic. Determining whether an applicant meets the criteria for citizenship is a form of sorting the civilised from the uncivilised and has racialising outcomes. The discretionary 'good character' test is, for instance, increasingly used as a means of refusing applications to naturalise.[94] Further, following the public outcry at the treatment of the Windrush generation, the government refused to include in the numbers of those wrongfully expelled so-called 'foreign criminals'.[95] The exclusion of people deported following criminal conviction from restitution measures marks them as uncivilised, as unworthy of legal rights because they have not met the standards for inclusion set by the colonial state. This is an example of the way in which British subjecthood, even in its contemporary forms, remains a fragile status for racialised people, who can be cast out, or treated as 'aliens' for legal purposes, when this suits the objectives of the colonial state.

Britain's relationship with its colonies was one of domination and exploitation and maintained for the economic and political advantages that accrued to Britain. Despite euphemistic descriptions of the British Empire adopted by some scholars, such as 'global institution',[96] it was no multi-racial paradise. Crucially, as Mawani notes, the British Empire 'was never founded on a centralized, unified, or contiguous authority emerging in the metropole and extending outward'. Instead, 'imperial authorities produced an assortment of jurisdictional spaces that held unequal claims to sovereignty, legality and political autonomy'.[97] The 1948 Act cannot therefore be understood as a recognition of the full humanity and entitlement to equal rights of racialised colony and Commonwealth citizens. Indeed, each instance of bestowal or extension of British subjecthood in any legal form is a colonial act, one that is necessarily reproductive of a white supremacist racial order. The 1948 Act was an attempt to reinforce Britain's position at the helm of its empire in the face of nationalist moves in various parts of the Commonwealth. British politicians themselves acknowledged the lesser worth of any citizenship status accorded to racialised colony and Commonwealth citizens.[98] Any recognition by the British government of its colonial subjects that flowed from the 1948 Act was designed principally to bolster colonial relationships of domination.[99] As will become apparent, as the British government's imperial ambitions waned in the face of the Empire's defeat, it quickly discarded the imperial lie of unity and equality and introduced racially exclusive immigration controls.

The Commonwealth Immigrants Act 1962: alienating subjects

In 1962 the first legislative steps were taken towards controlling the immigration of racialised colony and Commonwealth citizens and thereby physically depriving them of access to wealth accumulated via colonial dispossession located on the British mainland. While colonialism continued to exist following legislative changes to immigration and nationality law over the 1960s, 1970s and 1980s, British subjects were treated as aliens for legal purposes in the time-honoured fashion of expedient colonial rule. In this way, the 1962 Act, along with those that followed, are instances of colonial violence. Although informal measures had been introduced following the 1948 British Nationality Act in order to curb the movement of racialised people, the Commonwealth Immigrants Act 1962 was the first of a series of formal measures.

By the time Parliament came to discuss the Commonwealth Immigrants Bill in 1961, officials had already begun to speak of citizens of the United Kingdom and Colonies as immigrants rather than British subjects. Whereas previous Home Secretaries had been at pains to emphasise that those to whom the status introduced by the 1948 Act applied were subjects, in 1961 the Conservative Home Secretary Rab Butler spoke to the House of Commons of his fear of 'virtually limitless immigration'.[100] Of particular concern were people travelling to Britain from 'the West Indies, India, Pakistan and Cyprus, and to a lesser extent, from Africa, from Aden and from Hong Kong'.[101]

Butler made sure to convey the government's 'gratitude' to countries such as India and Pakistan 'who [had] tried to help' control outward movement to Britain via the introduction of 'fairly stringent measures'.[102] However, in spite of such efforts, he considered that 'a rapidly increasing number of immigrants [were] managing to come here from all these countries'.[103] Despite the language of 'immigration', prior to the 1962 Act there remained a legal distinction between Commonwealth and 'alien' migration since the former was not subject to control. Butler, aware of this distinction, clumsily used both categories in his speech.[104] The speech was aimed at convincing parliamentarians that Commonwealth citizens, a phrase that he said was 'synonymous with British subjects',[105] should be treated as aliens for the purpose of immigration control.

The shift in the official mindset from an imperial to a national concept of Britain was beginning to take hold in the 1960s. In contrast to the way in which relations with the Commonwealth were presented as being of the utmost importance when considering questions of legal status in 1948, Butler's presentation of the rationale behind the 1962 Act betrayed a tension between imperial and national interests. On the one hand he warned of the 'strain' on relationships between 'immigrants and resident British subjects' and the negative impact this might have on 'Commonwealth relations'.[106] At the same time, he expressed concern about the difficulty of integrating larger numbers of 'immigrants' into 'our national life'.[107]

While retaining the status of Citizenship of the United Kingdom and Colonies, the 1962 Act allocated the right of British subjects to enter Britain according to how their passports were issued.[108] The fragility of British subjecthood was revealed once again with the 1962 Act's stipulation that certain subjects would be treated as aliens for the purpose of immigration control. Subjects exempt from control were the (majority-white) citizens born in Britain or Ireland, or who held a British or Irish passport issued by either one of these governments, rather than one issued by a dependency government.[109] Butler described the 'objective' behind the Act as being to 'except from control – and, therefore, to guarantee their continued unrestricted entry into their own country – persons who in common parlance belong to the United Kingdom'.[110] It is clear from the exemptions set out above that the government considered such persons to be white. Although the Act did not specify the exclusion of racialised persons, they formed the vast majority of those whose right of entry was removed by the Act.

The Act required all those in possession of a Commonwealth passport and seeking to travel to Britain to apply for a work voucher from the Ministry of Labour.[111] Even those in receipt of work vouchers could be refused entry for a number of reasons. This echoed in several respects legislation designed to control the entry of 'aliens', discussed in the previous chapter. Rights of entry were subject to a significant degree of discretion granted to the Home Secretary. Entry could be denied where a medical inspector determined an individual to have a mental illness or to be otherwise deemed undesirable for health reasons.[112] Those suspected of having been convicted of a criminal offence subject to extradition,[113] or being a risk to national security[114] could be refused entry. A Commonwealth citizen aged above 17 and convicted of an offence punishable by imprisonment could be deported on recommendation by any court.[115]

The 1962 Act followed decades of official neglect of racialised people who had arrived from colony and Commonwealth countries. Despite being aware of the housing, employment and other racism-related issues they faced, the government refused to ameliorate the situation. They were expected 'to go it alone'.[116] The Cabinet Committee on Commonwealth Immigration considered that providing housing and other support and advice services would encourage more racialised people to travel to Britain. It stated that,

> as long as immigration remained unrestricted, the use of public funds for that purpose could only serve as an added attraction to prospective immigrants and would frustrate the efforts we were encouraging Commonwealth and Colonial governments to make to reduce the rate of emigration from their territories to the United Kingdom.[117]

Meanwhile British government ministers argued that legislation outlawing racial discrimination in Britain would be 'unworkable and unenforceable'.[118]

While British legislators considered how to go about reducing the numbers of racialised people in Britain, they monitored developments taking place in the United States with respect to the civil rights movement.[119] Fears about similar uprisings in Britain led to increased support among politicians for the introduction of immigration controls. Butler was of the opinion that 'some form of control was unavoidable if there was not to be a colour problem in this country on a similar scale to that of the USA'.[120] The 1958 attacks by the far right on West Indian communities in Nottingham and Notting Hill were ideologically constructed in terms of immigration, which had become code for race.[121] This racist street violence was crucial in laying the ground for the institutionalised racism that followed in the form of the Commonwealth Immigrants Acts of 1962 and 1968.[122]

Official and media responses to the attacks rarely made

explicit reference to 'racism either as a feature of British society or as a specific determinant of the riots'.[123] Some politicians presented the attacks on West Indian communities as evidence of the need for immigration control.[124] The Conservative MP Norman Pannell stated that

> [t]he Nottingham fighting is a manifestation of the evil results of the present policy and I feel that unless some restriction is imposed we shall create the colour bar we all want to avoid. Unless we bar undesirable immigrants and put out of the country those who commit certain crimes we shall create prejudice against the immigrants, particularly the coloured immigrants.[125]

Cyril Osborne, Conservative MP, argued that if all Commonwealth and colony immigration was not banned for one year there would follow 'serious unemployment' and

> the trade unions will impose the rule 'last in, first out' and there will be trouble. It will be black against white. We are sowing the seeds of another 'Little Rock' and it is tragic. To bring the problem into this country with our eyes open is doing the gravest disservice to our grandchildren, who will curse us for our lack of courage. I regard the Nottingham incident as a red light to us all.[126]

The Labour MP George Rogers was reported as having informed a government minister that the government was responsible for the violence because it had not dealt with the 'racial problem'.[127] He considered the major issues to be crime and overcrowded housing, 'which is badly needed by white people'.[128] Thus, rather than understanding racial violence in the US and Britain as being the product of colonial ideology, British politicians considered racism to be the result of the presence of racialised people in majority-white societies. Similarly, rather than understanding anti-colonial uprisings in the colonies and on the British mainland as struggles for freedom from oppression, such resistance movements were dismissed by the British authorities as racial conflict, and 'regarded as being inevitable by virtue of being biologically determined'.[129] Robert Miles has argued that the imperial ideology that divided colonised populations into physically distinct and culturally inferior 'races' and was used to legitimise colonial expansion 'came to constitute part of the common sense of all classes in Britain'.[130]

Even rationales that drove opposition to immigration control rested on colonial ideology and mythology. Hugh Gaitskell, leader of the Labour Party between 1955 and 1963, had an imperial military family history.[131] He had been passionately opposed to the introduction of the 1962 Commonwealth Immigrants Act, believing in the idea that a peaceful world was dependent on Britain retaining its status as a global power at the centre of a multi-racial Commonwealth system. Gaitskell feared a situation that would see Britain 'reduced to playing the role of a regional power', and thus firmly resisted any prospect of European Economic Community membership.[132] Some Conservative MPs, such as Robin Turton, also heavily opposed to European integration, tactically opposed the removal of entry rights for racialised colony and Commonwealth citizens, viewing this legislative move as the first step towards transforming Britain into 'a more European oriented nation'.[133] In the course of debate in the Commons on the 1961 Bill, one Labour MP interjected in protest, '[r]oll in the Common Market and our own people out'.[134]

The Conservative government's Commonwealth Immigrants Act 1962 was eventually passed. As mentioned above, it contained favourable conditions for white

Commonwealth migrants and exempted the Irish from control. The Act did not affect the Common Travel Area between Ireland and Britain.[135] However, the government secured the support of party backbenchers who had been opposed to the legislation in part by accepting that Irish citizens seeking to enter Britain from anywhere other than Ireland would be subject to control. The government considered that in reality Irish citizens would be granted entry by immigration officers who would assume that that they were travelling back to Britain after a holiday abroad or transiting to Ireland.[136] To understand how racism operated in the 1962 Act, it is helpful to draw on the work of Radhika Mongia. In her study of immigration legislation introduced to restrict the entry of Indian citizens to Canada, Mongia shows how racism is 'instituted by bureaucratic discretion'.[137] For the law to operate as intended, that is, to keep racialised Commonwealth citizens out, its 'spirit' must be given meaning through exercises of discretion by immigration officials. The 1962 Act, despite seeming to capture Irish citizens travelling to Britain from outside Ireland along with racialised colony and Commonwealth citizens, nevertheless produced a different effect for the Irish. The discretion granted to immigration officials, combined with the everyday assumptions made about who belongs in a British polity imagined as white, meant that Irish citizens would in fact cross the border with ease, whereas racialised subjects would not.

Figures on people entering Britain were approximate, consisting of annual Home Office estimates based on shipping and air transport passenger lists, as well as those calculated by bodies such as the Migrant Services Division of the Jamaican Colonial Government (until 1956), by the British Caribbean Welfare Service (until 1958) and by the

Migrant Services Division of the Commission in the UK
for the West Indies, British Guiana and British Honduras.[138]
These latter agencies, being concerned with welfare provision, concentrated on recording group arrivals and therefore tended to underestimate overall numbers of migrants.
Moreover, it was impossible to differentiate those who
remained long-term from those who were short-term visitors on the basis of available figures. Between 1955 and
1960, the Home Office estimated there to have been around
161,450 Caribbean entrants, 330,70 from India and 17,120
from Pakistan. In the two years prior to the coming into force
of the 1962 Act, the number of those entering Britain rose
considerably as individuals sought to pre-empt the restrictive effect of the Act: 42,000 Indians, 50,170 Pakistanis and
98,090 West Indians were thought to have arrived between
1 January 1961 and the pre-Act deadline of 30 June 1962.[139]
The statutory controls served to cut the total number of
annual racialised colony and Commonwealth entrants
from an estimated 136,400 in 1961 to an official 57,046 in
1963.[140] The passing of the Act meant the introduction of
an official documentation system consisting of the collec-
tion of annual official statistics under the terms of the Act.
However, the 1962 Act did not serve to prevent the entry of
colony and Commonwealth citizens altogether. Their overall presence in Britain increased throughout the decade. The
total number present in Britain by 1971 stood at 1,151,090
(2.4% of the general population), having risen from an estimated 522,933 in 1961.[141] As we will see in the following
section, officials' increasing focus on numbers operated to
produce the racialised migrant as a threat to white British
supremacy.

The Commonwealth Immigrants Act 1968:
a white Britain policy in the making

This country cannot take upon itself the whole legacy of the
Empire.[142]

In the late 1960s there was an increase in the number of East
African Asians entering Britain, many of whom possessed a
British passport issued by the Kenyan authorities.[143] This
movement followed the introduction of policies discrimi-
nating against Asians in Kenya by President Jomo Kenyatta.
British colonial authorities bore much of the responsibility for the divisions in Kenyan society.[144] Although Asians
had lived in East Africa for centuries, the majority arrived
as labourers and traders following the expansion of the
British Empire over the area.[145] In legal terms, the continued ability of Kenyan Asians to enter Britain following the
1962 Commonwealth Immigrants Act was a result of its
method of determining entry rights of citizens of the United
Kingdom and Colonies. Entry rights turned on the question of the authority under which passports were issued.[146]
Although formally, Kenyan Asians were subject to control
under the 1962 Act, when Kenya won independence in 1963
the colonial governor became the high commissioner. The
result was that passports that had been issued by the colonial governor were then issued under the authority of the
British government, meaning that their holders were not
subject to immigration control.[147]

According to some parliamentarians, this was not a legal
loophole but a pledge in operation. Those affected had
reportedly been promised by the previous British government that they could rely on their status as citizens of the
United Kingdom and Colonies should the need arise. As

a result, many East African Asians did not take up local citizenship. The Labour MP Sir Dingle Foot, in the course of the debate on the 1968 Commonwealth Immigrants Bill, queried

> [a]re we to tear up the obligations which we quite deliber-
> ately assumed in 1963, which we have recognised ever since,
> and upon which those concerned have relied. We are not
> dealing with a draftsman's error to be put right through sub-
> sequent legislation. In 1963 the Government knew perfectly
> well what they were doing.[148]

The existence of a pledge was disputed by Conservative MP Duncan Sandys, who argued that the Kenya Independence Act merely contained assurances that citizens of the United Kingdom and Colonies in Kenya would not be deprived of their status, but that this 'did not affect their position under the Commonwealth Immigrants Act [1962] one way or the other'.[149] There is no doubt that Kenyan Asians regarded the 1968 Act and British politicians' denial of the existence of a pledge as a betrayal. Placards held up at a protest against the 1968 legislation by Kenyan Asians at Nairobi airport were emblazoned with slogans such as 'Sandys – humanity will never forgive you!' and 'Great British Betrayal'.[150]

For all the talk of pledges, it is clear that those in Parliament who pushed hardest for control were concerned primarily about the entry of racialised Commonwealth and colony citizens as they watched the Empire being defeated. Thus, Sandys warned that

> we must bear in mind the problem which will arise when our
> other remaining Colonies become independent. It would, I
> suggest, be very difficult to refuse similar rights of entry to
> racial minorities in, say, Mauritius or Fiji ... We have to face
> the fact – and this is one of the inevitable consequences of
> the process of dismantling an empire – that once we have

granted independence to a Colony we are no longer in a position to look after the interest of its inhabitants as we did before.

After providing this skewed presentation of British rule as being about protection rather than exploitation, Sandys had the gall to present racist immigration controls as being 'in the interests of the immigrants themselves' to save them from experiencing racism in Britain.[151] Some supporters of the legislation were quite happy to acknowledge that the legislation was 'of course ... a question of colour', such as Labour MP Charles Pannell, who insisted that if it had been white Rhodesians (now Zimbabweans) seeking entry to Britain, it 'would have opened its gates to the lot of them'.[152]

Despite concern in some corners of the Cabinet about the prospect of legislation being seen by Commonwealth countries as 'a purely racial move',[153] and the effect this might have on the stability of the Commonwealth, the government moved swiftly towards legislation to bar the entry of Kenyan Asians. The Commonwealth Immigrants Act was passed on 1 March 1968 and supported by large majorities in the House of Commons from the incumbent Labour government and the Conservative opposition. It was rushed through in under three days, much as the 1914 Aliens Restrictions Act had been, though on this occasion, as Dallal Stevens notes, 'there was no war to justify the unusual haste'.[154] The 1968 Act made no mention of asylum, not surprisingly since its principal targets were people in flight from persecution. Kenyan Asians were not only citizens of the United Kingdom and Colonies, but were also refugees. Although the Labour Home Secretary, James Callaghan, denied that the Act was racist, preferring to describe the exclusive test adopted as 'geographical, not racial',[155] the fact that the legislation was racially targeted was clear from his reasoning that 'the problem' at issue was 'potentially much larger than that of the Kenya Asians. It includes all the Asians in other parts of Africa and this very much larger number of citizens totalling 1 million or more.'[156] Moreover, regardless of the views held by those who passed the legislation, or the terms in which it was expressed, its effects were racist. As Dingle Foot emphasised, the ancestry test deployed in the Act would ensure that 'the effect of this legislation, inevitably, will be that the great majority of Europeans who have not elected for Kenya citizenship will be able to come here. The overwhelming majority of Asians will not.'[157]

In 1967 there had been significant news coverage of Asians arriving in Britain. Public opinion data demonstrated majoritarian support for legislation restricting Kenyan Asians' entry to Britain.[158] Rather than seek to persuade the public to welcome them, Callaghan moved to restrict their entry. The usual procedure of referring the matter to a Home Affairs committee was not followed. Instead, Callaghan set up a special Cabinet committee on immigration, which he chaired. He was dismissive of his critics and 'dominated the proceedings'.[159] In a Cabinet memorandum, Callaghan argued for immigration controls by constructing them as quid a pro quo for protection from race discrimination in the form of the Race Relations Bill of 1965.

> Our best hope of developing in these Islands a multi-racial society free of strife lies in striking the right balance between the number of Commonwealth citizens we can allow in and our ability to ensure them, once here, a fair deal not only in tangible matters like jobs, housing and other social services but, more intangibly, against racial prejudice. If we have to restrict immigration now for good reasons, as I think we must, the imminent Race Relations Bill will be a timely factor in helping us to show that we are aiming at a fair balance all

round. Conversely, I believe that the reception of the Race Relations Bill will be prejudiced in many minds, and support for it weakened, if people think that the numbers entering are unlimited or unreasonably high.[160]

Much can be gleaned from Callaghan's reasoning and justification for stripping Kenyan Asians of their right of entry on racial grounds. Callaghan failed to understand that British racism is 'a product of imperial and colonial power'.[161] His presentation of racial prejudice as being an 'intangible matter' demonstrates his failure to understand racism as having serious material consequences for racialised people. The reasoning Callaghan deployed to justify the 1968 Act is perversely counter-intuitive in the trade-off presented as both necessary and desirable. His argument was that creating a 'multi-racial society free of strife' necessitated action consisting of yielding to racist demands by passing racist legislation. Essentially, he offered up the rights of racialised Commonwealth citizens in exchange for white Britons' acceptance of anti-discrimination laws. Callaghan's concern that the 1965 Race Relations Bill would garner less support without the imposition of racism in the form of immigration controls raises doubts about both the quality of protection contained in the Race Relations Bill and the ability of the British authorities to deliver protection from race discrimination. It further raises the question of the meaningfulness of the support of those who hold their willingness to abide by anti-racist norms conditional upon racist exclusion. The tactic of presenting a 'package deal' involving a tightening of immigration controls along with laws prohibiting racial discrimination in Britain had long been entertained by Harold Wilson's Labour government, in particular by a former Home Secretary, Frank Soskice.[162] Soskice had described the Race Relations Bill of 1965 as being part of a two-pronged government policy of achieving 'effective control of numbers' of racialised Commonwealth arrivals on the one hand, and the creation of 'one class of citizen each with equal rights' on the other.[163] A similar mantra would be repeated by many a Home Secretary to come.

The final line quoted from Callaghan above, that support for race relations legislation would be weakened 'if people think that the numbers entering are unlimited or unreasonably high', is revealing of the way in which numbers of racialised people were an object of fear in white supremacist Britain. The descriptor 'high' is in itself racist in suggesting that there is an ideal number of racialised colony and Commonwealth citizens who would be entering a predominantly white Britain. Frantz Fanon, in *Black Skin, White Masks*, challenged the racism of an interlocutor concerned with the number of black people in France, writing 'for you there is a problem, the problem of the increase of Negroes, the problem of the Black Peril'.[164] To illustrate the racism in white dominant societies' fears about the numbers of racialised people present, Fanon cynically imagines himself 'lost, submerged in a white flood composed of men like Sartre or Aragon', claiming he would like nothing better.[165] For Callaghan, it did not matter how many racialised people were actually entering Britain, but whether white British people would *think* the numbers were 'unlimited or unreasonably high'.

It is worth nothing that despite the racist hysteria apparent in the House of Commons debate on the Bill, Britain was experiencing a net outflow of migration at the time the 1968 Act was passed, a point commented on in the course of the debate on the Bill.[166] Those who made this point were ignored. For instance, the Liberal MP David

Steel argued that 'we are not an overcrowded island as is so often supposed', and tried to convince MPs not to pass controls, but instead to 'reassure the public mind about the state of immigration'.[167] In *Policing the Crisis*, Stuart Hall reflected on the structural relationship between the media and official discourse, observing that the important point is the establishment of the 'initial definition or *primary interpretation* of the topic in question'.[168] For example, he writes:

> once race relations in Britain have been defined as a 'problem of numbers' ... then even liberal spokesmen, in proving that the figures for black immigrants have been exaggerated, are nevertheless obliged to subscribe, implicitly, to the view that the debate is 'essentially' *about numbers*.[169]

In this way, the official and media reaction is not to any actual threat to society, but to 'a perceived or symbolic threat',[170] that is, what the racialised Commonwealth citizen was taken to represent: a threat to white British supremacy at home.

The 1968 Act provided that only Commonwealth citizens with an existing ancestral link with the country retained their right to enter Britain. For others, the Act put in place a quota system of entry vouchers. Section 1 removed the 1962 Act's exemption from control of citizens of the United Kingdom and Colonies with a passport issued by the British government. Not all citizens who had passports issued by dependency governments had taken local citizenship, and in some cases they were deprived of it in the course of independence processes.[171] The effect of the 1968 Act was to create a group of citizens of the United Kingdom and Colonies who did not have an immediate right of entry into Britain despite the fact that the only passports they held were British.[172] Two hundred thousand East African Asian British passport holders were abandoned, made stateless by the Act for lack of an alternative citizenship.[173] In general, the Act had wide cross-party support, despite its devastating consequences for Asians whose lives and futures depended on escaping persecution in Kenya. Tellingly, concern was raised about the preferential treatment of 'aliens' in comparison with Commonwealth citizens, betraying once again the fragility and deceptiveness of the distinction between subject and alien in imperial contexts. Lord O'Hagen, for instance, queried the government on

> what would happen if two British white sisters got engaged, one to a German, one to a Pakistani, and subsequently both pairs got married. Is not the position at the moment that the Commonwealth citizen would probably not be allowed to remain here, while in due course of time the alien probably might be?[174]

The 1968 Act accorded preferential treatment to white British settlers. Exempted from control were citizens of the United Kingdom and Colonies born in Britain or with at least one parent or grandparent born in Britain, people naturalised in Britain, or people who became citizens of the United Kingdom and Colonies by virtue of being adopted in Britain, or by registration under the British Nationality Acts in Britain or in a specified Commonwealth country.[175] The exemption granted to those with a parent or grandparent born in Britain meant that the 1968 Act effectively allowed (predominantly white) British settlers in any colony, protectorate or protected state to retain their right to enter Britain as a citizen of the United Kingdom and Colonies.[176] In this way lawmakers avoided the use of an explicit racial test for exclusion. Instead, the approach of legislators was to achieve their desired effect of racial exclusion by narrowing 'down the category of those who are deemed to "belong"' to Britain.[177]

The effect of the carefully crafted exceptions to immigration control set out in the Act was to deem white people as belonging to Britain to the exclusion of racialised colony and Commonwealth citizens. By 1967 government memoranda no longer referred to East African Asians as 'coloured' British citizens, but as 'citizens of the United Kingdom and Colonies who do not belong to the United Kingdom'.[178] The Act thus treated racialised citizens of the United Kingdom and Colonies as 'aliens' for the purpose of immigration control in the interests of protecting white British supremacy on the British mainland. Although the Act's primary target was East and Central African Asians, it deprived more than a million individuals worldwide of their right to enter Britain, including those in Malaysia, Singapore, South Yemen and the Caribbean.[179]

The 1968 Act was, for a minority of parliamentarians, 'the most shameful piece of legislation ever enacted by parliament, the ultimate appeasement of racist hysteria'.[180] The Act's genesis marked a significant departure in British politicians' attitudes towards the Commonwealth. The 1950s had been marked by official concern about the souring impact of immigration controls on relationships with the Commonwealth. By 1968 most Conservative and Labour party politicians were aligned in their eagerness to strip racialised colony and Commonwealth citizens of their right to enter Britain. In spite of their rallying around racist legislation, their hypocritical discomfort at being considered to be racists was very much on display in the course of the House of Commons debate on the Bill, along with an almost complete lack of acknowledgement of the British Empire's role in prompting the movement of colony and Commonwealth citizens to Britain. This was despite the presence in the Commons of parliamentarians such as Duncan Sandys, who made no secret of the fact that he was 'so closely concerned with the arrangements for Kenya's independence'.[181] His conclusion, ostensibly 'after much thought', was that 'it is not reasonable to expect us to open our doors to a vast number of people who have no direct connection with Britain and who do not in any way belong here'.[182] Sandys further considered that 'if they wish to leave Kenya, they should return to their countries of origin', a statement met with shouts of 'Where?' from MPs opposed to the legislation. In the time-honoured fashion of British politics – that of exporting 'problems', imperial by-products of its making – he gave the feeble reply: 'India and Pakistan'.[183] Quentin Hogg, the Shadow Home Secretary, asked the House, 'what have [we] done wrong and why [should] the right hon. Gentleman [Callaghan] be accused of being a racialist, when all that he is trying to do is to cope with a situation which he did not create'.[184] When faced with a question that pinpointed the origin of the persecution of the Kenyan Asians in 'the break-up of our own Empire', Hogg completely ignored it.[185]

The priority across the political spectrum was to pander to a growing far right and racist opposition to immigration of racialised colony and Commonwealth citizens. Hogg stated in the Commons that 'racial prejudice is often based on insecurity, and insecurity is largely the result of want of control, and want of control is precisely the thing which the Government are trying to get rid of by what admittedly is a measure which none of us like'.[186] This statement on 'control' evokes the slogan 'Take Back Control', which became the rallying cry of the anti-immigration Leave campaign in the course of the 2016 EU referendum. Rather than eliminating 'want of control', the 1968 parliamentarians' profound failure to understand racism as being a consequence of British colonialism, along with their misconception, whether genuine or otherwise, that the solution to racism lay in immigration control, had the effect of feeding the very racism that continues to drive demands for control. What is clear is that politicians, then and now, enact racism while denying that this is what they are doing and locating it instead in an imagined 'white working class'.

The 1968 Act demonstrated that British politicians were willing to weigh up the perceived domestic political costs of maintaining imperial ambitions. They came down on the side of mitigating those costs in an era in which the British Empire was facing defeat. As colonial populations ousted the British and won their independence, amnesia and disassociation from the British imperial project began to take hold in the British psyche. As though the white supremacist project of the British Empire had never existed, in 1968 Enoch Powell, in his infamous 'rivers of blood' speech, sought to differentiate the US from Britain in terms of the inevitability of the presence of racialised people: 'The tragic and intractable phenomenon which we watch with horror on the other side of the Atlantic but which is there interwoven with the history and existence of the States itself, is coming upon us here by our own volition and our own neglect.'[187] Powell conveniently skipped over the aspects of British history that have determined the presence of racialised people in Britain. Not only did Britain actively foster the idea of a British motherland in the course of its imperial expansion, but the wealth accumulated via colonial dispossession, both material and temporal, is located on the British mainland. British slave owners and the British economy reaped the financial proceeds of transatlantic slavery.[188] Wealth, resources and produce from the colonies was imported to Britain at the cost of the colonies.[189] As Ambalavaner Sivanandan has explained, 'colonialism and immigration were part of the same continuum ... The purpose of my aphorism "we are here because you were there" was to capture the idea of the continuum in a sentence intelligible to all.'[190]

Between 1970 and 1973 more than 200 East African Asians lodged complaints with the European Commission of Human Rights on the issue of the 1968 Commonwealth Immigrants Act's removal of their right to enter Britain.[191] In 1970, 31 such applications were declared admissible and for the first time the Commission issued a report in an individual case against Britain.[192] The Commission did not consider itself confronted with 'the general question whether racial discrimination in immigration control constitutes as such degrading treatment', but only whether the 1968 Act as applied in the cases before it 'discriminated on the ground of race or colour' and whether that treatment met the threshold of degrading.[193] Concentrating on the revocation of a previously granted right of entry for British subjects, the Commission found that Britain was in breach of Article 3 of the ECHR, which prohibits torture and inhuman or degrading treatment or punishment.[194] The Commission stated that race-based discrimination was 'a special form of affront to human dignity which, in aggravating circumstances, can amount to degrading treatment in breach of Art. 3'.[195] It found that the 1968 Act had 'racial motives and that it covered a racial group' and that 'it was clear that it was directed against the Asian citizens of the United Kingdom and Colonies in East Africa and especially those in Kenya'.[196]

Analysis of the Commission's report in the *East African Asians* case demonstrates that despite the apparent strength of its condemnation of the actions of the British government, the practical outcome and reasoning meant that its progressive content was limited.[197] The Commission refused to recognise the parity in the situation of British subjects and British Protected Persons denied entry to Britain.[198] It found that Article 3 was only breached in relation to the applicants who were citizens of the United Kingdom and Colonies. The Commission did not therefore consider 'whether a colonial power had some moral – and thus human and legal rights – duties towards her former colonial subjects'.[199] The Commission distinguished the situation of British Protected Persons from that of citizens of the United Kingdom and Colonies by stating that 'although not aliens, [they] are not British subjects', they had been made subject to immigration control under the 1962 Immigration Act, their position had not changed following the 1968 Act, and the 1968 Act 'did not distinguish between different groups of British protected persons on any ground of race and colour'.[200] Essentially, the Commission rubber-stamped Britain's alienation of British Protected Persons, a category of people with colonial connections to Britain but who had not been granted British subjecthood under the 1948 British Nationality Act. By contrast, the Commission was willing to reach its finding of a breach of Article 3 in the case of British subjects falling into the category of citizens of the United Kingdom and Colonies, despite this group also having been treated as 'aliens' for the purpose of immigration control via the 1968 Act.

It is possible to read the Commission's decision in the *East African Asians* case as reinforcing the position adopted by European colonisers of 'fierce and successful resistance to any claim that [they] should admit on their territory ex-colonial subjects-turned migrants'.[201] Marie-Bénédict Dembour has argued that the *East African Asians* case shows that '[o]nce colonialism had ended', the Strasbourg institutions were guided by the 'same exclusionary philosophy'.[202]

Yet colonialism has not 'ended'. The world remains colonially structured as do the domestic spaces of former colonial powers. Not only does Britain still have overseas colonies, but it is also the place where colonial spoils are located and disproportionately withheld from people with histories of colonisation both within and outside its borders. In such a context, legal status recognition processes, including those framed in terms of human rights, cannot respond adequately to reparative demands. The Commission thus limited itself to considering whether the 1968 Act was contrary to Article 3, leaving aside the broader questions of the legitimacy of processes of granting and refusing legal status in imperial contexts.

The Immigration Act 1971: whiteness as belonging

The Conservative Party's 1970 manifesto promised to 'establish a new single system of control over all immigration from overseas', declaring that the 'Home Secretary of the day will have complete control, subject to the machinery for appeal, over the entry of individuals into Britain'.[203] The stated purpose of the Conservative government's 1971 Immigration Act was to introduce 'permanent' immigration 'legislation of a comprehensive character' and to 'enable help to be given to those wishing to return abroad, and for services connected therewith'.[204] Its introduction was preceded by a persistent and violent campaign by the far right National Front.[205] The Act targeted racialised colony and Commonwealth citizens for further control, once again treating them as 'aliens' for the purpose of immigration control. The Home Secretary, Reginald Maudling, at times used the terminology 'coloured immigrant' when referring to colony and Commonwealth citizens whom he considered would be affected in various ways by the legislation during debate on the Bill in the Commons.[206] However, when it came to describing those exempted from control, primarily those born in Britain or with a parent born in Britain (the vast majority of whom were white), the government came up with a new word, 'patrial'. According to Maudling, 'the great advantage' of the term was to 'get away from' the word 'alien', which he claimed to have 'always disliked'. 'I do not think', he said, 'that it is sensible to describe other human beings as "alien" if one can avoid it.'[207] As though the British Empire had never existed, Maudling spoke of the need to have 'regard both to those who have always lived here and those who are here as immigrants'[208] (notice the use of this descriptor rather than that of subjects). Maudling talked of Britain as though it had always been a contained place rather than an empire which spanned continents. '[W]e must give assurance', he said, 'to the people who were already *here* before the large wave of immigration that this will be the end and that there will be no further large-scale immigration.'[209] However, the discourse of 'immigrants' was not wholly established. There were protestations in the Commons in the wake of the proposal that Commonwealth citizens should register their work permits with the police. On seeking to minimise what might look like a 'tyrannical' suggestion, Maudling stated that the 'condition of registration' had been accepted by '[a]ll Americans and Scandinavians who have come here over the years'. This statement was met with cries of 'They are not Commonwealth citizens', 'They are foreigners'.[210]

The 1971 Immigration Act definitively ended the right of colony and Commonwealth citizens to enter Britain, but granted the right of abode (the right to enter, live and work in Britain) to those already settled in Britain ('being ordinarily resident [for a period of at least five years in Britain at any time] without being subject under the immigration laws to any restriction on the period for which he may remain'). At the time the Act was introduced, Maudling claimed that one of its 'main objectives' was to 'reassure the immigrants already here as part of our community that they will have no loss of status under the Bill, that in this country there will be no first and second-class citizens'.[211] Yet following the introduction of the hostile environment policy and its implementation through the 2014 and 2016 Immigration Acts, there were numerous reports of people of the Windrush generation and their descendants facing unemployment, denial of access to healthcare, detention and expulsion because they could not prove their immigration status.[212] The 2014 Act removed the exemption from immigration control for Commonwealth citizens who were lawfully in Britain prior to 1973 after having been granted short-term stays for study or work, but who had since lost their status.[213] The 2014 and 2016 Acts required government agencies, public and financial service providers and private landlords to withhold services in the absence of proof of a secure legal status. Many people could not prove this for lack of documentation, in part due to Home Office actions.[214] The 1971 Act did not protect people from having to submit to the onerous and often impossible burden of proof. Indeed, it invited the devastating effects of the hostile environment, providing that '[w]hen any question arises under this Act whether or not a person is patrial, or is entitled to any exemption under this Act, *it shall lie on the person asserting it to prove that he is*'.[215]

Meanwhile, those exempted from control under the 1971 Act were primarily those born in Britain or with a parent born in Britain, thereby linking the right to enter Britain with whiteness.[216] The 1971 Act thus effectively made whiteness the primary basis for belonging in Britain. Citizens of the United Kingdom and Colonies who were 'patrials', those born in Britain or with a parent born in Britain, had a right of abode and therefore a right of entry and stay in Britain.[217] The effect of the requirement to show a 'patrial' connection was to discriminate against racialised colony and Commonwealth citizens. In 1971 a person born in Britain was most likely (98%) to be white.[218] This point did not escape the government of the day, though it nevertheless denied that the legislation was racially discriminatory:

> It is said that most of the people with patrial status will be white. Most of us are white, and it is completely turning racial discrimination on its head to say that it is wrong for any country to accord those with a family relationship to it a special position in the law of that country.[219]

Similarly, some parliamentarians, for instance James Callaghan, who was by then on the opposition bench, sought to argue that because in theory a racialised person could be a 'patrial' (if she or he was born in Britain for example), the law could not be described as racist.[220] The patriality provision in the Act was drafted so as to allow many citizens of Australia, Canada and New Zealand to retain the right to enter Britain, while racialised colony and Commonwealth citizens could not.[221] Irish citizens were exempt from control so long as they entered Britain through the Common Travel Area. Kathleen Paul has thus argued that the 1971 Act reconfigured British subjecthood by differentiating in legal terms 'between the familial community of Britishness composed of the truly British – those descended from white colonizers – and the political community of Britishness composed of people who had become British through conquest or dominion'.[222] The right of abode was also granted to people who had arrived in Britain from the Commonwealth or colonies with a labour voucher and had resided in Britain for five years.[223] However, they were the exception, and their position was not in reality secure. As I have argued, fragility of legal status disproportionately impacts racialised people. The 1971 Act's equating of Britishness to whiteness has haunted the administration of immigration law and policy, as the 2018 Windrush scandal demonstrates. The 1971 Act, along with the Commonwealth Immigrants Acts of the 1960s, demonstrate that in colonial contexts legal status differs in material terms according to whether and how a person is racialised. Although the British Nationality Act 1948 remained on the statute books in order to appease Commonwealth governments, its provisions were in large part replaced by the 1971 Act.[224] In response to the publication of the Bill, the Indian government ended visa-free travel for Britons.[225] Following the 1971 Act, the British government took further measures to deter the immigration of racialised Commonwealth citizens, including the introduction of 'virginity tests' which entailed forcing women arriving from India to be married in Britain to undergo vaginal examinations.[226]

The 1971 Act empowered the Home Secretary to set immigration rules before Parliament. Having failed to persuade Parliament to adopt the first set, the government set out revised rules on 25 January 1973. These treated Commonwealth citizens and non-Commonwealth citizens from outside the EEC as 'aliens' in relation to rights of entry and work, thereby assigning them a detrimental status as compared with EEC nationals.[227] Britain had finally joined the EEC in 1973, a process discussed in Chapter 5. The government implemented the provisions on the free movement of EEC workers through the immigration rules. Questions were raised in Parliament about the differential treatment between Commonwealth citizens and EEC nationals.[228] The government made assurances that people from Australia, Canada and New Zealand would not be in a worse position as regards their entitlement to enter Britain as compared with EEC nationals.[229] The original patrial provision in the 1971 Bill had entitled those with a grandparent, as well as a parent, born in Britain to a right of abode. After the clause was defeated in Parliament, the right was limited to those with a parent born in Britain. In spite of this, the clause's formulation inclusive of the grandparent connection, known as the 'UK ancestry route', was reinstated through the 1973 immigration rules and still exists today.[230]

The Ugandan Asian crisis

They said if you was white, should be all right.[231]

On 5 August 1972 the Ugandan leader, General Idi Amin, ordered the expulsion of all Asian British passport holders within 90 days. This order was the culmination of a series of measures which significantly restricted the rights of Asians to live and work in Uganda.[232] An estimated 60,000 Asians lived in Uganda at the time, half of whom held a British passport. Their ancestors had travelled to Uganda from all over the Indian subcontinent in the era of the British Empire, some as traders and others as indentured labourers.[233] Tellingly, the *Sunday Telegraph* referred to the Ugandan Asians as 'the white man's "heavy new burden"', betraying the prevalent British colonial psyche combined with ignorance of the history of the Asian presence in Uganda.[234] Although the Ugandan Asian crisis has been argued by some to have elicited a generous response from the British authorities,[235] the reality is that it was yet another instance of the British government's alienation of racialised citizens of the United Kingdom and Colonies, further illustrating the fragility of colonial legal status for racialised populations.

Edward Heath's Conservative government increased the British Asians quota from 1,500 to 3,000 in May 1971, but from this quota only 100 entry certificates were allocated to Ugandan Asians annually. Those who attempted to flee without securing an entry certificate to Britain found themselves 'rejected and shuttled around the world'.[236] In 1972 the Home Office set up a resettlement board to coordinate the reception of a number of Ugandan Asians.[237] In doing so, it sought to distance itself from the resettlement programme. The Heath government also called on 'local authorities and private individuals to volunteer vacant housing stock' while concealing the fact that state funding was being directed to the process.[238] The government introduced a policy that can accurately be described as racial segregation for the accommodation of Ugandan Asians who were resettled in Britain. It included the designation of dispersal zones as '"red" ("no-go") and "green" ("go") areas', zones which were previously described as 'black' and 'white' in internal communications.[239] Enoch Powell attacked the government's measures as a breach of their pledge not to allow further immigration.[240] Consistent with the correlative relationship between the violence of the colonial state and the racial terror this elicits on the ground, in August 1972 London's meat porters marched with National Front members chanting 'Britain is for the British' and 'Keep the Asians Out'.[241] Although public opinion fluctuated on the issue, only 6 per cent of respondents in the first public opinion poll supported the admission of Ugandan Asians with British passports, a figure that later rose to 54 per cent.[242]

Britain's reception of the Ugandan Asians has been widely understood as 'a humanitarian and morally laudable act of a former "mother country" to an expulsion of a racial minority'.[243] Anthony Lester has drawn attention to the difference in approach between Harold Wilson's administration, which passed the 1968 Commonwealth Immigrants Act in response to the arrival of Kenyan Asians, and 'the much more generous approach of Edward Heath's government' towards the 71,000 Ugandan Asians expelled.[244] However, Yumiko Hamai has demonstrated 'foot-dragging' in the British government's approach towards the Ugandan Asians for fear of public criticism, from the slow processing of entry certificates to the active discouragement of early departure by Asians seeking to flee prior to Amin's deadline of 7 November 1972.[245] The Home Office had delayed departures in the hope of securing alternative countries of destination and to allay the anti-immigrant sentiment of Heathrow airport staff who were refusing to process Asians arriving in Britain.[246] The British government asked more than fifty countries to take Ugandan Asians. Ultimately, Britain admitted only 28,608 citizens of the United Kingdom and Colonies from Uganda. Canada accepted around 6,000 and India 10,000, while New Zealand, Malawi and Kenya admitted hundreds.[247]

The capacity to treat subjects as 'aliens' for legal purposes is the colonial state's ultimate expression of power. The British government's position on Ugandan Asians who did not hold passports it had issued was that to accept them 'would be putting on this country a burden which is not ours'.[248] Despite being subject to immigration control pursuant to the Commonwealth Immigrants Acts of the 1960s and the 1971 Immigration Act, many of the Ugandan Asians were citizens of the United Kingdom and Colonies under the 1948 British Nationality Act. The British government's obligation under international law to accept the Ugandan Asians in the absence of alternative settlement options was thus of little practical consequence in light of the immigration control measures in place.[249] Instead, the government sought to present the Ugandan Asians as 'unfortunate refugees' and a 'burden' to be shouldered internationally. A Home Office civil servant noted at the time that 'it seems preferable to accept the [Asians] from Uganda on the basis that they are "refugees" whether or not they are technically refugees'.[250] The refugee category was thus invoked out of convenience by an administration wishing to frame its actions towards the Ugandan Asians as charitable or humanitarian, rather than in terms of legal or reparative obligation.[251]

The treatment of white subjects in the course of successful independence movements can be usefully juxtaposed with that of the Ugandan and Kenyan Asians. As Gurminder Bhambra and John Holmwood note, 'considerable sympathy' was shown for '"patrial" white settlers in South Africa and Rhodesia/Zimbabwe', in comparison to that proffered to South Asians.[252] The British government's approach towards Ugandan residents with ancestral links to Britain is illustrative of how the legal status of Citizenship of the United Kingdom and Colonies applied differently in material terms to white subjects. White Ugandan residents comprised a group of 7,000, and were known by British officials as 'belongers'.[253] Unlike racialised subjects, their whiteness gave rise to an automatic relationship of belonging to the British polity. With belonging came material privileges in the form of protection, including an evacuation plan. Although Idi Amin had not expelled white Ugandan residents, the British government's preparation for their departure began early and the plan was constantly revisited. The government even countenanced military intervention should the risk to white residents' safety escalate.[254]

The British Nationality Act 1981: the final act of colonial appropriation

It is time to dispose of the lingering notion that Britain is somehow a haven for all those whose countries we used to rule.[255]

In 1981 the Home Secretary William Whitelaw declared that a new articulation of British citizenship was necessary so that holders of the status of Citizenship of the United Kingdom and Colonies 'may not unnaturally be encouraged to believe, despite the immigration laws to the contrary, that they have a right of entry' to Britain.[256] The 1981 British Nationality Act, passed by Margaret Thatcher's Conservative government, was ostensibly about defining a legal status of British citizenship for those who are 'closely connected' with Britain and who 'belong' to Britain 'for international or other purposes'.[257] Previous iterations of immigration control had made clear that Commonwealth citizens who were 'closely connected' to and deemed to 'belong' to Britain were white. The 1981 Act continued this process of racial exclusion by constructing British citizenship on the foundation of the 1971 Act's concept of patriality, tying citizenship to the right of entry and abode.[258] In a manner that denied the relevance of the British Empire in producing the category of Citizenship of the United Kingdom and Colonies, Whitelaw denied these citizens 'close ties' with Britain, claiming that they did not 'actually belong' in Britain.[259]

The popularity of the National Front was at its peak in the lead-up to the passing of the 1981 Act.[260] Despite being couched in terms of citizenship and nationality, the 1981 Act was an immigration control measure designed to deliver on the Conservative Party's 1979 election manifesto promise of firm immigration controls targeting racialised Commonwealth migration to Britain.[261] This was underlined by the need for Commonwealth citizens to register as British citizens within five years of the Act coming into force or lose their entitlement to citizenship.[262] Immigration control was once again presented as a prerequisite for the enactment of race relations legislation.[263] Although the 1981 Act retained the quota system for Commonwealth immigration set out in the 1968 Act, the criteria were strict and there was a cap of 5,000 per year.[264]

The 1981 Act repealed the British Nationality Act 1948, all but abolishing the status of British subject.[265] British citizenship was tied to membership of a British polity exclusive of the colonies and Commonwealth. Dora Kostakopoulou and Robert Thomas have argued that '[t]he consolidation and legitimation of modern states' depends on the 'drawing of firm boundary lines which delimited the area of the state's jurisdiction'.[266] While in reality Britain's jurisdiction continues to extend over its remaining colonial territories, the 1981 Act drew a hard border around 'the motherland', effectively announcing Britain as post-colonial, making it impermeable to its former racialised subjects. Geographically the Act limited British citizenship to the landmasses known as England, Scotland, Wales and Northern Ireland.[267] The Act thus conjured up a post-colonial notion of Britain and British citizenship in order to divorce Britain conceptually and physically from its former empire. By linking citizenship with a right of abode granted to those with a patrial connection to Britain, the 1981 Act reinforced the idea that Britishness is commensurate with whiteness. Whiteness as an 'embodied national identity' is, as Karen Wells and Sophie Watson have argued, a 'highly exclusionary notion of Britishness that essentially conflates being British/English with being white, Anglophone and Christian'.[268] There was objection at the time from members of the Labour opposition and the Church of England, whose bishops released a statement in which they argued that '[a]ny new nationality law should state as a matter of principle that our national identity is multi-racial, thereby avoiding the potential racial conception of national identity'.[269] In drawing a border around Britain as we know it today, the 1981 Act embodied an assertion of white possession of the spoils of colonialism, whether in the form of wealth, infrastructure, healthcare, security, employment or opportunity. The Act, in barring access to Britain for colonised populations, was a final act of seizure of stolen colonial wealth.

The 1981 Act introduced the status of British citizen and defined the conditions for its acquisition. Those with a right of abode were granted British citizenship. Under the Act, a person born in Britain is a British citizen if at the time of birth her father or mother is a British citizen or is settled in Britain.[270] The Act thus removed the automatic right of acquisition of citizenship for those born in Britain, thereby excluding from the post-imperial British polity many racialised subjects already living in Britain and children born to them. Its exclusionary effect would fall primarily on racialised people, yet the government denied that the legislation was racially discriminatory.[271] Roy Hattersley, shadow Home Secretary, criticised the position of the government:

> What is racist is that the difference between the two categories always works out, or almost invariably works out – or 90 per cent of the time works out – in a way which disadvantages the black community and gives corresponding

advantage to the white. That is why I again describe the Bill, irrespective of the Home Secretary's good intentions, as racist in outcome.[272]

The Act introduced a 'good character' requirement for the acquisition of citizenship, thereby 'extending the border from the point of entry and admittance into the nation-state to a more fluid point of inclusion/exclusion encroaching into everyday life of racially marginalised communities'.[273] The Act abolished the status of Citizenship of the United Kingdom and Colonies. Persons who had fallen into this group were divided into three categories: British citizens, which included citizens of the United Kingdom and Colonies with the right of abode in Britain; British Dependent Territories citizens, which applied to persons in territories that were still British colonies at the time (Hong Kong, Bermuda, the British Virgin Islands, Gibraltar and the Falkland Islands) – this group could register as British citizens after five years' residence in Britain; and finally, British Overseas citizens, which comprised all citizens of the United Kingdom and Colonies to whom neither of the other statuses applied. These comprised approximately 190,000 individuals who had no right to enter Britain and were treated as 'aliens' for the purpose of immigration control and naturalisation.[274] Primarily they were stateless East African Asians and persons in Malaysia seeking entry to Britain.[275] For Hattersley, the category of British Overseas citizenship was 'not so much a status as subterfuge'.[276] Although it included former citizens of the United Kingdom and Colonies living in former British colonies, 'it offer[ed] them virtually nothing'.[277] Once again we see the fragility of colonial legal status, which not only marks its subject as colonised, but can also be emptied of meaningful content at the whim of the colonial state. The defeat of the

British Empire allowed Enoch Powell to say in the course of parliamentary debate on the 1981 Bill that the 1948 British Nationality Act had been a 'disastrous error' and to express surprise at the fact that colonial statuses such as British Overseas and British Dependent Territories citizenship did not 'correspond to States'.[278] Yet it is not in the least surprising that they do not correspond to states. They correspond to an empire, the memory and acknowledgement of which was fast fading, even by those closely connected with its administration. Powell himself had long harboured a dream of being Viceroy of India, dashed when India won its independence in 1947.[279]

The effects of the changes to immigration and nationality legislation outlined above came into stark view in 2018 in the course of the Windrush scandal. In its submission to the Windrush review in 2018, Amnesty International pointed out that the 'injustice done' by changes to immigration and nationality legislation in the 1960s, 1970s and 1980s 'was compounded' because not enough was done to 'ensure that people were aware of the changes; understood they were affected ... and how; and assisted and enabled to exercise, where these were available, rights to mitigate the changes and their effects'.[280] For a number of reasons many people who were eligible to register as British citizens under section 7 of the British Nationality Act did not take up this right. As Amnesty International pointed out:

> Some people were not aware of their right or need to do so because they continued to believe themselves to be British or saw no immediate change to their day to day lives, unaware of the future implications of not doing so by reason of legislative, policy and operational developments they could not possibly have predicted. Other people were deterred from doing so by the fee or by the bureaucracy. Some people were simply insulted at the demand that they register as British

(citizens), including paying a fee, given their arrival in the UK as British (subjects) and their contribution to British society and public service.[281]

Under the 1971 Immigration Act people with a settled status had an ongoing right of re-entry regardless of the duration of their absence from Britain. It is possible that the existence of this right led some people to choose not to register as British citizens following the 1981 Act, considering that there was a cost attached to doing so. However, this right of re-entry was subsequently removed by the Immigration Act 1988 for those absent continuously for two years.[282]

The 1981 Act, together with previous post-war immigration controls, crafted as white supremacist a Britain as possible, short of introducing an explicit 'White Britain policy'. Through the 1981 Act racialised colony and Commonwealth citizens were told that their present or historical connections to the British Empire neither entitled them to Britishness as an identity nor to access Britain as a place. Much more than merely the right to cross a border is at stake in the enactment of immigration controls. Depriving colonised populations of the right to enter Britain simultaneously deprives them of access to stolen colonial wealth as it manifests in Britain, in the form of infrastructure, employment, healthcare, welfare, safety and opportunity. Colonialism entailed the extraction and accumulation of material and temporal resources. Colonial theft of intangibles such as economic growth prospects, opportunities, life chances and futures is difficult to discern in colonial relationships which are traditionally understood to have come to an end. Yet Britain, built on wealth accumulated via colonial dispossession, *is* the spoils of colonialism. Immigration law, in this way, is the modality through which Britain transitioned from being a colonial power in the traditional overseas extractive sense, to a space of domestic colonialism masquerading as a post-colonial nation.

Britain, in being the place where colonial spoils are located, must be understood as a live colonial space, and one that is necessarily contested. There is nothing clear-cut about the idea that Britain is a place first and foremost for white British people. The notion that Britain is a contested space is even invoked by the staunchest of right-wing, anti-migrant ideologues. Enoch Powell, for instance, stated that '[i]t is ... truly when one looks into the eyes of Asia that the Englishman comes face to face with those who would dispute with him the possession of his native land'.[283] The argument for a white Britain is thus repeatedly made by racist nationalists precisely because its history would suggest otherwise.

As a consequence of Britain's transition from an empire to a nation-state, and its constitution of itself as white, the presence, and claim to Britishness, of racialised persons already on the British mainland has since been in question. This is evident in official and scholarly discourse which continues to refer to the descendants of racialised British citizens as 'second-', 'third-' and 'fourth-' generation migrants, terminology that is not applied to the descendants of white European post-war migrants.[284] The questioning of racialised people's entitlement to be present in Britain also manifests in mutually reinforcing street and institution-alised forms of racial violence. The 1981 Act's declaration that Britain was a physically distinct and legitimately bordered space populated by white British citizens required the implementation of colonialism domestically. The same power relationships that underpinned the British Empire were relied on to ensure that wealth accumulated via colonial conquest and located in Britain was seen to be in its rightful place. Colonialism was configured domestically so as to maintain the white supremacist order of the British Empire within the post-1981 borders of Britain. The enactment of immigration and nationality laws that excluded racialised colony and Commonwealth citizens from the British polity was thus a crucial transitional move from primitive accumulation via overseas extractive colonialism to colonialism in the imperial metropole.

Britain, in its post-colonial iteration, has long projected a notion of itself as being under siege by racialised colony and Commonwealth citizens. Paul Gilroy writes, 'black settlement has been continually described in military metaphors which offer war and conquest as the central analogies for immigration'.[285] Such descriptors have included 'unarmed invasion, alien encampments, alien territory and the new commonwealth occupation'.[286] As Bhambra and Holmwood note, 'it was precisely the idea of an "immigrant-descended", non-white, population that came to be regarded as a threat to national identity'.[287] The idea that racialised people posed a threat to Britain carried consequences for Commonwealth and colony citizens on the inside. Once 'alien cultures' came to 'embody a threat, which in turn, invited the conclusion that national decline and weakness have been precipitated by the arrival of blacks', this not only provided the impetus for expulsion, but also for the enactment of internal forms of racial exclusion in respect of those who could not easily be removed.[288] Internal bordering became a new mode of colonialism, producing and sustaining the post-colonial project of a white Britain. This has occurred in part through the institution of policy and legal regimes which effectively construct 'a border in every street'.[289]

Chapter 4

Migrants, refugees and asylum seekers: predictable arrivals

Several works exist that compare British governments' responses to refugees over time.[1] Each traces the arrival and reception of groups of refugees, demonstrating how each was treated differently, offering explanations for governments' varying levels of 'generosity'. Yet refugee movements are not appropriate for comparison when divorced from the context of Britain's colonial identity. The relevance of Britain's contemporaneous identity as an empire, and the connection between this global white supremacist project and the domestic response to refugee movements, is frequently overlooked in the refugee law literature. The rhetoric of 'compassionate cases' and the international refugee law structure underpinning it provides a convenient path for Britain to frame itself as a generous host state and shed the association between its colonial history and the migration of its former subjects. As asylum applications increased, British officials claimed that they were being made by 'economic migrants' abusing the system. After briefly addressing international refugee law and tracing early attempts at legislating asylum in Britain, I analyse a number of Supreme Court cases. I show how the pre-eminence of the principle of state sovereignty and courts' inability to question governmental power to grant or refuse legal status further goes to show the limitation of recognition-based approaches to migrant solidarity and racial justice.

Asylum as a post-imperial category

We do have to hold out the prospect of an end of immigration, except of course, for compassionate cases.[2]

The removal of entry rights for racialised colony and Commonwealth citizens over the course of the 1960s, 1970s and 1980s produced the asylum route as one of the few means for historically dispossessed people to access Britain. The vast majority of asylum seekers in Britain are from its former colonies.[3] As Marie-Bénédicte Dembour has noted, '[m]igration patterns to Europe in the decades following independence very much followed colonial connections with, for example, Nigerians seeking to go to the UK, Algerians to France, and Zairians/Congolese to Belgium'.[4] At the same time, officially, legally and in the public conscience 'there was no sense in Europe that something was owed to these new migrants because of the colonial past'.[5] Dembour describes European colonisers' abandonment of their former colonial subjects as 'postcolonial dereliction', originating in 'the leftovers of ideology which saw nothing wrong in colonising other people, described as primitives, and thinking that the economic and political benefits which were drawn from this were rewards for the "burdens of empire"'.[6] The invocation of asylum and refugee law and the acceptance of the distinction between categories such as 'refugee' and 'migrant' allows Britain to conceal its colonial history beneath a veneer of humanitarianism. In 1978 Margaret Thatcher, then leader of the Conservative opposition, unwittingly illustrated the way in which refugee law is existentially and ideologically bound up and compatible with the racial and colonial violence of immigration control.

> [P]eople are really rather afraid that this country might be rather swamped by people with a different culture and you know the British character has done so much for democracy, for law and done so much throughout the world that if there is any fear that it might be swamped, people are going to react and be rather hostile to those coming in. So, if you want good race relations, you have got to allay peoples' fears on numbers ... We do have to hold out the prospect of an end of immigration, except of course, for compassionate cases.[7]

Thatcher presents a confused justification for contemplating an end to 'people of the new Commonwealth or Pakistan' migrating to Britain.[8] She holds up a distorted picture of British colonialism as a humanitarian mission and unintelligibly offers this as a reason for anti-immigrant sentiment among white Britons. She rehearses former Home Secretary James Callaghan's justification for introducing immigration controls as being to enhance 'race relations' by allaying 'peoples' fears on numbers', code for the maintenance of Britain as a white supremacy. Finally, Thatcher holds out the exceptional category of 'compassionate cases' to whom access might be granted, demonstrating the way in which refugee law allows Britain to present itself as a generous host – rather than colonial state.

In the 1980s people travelled to Britain in search of asylum in increasing numbers. An asylum seeker is traditionally understood to be a person travelling in search of a place of safety from persecution, but who has not yet been legally declared a refugee according to an asylum procedure. People seeking asylum need leave to enter, which can only be granted once a claim has been processed and so are usually given a temporary admission status.[9] Entry into Britain is invariably made difficult, and asylum seekers can be detained for indefinite periods. While the majority are fleeing persecution as legally defined in international refugee law,[10] the colonial context of migratory movements must be acknowledged. People who arrived in Britain seeking protection in the 1980s are often misleadingly referred to as 'spontaneous arrivals'.[11] The term suggests that there was an element of unpredictability and suddenness in their arrival. The descriptor 'spontaneous' feeds an ahistorical understanding of contemporary migratory movements, erasing the connection between migration and colonialism. Britain's colonial history and identity makes it entirely predictable that former colonial subjects would seek to travel to Britain. Teresa Hayter has thus argued that

> imperialism created links between the colonies and the metropolis ... it can be argued that some [wars, conflicts and repression] arise from centuries of imperialist control, and in particular the imperialists' divide and rule tactics and the boundaries they drew on maps. Imperialism in its modern guise has created new forms of impoverishment, which may exacerbate existing nationalist and ethnic tensions.[12]

The 1951 Refugee Convention: legitimising the post-imperial lie[13]

After the Second World War, a high degree of management and coordination between states was considered necessary in view of the millions of displaced persons across Europe.[14] International efforts were not, however, directed at addressing the situation of displaced persons in European colonies where fighting had taken place.[15] The Refugee Convention was agreed on 28 July 1951, and signed and ratified by Britain in 1954. While Britain participated in the negotiations on the Convention, pledging to protect European refugees and insisting on the exclusion of colonial subjects from the scope of the Convention,[16] colonial populations were fighting for independence from British rule. Transitions to independence resulted in large-scale forced displacement. It is estimated that the partitioning of India led to the forcible displacement of 15 million people.[17] Nevertheless, despite post-war and post-independence large-scale displacement in the colonies, the Convention's scope was geographically limited to refugee movements 'resulting from events occurring in Europe' prior to 1 January 1951.[18]

The Convention definition of a refugee was formulated on the basis of a contrived image of an individual deserving of protection. It was moulded to fit 'existing refugees' already on European states' territories.[19] Its rhetoric of 'profound concern for refugees'[20] is still celebrated today for its universalistic and inclusive approach to refugee protection, despite having been written with only white European refugees in mind.[21] Lucy Mayblin has observed that the exclusion from the scope of the Convention of non-European refugees 'occurred despite extensive and protracted resistance from the representatives of formerly colonised states'.[22] In time the Convention was to provide a convenient legitimising framework for Britain, enabling it to construct itself as a post-colonial host state rather than as a colonial space.

Patricia Tuitt has argued that '[w]hat distinguishes the Geneva Convention definition from other legal definitions of the refugee is its position of dominance – formal at least over other definitions – and its continued dominance in Europe in spite of the fact that few refugees seeking asylum in Europe fall within the Article 1(A)(2) definition'.[23] This is in part due to the definition's narrow construction. Traditionally, the essential quality of a refugee was seen to be their presence outside their own country as a result of political persecution.[24] The definition of a refugee eventually settled on in the 1951 Refugee Convention defined a refugee as a person who,

> owing to a well-founded fear of being persecuted for reasons of race, religion, nationality, membership of a particular social group or political opinion, is outside the country of his nationality and is unable, or owing to such fear, is unwilling to avail himself of the protection of that country; or who, not having a nationality and being outside the country of his former habitual residence as a result of such events, is unable or, owing to such fear is unwilling to return to it.[25]

Recognition as a refugee therefore requires an individual to have crossed an international border and to have suffered some sort of discriminatory human rights breach. Proof of persecution alone is not sufficient to establish refugee status; the threat to the individual's life or liberty must have a discriminatory impact on the basis of 'race, religion, nationality, membership of a social group or political opinion'.[26] Though persecution is not itself defined, certain types of harm have traditionally been seen as falling within its scope of meaning, while others have not. For example, individuals fleeing poverty or climate-change-induced environmental degradation are not considered deserving of asylum. Traditionally, the dominant discourse has considered that '[t]he solution to their problem, if any, lies more within the province of international aid and development, rather than in the institution of asylum'.[27] This is, of course, a convenient position to adopt for countries with colonial histories involving large-scale land and resource dispossession, exploitation and extraction. Poverty and environmental degradation can be conceived of as subtle but grindingly powerful forms of persecution if we consider that they are frequently the consequence of histories of resource extraction and ongoing 'economies of dispossession'.[28] Tuitt has noted that '[i]nevitably once a demand is made to prove that persecution was for a specified and recognised reason, then one introduces judgements which crudely are about when it is and is not justifiable or acceptable to persecute someone'.[29] The system becomes a 'lottery of state humanitarian protection'.[30] Placing the 1951 Convention definition in its historical context allows us to see that the persecution standard is reflective of the threat that Anglo-European countries perceived as emanating from eastern Europe – '[i]n short, it demonstrates the political goals of Western states who were largely instrumental in the drafting of the Geneva Convention'.[31]

The 1967 New York Protocol gave states the option of removing the geographical and temporal limitation attached to the 1951 Convention. Today, only four parties to the Convention retain the geographical limitation.[32] Britain signed the Protocol in 1968. After two years, the 1967 Protocol had been signed by 27 states, and by 1972, 52 states had ratified it.[33] However, as Mayblin points out, 1967 was not 'a moment of "peak rights" for asylum seekers'.[34] The main reason for the 1967 Protocol was to permit the United Nations High Commissioner for Refugees (UNHCR) to intervene in Africa, Asia and Latin America.[35] The lifting of the limitation was thus not designed to include colonial and former colonial populations within the scope of the

Convention, nor to invite them to seek asylum in European countries.

Traditionally the refugee debate has been depoliticised in being forced to sit on the narrow ethical basis of sanctuary from persecution for an undefined period of time. In this way, questions of historical injustice are ignored.[36] Tuitt has argued that refugee determination decisions are opportunities for the state to reassert its borders and the legitimacy of the nation-state system as a whole.[37] Human rights and refugee law processes can be seen as buttressing the idea that colonialism is in the past while also reinscribing those very colonial relations. As Sarah Keenan writes, refugee law 'conceptually confirms' a former colonial power's 'status as a space of modernity, cultural tolerance and political superiority, and that of the country of origin as a space of primitiveness ... and inferiority'.[38] Such processes of status recognition have the effect of reinforcing 'hierarchies of race, gender and sexuality and colonial landscapes of "good" and "bad" states'.[39] Refugee law helps to erase the role of colonialism in causing instability in social and economic structures in former colonies, as well as providing 'ideological legitimation for [contemporary] imperialist projects'.[40] This points to the limitations of legal recognition processes, which while accommodating certain individual claims to status, embody an assimilationist logic and have the effect of delegitimising the claims to redistributive and reparative justice of the vast majority of people with geographical or ancestral histories of colonisation.

From refugee to economic migrant

The 1971 Immigration Act made no mention of refugee protection, which remained a 'traditional and jealously guarded prerogative' of the government.[41] The accompanying 1973 immigration rules, issued by the Home Secretary, addressed the question of asylum, which meant that the system was administrative and highly discretionary.[42] Until 1992 they could be amended by the Home Office without informing Parliament. The immigration rules made a footnote reference to the Refugee Convention:

> A passenger who does not otherwise qualify for admission should not be refused leave to enter if the only country to which he can be removed is one to which he is unwilling to go owing to a well-founded fear of being persecuted for reasons of race, religion, nationality, membership of a particular social group or political opinion.*

> *The criterion for the grant of asylum is in accordance with Article 1 of the Convention relating to the Status of Refugees[43]

The Convention's confinement to discretionary immigration rules meant that for two decades asylum remained an exclusive prerogative of the government, beyond the scrutiny of Parliament and the judiciary. It existed as a separate protection category from that of refugee status until 1979, and tended to be considered more suitable than refugee status for 'Commonwealth citizens', indicative of its post-colonial character.[44] After 1979, although secondary statuses remained in use, all those granted asylum were recognised as refugees.[45]

The increasing numbers of people seeking protection prompted the British government to reconsider the workability of its discretionary regime. Robert Thomas has observed that, although these 'club government' traditions were able to administer the 4,000 asylum claims made yearly during the 1980s, they have since proved deficient.[46] In 1984 2,905 asylum applications were lodged in Britain, and in 1985, 4,500. Claims had remained under 4,500 until 1989 when they increased to 11,640, 'a reflection of the global increase'.[47] The majority of these applicants came from former British colonies or protectorates, such as Sri Lanka (1,790), Somalia (1,850) and Uganda (1,235).[48] The government resorted to legislation and discretionary rule-making powers, targeting those seeking protection with control measures.[49] Asylum seekers were constructed as being 'illegals' and 'scroungers' in order to justify their exclusion from access to territory as well as social provision.[50]

The government sought to preclude and deter applicants as well as to quickly remove those whose claims failed, arguing that people without a legal right of entry make asylum claims in order to be able to remain in Britain for economic reasons.[51] Visa requirements were placed on countries from which asylum seekers travelled. Countries are added to the visa list when the numbers of asylum claims are expected to increase.[52] Tuitt has argued that the imposition of visa requirements 'place[s] refugees in a position whereby, if they are to seek any form of territorial protection in Western European states, they are forced to comply with the image of the fraudulent refugee which Western states have constructed'.[53] In May 1985 such requirements were imposed on Sri Lanka, a former British colony, after an increase in the numbers of Tamils seeking protection in Britain. It had become commonplace to characterise asylum seekers as 'manifestly bogus', 'economic migrants' and 'liars, cheats and queue jumpers, as one MP described the Tamils'.[54] Visa requirements on other countries soon followed, many of which were former British colonies.[55] Following an increase in asylum claimants from Zimbabwe between July and September 2002, the Home Secretary placed Zimbabwe on the visa list.[56] On 11 February 2003 Britain suspended its party status to the 1959 Council of Europe Agreement on the Abolition of Visas for Refugees, justifying the move on the basis that refugees were travelling to Britain and 'either remaining illegally or making asylum applications under false identities in order to access the benefits system'.[57] Anderson has argued that it is the 'erasure of imperial history' that allows for a discourse of choice around the reasons why people from Zimbabwe, Sri Lanka and Kashmir travel to Britain, reflecting a 'dehistoricized present rather than post-colonial legacies'.[58]

The restrictive effect of visas is intensified when coupled with the impact of carrier sanctions, a system of imposing penalties on companies that bring undocumented persons across a border. The Immigration (Carriers' Liability) Act 1987 established a system whereby any ship or aircraft would be fined £1,000 for each undocumented passenger. The Home Secretary, Douglas Hurd, emphasised that the reason for the legislation was the increasing number of asylum claims, stating that '[t]he immediate spur to this proposal has been the arrival of over 800 people claiming asylum in the three months up to the end of February'.[59] Control measures that are implemented within a framework of private liability reallocate the task of immigration control from the state to private actors, such as airline and ferry personnel, thereby outsourcing the policing of borders to third parties.[60] The increase and diversification in such practices since the 1980s has resulted in the proliferation of sites at which the fate of people seeking entry to Britain is determined.

The official narrative put forward to justify control measures against people seeking asylum was that Britain's resources were limited and asylum seekers were a threat. This discourse helped to give currency to the idea that colonially secured wealth located in a post-colonial Britain belonged to people categorised as British citizens pursuant to the 1981 British Nationality Act. Dora Kostakopoulou and Robert Thomas have shown how 'the exclusionary power of national state, cultural and identity related aspects of territoriality have been combined with the material powers of territory', leading to people seeking asylum being seen not only as 'culturally other and a threat to the identity of the nation' but also as 'responsible for the depletion of the material resources needed for the sustenance of the nation'.[61] Asylum seekers' alien rather than subject status is historically contingent. Their alienation was effected through changes to immigration and nationality laws, a process that entailed the removal of their entry rights to Britain.

Legislating asylum: excluding former subjects

The Asylum and Immigration Appeals Act 1993, introduced by John Major's Conservative government, represented Britain's first attempt at detailed asylum legislation. In 1992, in spite of the very recent legislative history of the alienation of British subjects, including the deflection of Kenyan and Ugandan Asians in flight from persecution, the Conservative Home Secretary Kenneth Clarke introduced the Bill by emphasising the 'long and honourable tradition in the United Kingdom of offering political asylum to those who flee to this country'.[62] He spoke of the Bill as being about 'strengthen[ing] our system of controlling entry and excluding people not entitled to be here'.[63] He used the same rationale for 'strict immigration control' as his predecessor Home Secretaries, claiming that 'good race relations' depended on it, as though institutionalised state racism begets anti-racism.[64] Clarke spoke generally of deflecting people from 'third-world' and 'troubled' countries,[65] some of which would have been former British colonies but were not acknowledged as such.

Roy Hattersley, the shadow Home Secretary, who had spoken against the racism of the 1981 British Nationality Act, reminded the House of Commons of the connection between Britain's colonial past and contemporary immigration and encouraged the government to take on the 'responsibility of empire'.

> Our immigration relationship is different from that of the rest of Europe as we have an imperial inheritance, the responsibility of empire and a duty to Commonwealth citizens who came to this country 30 or 40 years ago at the invitation of the Government, and who are denied the right for their families to visit them. That is a disgrace and I shall vote against the Bill with as much enthusiasm as I have voted against any Bill, because it is one of the most squalid measures ever to be put before the House.[66]

His position was not a popular one. People seeking asylum were described by Clarke and other parliamentarians as having arrived in Britain 'suddenly', 'unpredictably' and 'unexpectedly'.[67] Yet, as Hattersley had tried to point out, their arrival was entirely predictable both as a result of the impact of British imperial rule and the manner in which subjects had been alienated through successive immigration laws.

The Act set out the procedural rules governing people seeking protection and their dependants. It amended provisions on rights of appeal contained in the Immigration Act 1971 and extended the provisions of the Immigration (Carriers' Liability) Act 1987 to transit passengers. The 1993 Act effectively incorporated the 1951 Refugee Convention into domestic law. It was stated that '[n]othing in the immigration rules (within the meaning of the 1971 Act) shall lay down any practice which would be contrary to the Convention'.[68] Prior to the 1993 Act, the decision to remove a person seeking protection was a matter of administrative discretion, requiring only observance of the principle of *non-refoulement*, that people must not be sent back to places where they risk persecution, as per the 1951 Refugee Convention.[69] Although the Act introduced an in-country right of appeal for asylum applicants, overall it was restrictive, curtailing the socio-economic rights of asylum applicants and removing their right to permanent accommodation provided by the local authority.[70]

The 1993 Act followed pressure from NGOs and courts to make the procedure for dealing with asylum claims more structured.[71] Although no mention of European norms was made in the Act, its content was heavily influenced by European intergovernmental cooperation. European interior ministers cooperated in secret on matters considered to affect internal security, including irregularised migration. This highly restrictive context was Britain's first experience of legislating specifically on asylum. The 1993 Act was to a large extent a product of the non-binding agreements reached in the course of intergovernmental cooperation, such as the London Resolutions, a set of concepts including the 'safe third country', the 'safe country of origin' and 'manifestly unfounded claims' – all designed to deflect people seeking protection and limit access to territory and procedures.[72] Amnesty International reported in 1995 that individuals returned under 'safe third country' rules were frequently subjected to chain-*refoulement* whereby the country to which they were returned refused responsibility for examining their claims. The Home Office's response was that it 'does not consider it either necessary or advisable to seek guarantees from other States' and that it is not the government's 'policy to do so'.[73] This approach was adopted in the immigration rules, which stated that in cases where the Home Office has refused an asylum application on safe third country grounds, the Home Office 'is under no obligation to consult the authorities of the third country before the removal of [the] applicant'.[74]

In 1995, echoing the tired rationale of previous Home Secretaries, Michael Howard introduced the Asylum and Immigration Bill by declaring that 'good race relations' depended on 'firm but fair immigration controls'.[75] Once again, racism was presented as the result of the presence of racialised people in Britain and its amelioration held up as a quid pro quo for immigration control. The Race Relations (Amendment) Act 2000 extended anti-discrimination legislation into the public sector, but excluded from its scope decision making on immigration.[76] The Asylum and Immigration Act 1996 introduced new criminal offences including knowingly assisting asylum seekers to gain entry into Britain, and knowingly helping someone to obtain leave to remain through deception.[77] Penalties for immigration offences were extended,[78] as were police and immigration officials' powers to search and arrest.[79] It became a criminal offence for employers to hire a person subject to immigration control and who requires permission to enter or to remain, or who is prevented from undertaking employment due to a condition attached to their entry or admission.[80] The Act introduced a penalty of £5,000 where an employer could not prove an employee's right to work.[81] The Refugee Council reported in 1999 that these provisions affected employers' willingness to hire asylum applicants and refugees as a result of the burdensome documentation requirements and the risk of penalty in cases of error.[82]

The 1996 Act, like the 1993 Act, contained provisions modelled on developments that were taking place at the European level. Colin Harvey has commented on the contrast between the British government's general scepticism towards European integration and its enthusiasm for European asylum norms agreed intergovernmentally.[83] The Act included a power for the Home Secretary to designate countries in which there is 'in general no serious risk of persecution',[84] a concept taken directly from the 1992 London Resolutions.[85] It denied 'safe third country' applicants an in-country right of appeal, thereby reversing the general in-country right of appeal granted to asylum applicants in the 1993 Act.[86] Under the Act a 'state of upheaval' declaration could be made in relation to a specific country 'subject to such a fundamental change in circumstances that [the Home Secretary] would not normally order the return of a person to that country'. The Democratic Republic of Congo (formerly Zaire), a former Belgian colony, was the first country to be designated as being in a 'state of upheaval'. The second was Sierra Leone, a former British colony.[87]

Courts and colonial power

Courts operate within a framework of state sovereignty within which the legitimacy of borders and immigration control is assumed. Fundamentally, the capacity for the judiciary to effectively review immigration and asylum decisions is structurally limited due to the courts' inability to question the government's claim to sovereign power to grant or refuse legal status. This point is illustrated in what follows with reference to three Supreme Court cases: the 1987 case of *Bugdaycay* v. *Secretary of State for the Home Department*,[88] which was the first time the 1951 Refugee

Convention was considered by the Supreme Court; the 2018 case of *Rhuppiah* v. *Secretary of State for the Home Department*[89] on the meaning of a precarious immigration status where a claimant seeks to rely on Article 8 of the ECHR on the right to a private life in challenging a removal decision; and the case of *N* v. *Secretary of State for the Home Department*[90] on the scope for reliance on Article 3 of the ECHR by claimants challenging removal where their life depends on access to healthcare in Britain.

The legal and administrative developments of the 1970s, 1980s and 1990s resulted in a burgeoning and increasingly formalised immigration and asylum bureaucracy. One consequence of the formalisation of the asylum system was that the judiciary assumed a significant role in monitoring official decision making.[91] Legal representatives and judges were able to invoke formalised norms, providing some scope for scrutiny of executive decisions relating to individual rights. Despite the limited scope for judicial review of immigration and asylum decisions at the time, these cases made up 72 per cent of the caseload between 1987 and 1989.[92] Judges can only review the merits of an administrative decision when hearing appeals, but not in the course of judicial review. For these applications, only procedural aspects of administrative decision making can be revisited on grounds of illegality, irrationality, or procedural impropriety. As numbers of judicial review applications increased, the judiciary's response became increasingly conservative.[93] Despite the courts' habitual adoption of a highly deferential approach to immigration decisions, thereby allowing the executive to exercise 'a wide power to develop and administer asylum policy',[94] they nevertheless tend to be assumed to have an overall progressive effect on the field. While this might be true incrementally, it is difficult to draw overall conclusions about courts' attitudes to migrant applicants. This is because of the rights-based nature of the immigration and asylum docket. Even if courts only find in favour of a small percentage of applicants, the overall effect can seem progressive because it is always the individual claimant who is appealing an initial refusal by the Home Office, which only appears in court to defend its position. Further, the response of governments to the practical effects of court decisions has been to limit as far as possible access to courts in order to pre-empt judicial intervention. Ad hoc legislative responses are used to nullify court decisions that go against it.

Bugdaycay v. *Secretary of State for the Home Department*: adjudicating the impossible

Bugdaycay concerned four conjoined appeals, all applicants from former British colonies challenging refugee status refusal decisions. In 1987 judicial review was the only means by which immigration and asylum decisions could be challenged. The court refused to review the decision to reject the asylum claims in the first three cases despite the appellants' claims that they would face political persecution if returned to Pakistan. The court made this decision on the basis that the appellants had obtained leave to enter by falsely stating that they were visitors when their intention was to claim asylum. It held that it would not question the fact finding of a discretionary decision by the Home Office regarding an application for asylum, except on grounds of irrationality. Lord Bridge emphasised that 'the resolution of any issue of fact and the exercise of any discretion in relation to an application for asylum as a refugee lie exclusively within the jurisdiction of the Secretary of State subject only to the court's power of review'.[95]

In respect of the fourth applicant, Musisi, a Ugandan who had arrived in Britain having travelled through Kenya, the court reviewed the decision on the basis that the procedures to which the applicant's claim was subject were inadequate. Not only was the immigration officer who had interviewed the applicant not aware of the situation in Uganda, the Home Office had also failed to ascertain whether Musisi would be returned to Uganda if sent to Kenya. Lord Bridge made the since oft-quoted declaration that the courts are entitled, within limits, 'to subject an administrative decision to the more rigorous examination, to ensure that it is in no way flawed, according to the gravity of the issues which the decision determines'. 'The most fundamental of all human rights', he continued, 'is the individual's right to life and when an administrative decision under challenge is said to be one which may put the applicant's life at risk, the basis of the decision must surely call for the most anxious scrutiny.'[96]

Lord Templeton similarly considered that 'where the result of a flawed decision may imperil life or liberty a special responsibility lies on the court in the examination of the decision-making process'.[97] These statements have been said to represent an 'unequivocal recognition of the need for stricter scrutiny of administrative discretion where fundamental human rights are at stake, and of the need to protect those rights'.[98] Yet a close reading of the case demonstrates the limits of the review undertaken as well as the extent of judicial deference to immigration decisions and the legal frameworks within which they are made. According to Lord Bridge,

> all questions of fact on which the discretionary decision whether to grant or withhold leave to enter or remain depends must necessarily be determined by the immigration

officer or the Secretary of State in the exercise of the discretion which is exclusively conferred upon them by section 4(1) of the [Immigration] Act [1971]. The question whether an applicant for leave to enter or remain is or is not a refugee is only one, even if a particularly important one required by paragraph 73 of HC 169 to be referred to the Home Office, of a multiplicity of questions which immigration officers and officials of the Home Office acting for the Secretary of State must daily determine in dealing with applications for leave to enter or remain.[99]

This paragraph marks a change in tone whereby the life and death question of whether someone is a refugee becomes 'only one', albeit important, matter for immigration officers and the Home Office to consider when determining whether a person is to be granted permission to enter and remain in Britain. Section 4(1) of the Immigration Act 1971 to which Lord Bridge refers stipulates that the power to grant or refuse leave to enter Britain lies with immigration officers, and that the power to grant leave to remain or vary its duration or conditions lies with the Home Secretary. Thus, despite calling for 'anxious scrutiny' of administrative decisions which have the potential to affect an individual's right to life, Lord Bridge is nevertheless deferential towards the 1971 Act and the ultimate discretion it grants the executive as regards entry decisions.

Although it is unsurprising that the overarching power of the British government to recognise or refuse legal status has been deemed to lie beyond the scope of judicial scrutiny, the assignation of non-justiciability in this context draws attention to the limited potential for court processes to lead to racial justice outcomes. It is difficult to imagine the Supreme Court ruling that Parliament could not have intended to deprive colony and Commonwealth citizens of the right to enter and remain in Britain through the

1971 Act. Yet Britain's jurisdiction was not exclusively a national one at the time of *Bugdaycay*. Britain remained a colonial power with subjects in colonies overseas. Indeed, the existence and work of the Judicial Committee of the Privy Council daily calls into question the boundaries of British jurisdiction. The Privy Council is staffed by Supreme Court judges along with other senior British judges and those of Commonwealth nations. It is the highest appeal court for a number of Commonwealth countries, the British Overseas Territories and the British Crown dependencies. Its rulings form precedents in England and Wales as well as other common law jurisdictions. While not the most visible court, the Privy Council is a fully operational relic of the British Empire. It now shares a building with the Supreme Court, unavoidably raising the question of where British legal jurisdiction begins and ends. In the absence of scrutinising Parliament's legislative intentions in *Bugdaycay*, the Supreme Court would have had to do the impossible and acknowledge the 1971 and 1981 Acts for what they were: acts of colonial theft. In order to do this, it would have had to recognise all claims of former colonial subjects as legitimate claims to entitlement to stolen colonial wealth and resources located within Britain's newly drawn national boundaries. The fact that no conventional legal basis exists that would permit such a reparative-oriented decision points to the limits of the legal system for achieving racial justice. The Supreme Court cannot grapple with the broader questions of justice at stake in the 1971 and 1981 Act's cordoning off of colonial spoils without calling into question Britain's existence as a sovereign nation-state, and by implication its own power of adjudication.

Rhuppiah v. *Secretary of State for the Home Department*: recognising precarity

The 2014 Immigration Act, which implemented the hostile environment, sought to constrain judicial scrutiny of status refusal and removal decisions. The Act inserted into Part 5A of the Nationality, Immigration and Asylum Act 2002 section 117B(5), entitled 'Article 8 of the ECHR: Public Interest Considerations'. This provision stipulates that little weight should be given to a private life that is established at a time when a person's immigration status is 'precarious'. In 2018 the Supreme Court delivered its judgment in the case of *Rhuppiah*, in which it ruled on what it means to occupy a precarious legal status in Britain. Ms Rhuppiah had travelled to Britain from Tanzania, a former British colony. After living and studying in Britain for several years she found herself facing removal following the denial of her application for indefinite leave to remain. Ms Rhuppiah had formed a long-standing friendship and relationship of primary care with Ms Charles, who suffered from a debilitating illness. Ms Rhuppiah sought to rely on Article 8 of the ECHR[100] in challenging her removal, arguing that it would amount to a disproportionate interference with her private life. Article 8 of the ECHR protects the right to private and family life:

> 1. Everyone has the right to respect for his private and family life, his home and his correspondence.
> 2. There shall be no interference by a public authority with the exercise of this right except such as is in accordance with the law and is necessary in a democratic society in the interests of national security, public safety or the economic well-being of the country, for the prevention of disorder or crime, for the protection of health or morals, or for the protection of the rights and freedoms of others.

Article 8 thus allows for interference with the right by a public authority in the instances set out in Article 8(2). The European Court of Human Rights has held that the meaning of 'private life' is not confined to a narrow understanding of a person's personal life and includes 'to a certain degree the right to establish and develop relationships with other human beings'.[101]

Section 117B(5) instructs courts or tribunals tasked with determining whether a removal decision is an unlawful interference with Article 8 on the question of what is to be considered 'in the public interest'. It begins with the statement that 'the maintenance of effective immigration control is in the public interest'.[102] It is clear that the 'public' is conceptualised as encompassing people legally recognised as British citizens, since 'effective immigration controls' are not in the interests of those excluded from the post-1971 and 1981 conceptualisation of the British public. Also deemed to be 'in the public interest, and in particular in the interests of the economic well-being of the United Kingdom' is that 'persons who seek to enter or remain in the United Kingdom are able to speak English, because persons who can speak English are less of a burden on taxpayers, and are better able to integrate into society'.[103] The same set of interests are also considered to be protected where people seeking to enter and remain in Britain are 'financially independent' because such persons will not be a 'burden on taxpayers' and are better able to integrate into society.[104] The invocation of the interests of the 'English-speaking taxpayer' feeds the mythology of a post-colonial Britain whose riches belong in the first instance to white Britons. Erased is the history of Britain's economic progress, which was made possible through processes of colonial dispossession.

The particular provision under consideration by the court in *Rhuppiah* was Section 117B(5), which states that '[l]ittle weight should be given to a private life established by a person at a time when the person's immigration status is precarious'. Thus, in the balancing act entailed in determining whether Article 8 rights have been unlawfully interfered with, courts and tribunals are to attach little weight to a private life established at a time when such a person's immigration status is *precarious*, and not only when a person is present unlawfully. The effect of Section 117B(5) is to make it much more difficult for claimants to rely on Article 8 when fighting removal decisions. Embodied in the amendments introduced in the 2014 Immigration Act is both the reification of secure status in the form of citizenship, and the precaritisation of racialised life whereby people who do not have a secure status, disproportionately racialised people, live under the threat of expulsion.

The Supreme Court, in determining the meaning of 'precarious', held that 'everyone who, not being a UK citizen, is present in the UK and who has leave to reside here other than to do so indefinitely has a precarious immigration status for the purposes of section 117B(5)'.[105] The decision in *Rhuppiah* means that people who had a temporary status in Britain could not argue that their status was not precarious because they assumed it would be renewed and eventually made permanent. The effect of Section 117B(5) is that a private life, which includes familial and close personal relationships such as those of Ms Rhuppiah and Ms Charles, cannot be safely created by those with a temporary status. People residing in Britain on a temporary status are at the constant mercy of the state. Hanging over them is the threat of losing their status and of a court attaching little weight to the private life they established while holding that temporary status.

Although the court's interpretation of the meaning of precarious immigration status relates to the application of Section 117B(5), for many racialised people their legal status, even where they are naturalised citizens, is precarious. The court left indefinite leave to remain outside the scope of 'precarious', yet this is also an insecure status since it can be lost when a person lives outside Britain for more than two years and can be withdrawn on grounds of public security, public health or public policy. Section 117B(5) reflects in law the idea that colonial spoils, broadly conceived so as to include the freedom to make everyday choices about how to live one's life, are predominantly a privilege attached to being white and British. The Home Office insists that citizenship 'is a privilege not a right'.[106] While the privileges attached to citizenship extend to racialised Britons, they are in a minority and are especially vulnerable to having their citizenship revoked under citizenship deprivation laws.[107] Under Section 40(2) of the British Nationality Act 1981 the Home Secretary 'may by order deprive a person of a citizenship status if the Secretary of State is satisfied that deprivation is conducive to the public good'. However, where a person would be made stateless pursuant to the revocation of their citizenship, the Home Secretary may not make such an order, unless there are 'reasonable grounds for believing that the person is able, under the law of a country or territory outside the United Kingdom, to become a national of such a country or territory'.[108] Racialised Britons are therefore at disproportionate risk of having their citizenship revoked because they are more likely than white Britons to have dual nationality or the possibility of acquiring another nationality. Home Secretaries have shown increasing willingness to revoke citizenship in situations that risk making people stateless, sometimes with fatal consequences, as we saw in relation to the case of Shamima Begum in 2019, whose newborn baby died after then Home Secretary, Sajid Javid, deprived her of her British citizenship.

The use of the term precarious in Section 117B(5), together with the wide scope of meaning attached to it by the Supreme Court, have the effect of reifying citizenship. Meanwhile, measures have increasingly been introduced which make it more difficult for racialised people to attain the threshold required to be granted citizenship and make it easier for the status to be withdrawn. Alongside citizenship deprivation laws, there has been an increase in the number of passport removals and denials of naturalisation, particularly through the operation of the 'good character' test, which has been the main reason for citizenship refusal decisions in recent years.[109] Nisha Kapoor and Kasia Narkowicz note that while the denial of citizenship through the refusal of naturalisation applications does not result in the withdrawal of residency rights, it does 'maintain a position of precariousness for those refused, restricting freedom of movement for those with no viable passport and preserving a sustained possibility for deportation at future dates'.[110] The scope of the 'good character' test has expanded beyond consideration of criminal behaviour so as to include scrutiny of 'non conducive, adverse character, conduct or associations' in the course of decision making on applications for leave to remain and citizenship.[111] Kapoor and Narkowicz argue that the effect of such measures is to 'starkly illuminate the extension of the border beyond the point of immigration so that marginal subjects who possess legal citizenship remain vulnerable and in positions of precarity through maintained raced and classed structures of exclusion'.[112] Home Office guidance states that the (non-exhaustive) factors that suggest that a person will 'not normally' be considered to be of good character include criminality and suspected criminality, 'financial soundness', 'notoriety' – that is, their activities have 'cast serious doubt on their standing in the local community' – and 'immigration-related matters'.[113] The countries from which nationals are most likely to be refused citizenship on character grounds tend to be those from which a high proportion of asylum applicants originate, as well as those experiencing post-colonial instability in the form of civil war or imperialist invasion in which Britain has been directly on indirectly involved.[114]

Racialised people are disproportionately represented in the 'precarious' status category. The broad definition attached to 'precarious' in *Rhuppiah* narrows further the already limited scope for racial justice via processes of legal status recognition within the colonial state. As Kapoor and Narkowicz have argued with respect to the use of the 'good character' test to refuse naturalisation, it 'cements an impossible threshold' for racialised people seeking citizenship status.[115] Determining whether an applicant meets the criteria for a secure status thus feeds the colonial civilised/uncivilised dichotomy. In this way status recognition regimes operate according to a colonial logic. A failure to pass the 'good character' test becomes equivalent to a finding of barbarousness, which, in the era of the British Empire, legitimised outright dispossession of land and rights.[116] Such a finding in the context of refusal of naturalisation ultimately renders the applicant vulnerable to removal. The 'good character' test thus has racialising outcomes. Those found not to be of good character are constructed as racially inferior and as deserving of the position of vulnerability in which they subsequently find themselves. Meanwhile, white Britons are for the most part understood to be the authentic holders of British citizenship, as per the parameters of the 1981 British Nationality Act. It is white Britons who are effectively invoked as the 'public' in need of protection via 'the maintenance of effective immigration control' in Section 117B(1). It is in their name that access to citizenship is so fervently policed through the application of the 'good character' test. It is therefore unsurprising that white Britons come to understand themselves as especially entitled to the privileges associated with secure status.

Although *Rhuppiah* entailed a ruling on private and not family life and on having a 'precarious' and not an unlawful immigration status, there are broader points to be gleaned from Section 117B. It is possible when regularly reading case law to become too familiar with terms such as 'private', 'family life' and 'interference', and for them to lose meaning other than that which is legally designated. If we pause to consider what 'family life' is and what 'interference' is, the violence of Section 117B more broadly becomes palpable. Section 117B(4) states that '[l]ittle weight should be given to (a) a private life, or (b) a relationship formed with a qualifying partner, that is established by a person at a time when the person is in the United Kingdom unlawfully'. The law thus demands that people unlawfully present in Britain either place their lives on hold or heed the racist dictum, 'Go home', which in 2013 emblazoned vans commissioned by the Home Office to drive around areas of London in which racialised people live. The effect of Section 117B(4) is that a family life cannot be safely created by those unlawfully present in Britain. The law's effective instruction to those present in Britain unlawfully or with an insecure status is to be wary about living their lives, about forming loving relationships, about having children. They cannot assume the safety of the familial and personal relationships that people with secure statuses take for granted. Thus, the descriptor 'interference' becomes apparent for the euphemism that it is. Legitimate interference with the right to a private and family life constantly sees families separated. It has been held, for instance, to include the removal of a British citizen's Jamaican husband who was in Britain unlawfully at the time they were married.[117] Legitimate interference becomes tantamount to racially targeted destruction of the loving relationships that make life meaningful, a colonial practice with a long history. Colonial authorities destroyed racialised families in multiple ways, stealing children from their parents[118] and selling enslaved members of the same family separately.[119] Colonial states continue to 'interfere' with racialised families' loving relationships by disproportionately scrutinising their marriages,[120] deporting their members,[121] separating them,[122] refusing family reunification[123] and incarcerating them.[124]

Asylum seekers and the welfare state: eliding the colonial

On introducing the 1996 Asylum and Immigration Act, Michael Howard had explicitly linked asylum with welfare, arguing that Britain 'is far too attractive a destination for bogus asylum seekers and other illegal immigrants. The reason is simple: it is far easier to obtain access to jobs and benefits here than almost anywhere else.'[125] Howard thus peddled the notion that people travel to Britain to access resources to which they are not entitled. This history-effacing narrative has long provided the justification for the introduction of measures which make it more difficult for people to access vital support services after arriving in Britain. In a precursor to the hostile environment policy introduced by Theresa May in 2014, in 1995 Howard called for the NHS to 'find better ways of controlling access to free medical treatment ... and to improve procedures to enable providers of benefits and services to identify ineligible persons from abroad'.[126] Limitations imposed on asylum seekers' access to support and welfare services operate 'on the assumption that the majority of asylum seekers are "bogus" and "undeserving", while the minority granted Convention status are the "deserving"'.[127] In 2002 Rosemary Sales could write that such legal developments 'have intensified differences among migrants, with a widening gap between the rights of the most precarious, including asylum seekers, compared to long term secure residents'.[128] Yet, as the 2018 Windrush scandal demonstrated, following the 2014 and 2016 Immigration Acts' implementation of the hostile environment policy, the security of long-term residents' rights and legal status has increasingly been called into question.

The 1996 Act limited access to welfare for persons seeking protection. There were media reports in the 1990s of hospitals refusing treatment to Kurdish people without documentation proving their protection status.[129] In 1996 the Home Office Immigration and Nationality Directorate (IND) issued guidelines targeted at welfare departments concerned with housing, student bursaries and council tax benefits, inviting 'local authorities to use facilities offered by the IND in identifying claimants who may be ineligible for a benefit or service by virtue of their immigration status; and to encourage local authorities to pass information to the IND about suspected immigration offenders'.[130] The Conservative government had previously enacted measures which removed access to welfare for asylum claimants who did not make their claim at the border, and from persons who had their claims refused at first instance.[131] The rules were the subject of a court challenge. Lord Justice Simon

Brown held that 'Parliament cannot have intended a significant number of genuine asylum seekers to be impaled on the horns of so intolerable a dilemma: the need either to abandon their claims to refugee status, or to maintain them as best they can but in a state of utter destitution.'[132]

The government's response was to include a provision in the 1996 Act that had the effect of reversing the Court of Appeal's ruling.[133] The Act's removal of access to social housing and financial welfare led legal representatives to rely on local authority administered legislation to ensure support for asylum claimants. Section 21 of the National Assistance Act 1948 required local authorities to provide 'welfare arrangements' for the 'blind, deaf, dumb and crippled', and provided for 'residential accommodation for persons aged eighteen or above who by reason of age, infirmity or any other circumstances are in need of care and attention which is not otherwise available to them'.[134] A court upheld the application of this provision to local authority responsibility for asylum applicants. The result was that adult asylum seekers were granted housing and subsistence in the form of vouchers.[135] Initially a cashless voucher scheme was in place whereby Sodexo, a French company, provided vouchers that were only exchangeable at designated supermarkets. Under the scheme, checkout operators were required to check the eligibility of people using the vouchers and ensure that purchases did not include prohibited items such as cigarettes and alcohol.[136] Alice Bloch and Lisa Schuster documented the way in which the voucher system 'resulted in the stigmatisation of asylum seekers by marking them out clearly as different and dependent'.[137] This legal measure, though abolished after a Home Office review in 2000,[138] in singling out racialised welfare users for the voucher scheme, served to make them hyper-visible and construct them as underserving as compared with white British recipients of welfare.

In 1997 the newly elected Labour government quickly busied itself with attempting to curb growing numbers of persons seeking asylum in Britain. Asylum applications grew by around 4,000 a year in 1988 to over 32,000 in 1997.[139] Numbers continued to rise in the late 1990s, with 71,160 applications in 1999, primarily as a result of war in Yugoslavia and the Kosovo crisis.[140] Applications peaked at 84,000 in 2002.[141] The Immigration and Asylum Act 1999 followed the 1998 White Paper *Fairer, Faster, Firmer – A Modern Approach to Immigration and Asylum*. Jack Straw, the Home Secretary, introduced the White Paper by regretting the 'piecemeal and ill-considered changes' that had been made to the country's asylum regime 'over the last 20 years'. He described the system as being 'too slow' and suffering from 'huge backlogs'.[142] On 31 May 1998 the number of applications yet to be determined at the initial stage stood at 52,000; 10,000 of these had been lodged more than five years previously.[143] The White Paper was replete with fears about the rising cost of processing and supporting asylum applicants. The estimated cost of the administration of the asylum system was £500 million a year.[144] While £100 million was spent on processing individual applications, about £400 million was spent on the social, health and educational support provided to applicants, expected to double within five years 'unless action is taken to rationalise those arrangements and deal with asylum applications more quickly'.[145] The major concern in the White Paper was ostensibly to limit the costs of administering the system. In spite of this, a system of collectively determining claims was not considered in place of the individualised method of deciding applications.

A large measure of the Immigration and Asylum Act

1999 was reliant on secondary legislation to be introduced at a later date and not subject to parliamentary debate.[146] The 1999 Act made use of the criminal law in the regulation of asylum, making it an offence 'if, by means which include deception by him', a person 'obtains or seeks to obtain leave to enter or remain in the United Kingdom' or 'secures or seeks to secure the avoidance, postponement or revocation of enforcement action against him'.[147] The 1999 Act conferred on the Home Secretary new powers and created new possibilities for the search, arrest and detention of asylum applicants.[148] The legislation contributed, as Sales has argued, to the creation of 'a new social category of asylum seeker', separating the asylum seeker both in policy and popular discourse from recognised refugees.[149] A voucher scheme was imposed on all claimants,[150] and a system of forced dispersal put in place.[151] The aim of dispersal was to reduce the number of asylum applicants in London and Kent.[152] The policy is effectively one of racial segregation designed to reduce the appearance of the scale of asylum by distributing racialised people across Britain. Through dispersal, asylum applicants are made invisible by being removed and excluded from certain places, yet are also made hyper-visible through their forcible insertion into white-dominated spaces in which they represent diminutive minorities. The cumulative effect of dispersal policies has been that asylum seekers are exiled to the poorest parts of Britain.[153] Access to support is based on coercion, requiring asylum seekers to agree to dispersal in order to avoid destitution. In this way the movement of racialised people is continually subject to coercion, from their initial flight and mode of travel, to their forced displacement within Britain. Just as the label of 'Commonwealth citizen' had symbolised a threat to white supremacy and was invoked to justify racially exclusive measures in Britain in the 1960s and 1970s, its new iteration, that of 'asylum seeker', had assumed this role by the 1990s.

Fiona Williams has shown how 'racism has operated in specific ways over the historical development of the welfare state', arguing that the relationship between race and welfare articulated through restrictions on access for asylum seekers represents 'a nationalism and racism intrinsic in the provision of welfare'.[154] The omission in mainstream discourse of the colonial context for the presence of asylum seekers and other people without a legal status in Britain enables them to be presented as a drain on resources understood as belonging to Britons. Bhambra and Holmwood have criticised the habitual construction of immigration as having 'undermined the solidarity necessary to recognise the claims of fellow citizens to social rights' and called for acknowledgement of the connections between modern welfare states and histories of colonial dispossession.[155] They argue that colonialism was intrinsic to the historical trajectories of European welfare states, and show how the welfare state in Britain was 'dependent on a political economy of Imperial and (subsequently) Commonwealth preferences which was designed to enrich the British state while restricting the rights extended to subjects throughout its territories'.[156] Understanding the British welfare state as a product of colonialism and being cognisant of the continuum between colonialism and contemporary migratory movements to Britain enables us to see how measures that restrict access to welfare for asylum seekers feed the assertion, given legal force through the 1981 British Nationality Act, that white Britons are exclusively entitled to the wealth and resources accumulated via colonial dispossession.

N v. *Secretary of State for the Home Department*: deathbed access only

> The general principle is that a person cannot avoid return on the basis that they should continue to benefit from medical, social or other form of assistance provided in the UK.[157]

The cases that perhaps best demonstrate the way in which access to colonial spoils is withheld from people with geographical or ancestral histories of colonialism are those that involve people whose lives depend on being granted permission to remain in Britain so that they can continue accessing vital healthcare. Such cases are based on Article 3 of the ECHR which provides that 'No one shall be subjected to torture or to inhuman or degrading treatment or punishment.' Despite the absolute terms of this provision, it has been held to apply to medical treatment cases only in 'very exceptional circumstances'.[158] The result is that the courts regularly preside over the sending of people back to certain death. In the case of *N* v. *Secretary of State for the Home Department*, which remains the authority,[159] the Supreme Court set out the test as being

> whether the applicant's illness has reached such a critical stage (i.e. he is dying) that it would be inhuman treatment to deprive him of the care which he is currently receiving and send him home to an early death unless there is care available there to enable him to meet that fate with dignity.[160]

N, from Uganda, a former British colony, was receiving treatment for HIV/AIDS when she faced removal from Britain. She was not dying in the sense that the medical treatment she was receiving in Britain was effective. However, as she argued, if she were to be returned to Uganda her rights under Article 3 would be breached because she would not have access to the medication she required in order to stay alive and she would die a very painful death. The Supreme Court judges who considered her case were well aware of this fact. Lord Nicholls stated that N's

> doctors say that if she continues to have access to the drugs and medical facilities available in the United Kingdom she should remain well for 'decades'. But without these drugs and facilities her prognosis is 'appalling': she will suffer ill-health, discomfort, pain and death within a year or two.[161]

According to Lord Hope, N's prospects for surviving for more than a year or two if she were returned to Uganda were

> bleak. It is highly likely that the advanced medical care which has stabilised her condition by suppressing the HIV virus and would sustain her in good health were she to remain in this country for decades will no longer be available to her. If it is not, her condition is likely to reactivate and to deteriorate rapidly. There is no doubt that if that happens she will face an early death after a period of acute physical and mental suffering.[162]

Nevertheless, the Supreme Court deemed the Article 3 threshold not to have been reached in N's case. While the judges considered the pain, suffering and death that N would experience should she be removed as being of the utmost humanitarian concern, they nevertheless found that the Convention does not *oblige* states to grant the right to remain to people in order to avoid such outcomes. Precisely because N was receiving effective treatment and was not on her deathbed, her case fell outside the scope of Article 3. Lord Nicholls described N's removal as tantamount 'to having a life-support machine switched off',[163] an entirely inappropriate comparison since life-support machines are switched off in cases where there is no hope of recovery, whereas N could have lived a long and healthy life had she been permitted to stay in Britain and access the medication she needed. Lord Hope stated that '[t]he question must always be whether the enlargement [in interpretation of the ECHR] is one which the contracting parties would have accepted and agreed to be bound by'.[164] By confining the question before them to one of 'the extent of the obligations' under Article 3, the court could omit consideration of what a humanitarian approach required, as well as what justice demanded. A just approach, for example, might see states' obligations towards the populations of their former colonies as being reparative.

It is clear that the Supreme Court's decision was driven by specific policy goals rather than the wording of Article 3 of the ECHR. There is no doubt that the conditions N faced on removal fell within the ordinary meaning of the terms 'inhuman and degrading'. For the court, the policy question at issue was one of access to resources understood as belonging to those legally entitled to be in Britain and at risk of depletion on account of immigration. Article 3 could not be allowed to function as a route to an immigration status. Lord Hope thus considered that a finding in N's favour would 'risk drawing into the United Kingdom large numbers of people already suffering from HIV in the hope that they too could remain here indefinitely so that they could take the benefit of the medical resources that are available in this country'.[165] The court understood the dilemma it faced as being a choice between

> allowing the patient to remain in the host state to enjoy decades of healthy life at the expense of that state – an expense both in terms of the cost of continuing treatment (the medication itself being said by the Intervener to cost some £7,000 per annum) and any associated welfare benefits, and also in terms of immigration control and the likely impact of such a ruling upon other foreign AIDS sufferers aspiring to

these benefits – and deporting the patient to a life of rapidly declining health leading to a comparatively early death.[166]

By contrast, the dissenting judges made short shrift of the floodgates argument, stating that 'when one compares the total number of requests received (and those refused and accepted) as against the number of HIV cases, the so-called "floodgate" argument is totally misconceived'.[167] Further, unaddressed in the N decision is the question of how Britain came to be so rich in resources and to have one of the most advanced healthcare systems in the world. There is no mention of the resource and labour extraction entailed in colonisation and the fact that Britain's economy and infrastructure are products of this history.[168] Colonisation and ongoing forms of racial capitalist exploitation systematically destroyed vital means and methods of sustenance in Uganda and more widely in East Africa, severely affecting the health of local populations.[169] Lord Hope characterises African countries as 'still suffering so much from the relentless scourge of HIV/AIDS'.[170] It is easy to put African countries' problems down to AIDS, which as Cindy Patton points out is 'not a problem of Africa', but a 'problem of Western ethnocentrism'.[171] What Lord Hope does not say is that African countries are still suffering from the relentless scourge of colonialism. Another way of looking at N's case would have been to acknowledge that the resources in Britain that were keeping N alive in fact rightfully belong to her. Although the absence of such a critical discourse in the courtroom is unsurprising, a decision like that in N must be understood as ongoing colonial violence. The judges acknowledged that N's presence in Britain was what was keeping her alive, but through the application of human rights law they legitimised her removal, sending her to her death. N died within three months of her expulsion to Uganda.[172]

The judges construct wealth disparity and illnesses as unfortunate or natural occurrences rather than products of a colonially structured world. Lord Brown thus characterises the suffering to be faced by N on removal as flowing from 'a *naturally* occurring illness'.[173] Lady Hale acknowledges that in Britain, 'HIV is a long term but treatable illness whereas in sub-Saharan Africa for all but the tiny minority who can secure treatment it is a death sentence'.[174] This is a jarring description since the European Court of Human Rights decision in the case of *Soering* prohibits the return of individuals to countries where they face the death penalty.[175] In the court's ruling in *N* it was deemed that 'the alleged future harm would emanate not from the intentional acts or omissions of public authorities or non-State bodies, but instead from a naturally occurring illness and the lack of sufficient resources to deal with it in the receiving country'.[176] Yet the political cannot be bounded off in this way. The effect of constructing HIV and its lack of treatment in former colonies as a natural occurrence is to depoliticise the context of deep disparities in wealth and healthcare. The mass murder of colonised populations occurred not only through direct killings, but also as a result of resource deprivation, famine and the spread of disease.[177] Recurring famines in India, such as the Orissa famine in 1886, killed one in three people in the region.[178] The response of the British government was to do nothing. Colonial authorities prevented individuals from providing relief and exported 200 million pounds of rice to Britain. The colonial authorities argued that excessive deaths were nature's way of responding to overpopulation.[179] Yet deaths as a result of famine were not a natural occurrence. They followed the East India Company's destruction of the

Indian textile industry and the forcing of people into agriculture, an industry dependent on the weather. Ultimately, the effect of the ruling in *N* is to reproduce the 'let die' logic of colonialism which saw colonial administrations construct the murderous spread of disease and famine as nature's way of dealing with so-called surplus populations.

The European Convention on Human Rights: exclusive humanitarianism

It is clear from the above discussion that the framework of the European Convention on Human Rights has failed to protect the human rights of people categorised as migrants.[180] At the time the Convention was agreed, five states parties, including Britain, were colonial powers.[181] This colonial context was the foundation upon which the European human rights regime was constructed.[182] None of these colonial states would have ratified the Convention had it not provided them with the possibility of excluding their colonial subjects from its scope of application. The long-term British resistance to the application of the Convention was in part driven by colonial exigencies. In 1950 the Colonial Secretary, James Griffiths, expressed his opposition to the Convention in a manner that both revealed the racist paternalism of colonial rule and made clear the prevalence of ongoing colonial ambitions within the British government. He considered that the introduction of a system of individual petitions would 'cause considerable misunderstanding and political unsettlement' in colonial territories because '[t]he bulk of the people in most Colonies are still politically immature and the essence of good government among such people is respect for one single undivided authority'.[183] Following pressure exerted by British delegates, the 'colonial clause' was framed so as to protect the interests of colonial powers concerned not to extend human rights protections to colonial subjects.[184] The clause left it to their discretion whether to extend the Convention's application to colonial territories.[185] For states that submitted to the possibility of individual petitions to the European Court of Human Rights, the clause made it possible for colonial powers to exclude subjects in overseas colonies from being able to make such petitions.[186] It was not until 1998 that Protocol No. 11 abolished the optional clauses.[187] Britain ratified the Convention in 1951 and grudgingly extended its application to 42 of its colonial territories in 1953. This was done with the purpose of keeping at bay domestic and international criticism of British colonial rule.[188] However, the effect of this extension was limited, since Britain did not submit to its supervisory aspect until 1966. By this time the then Labour government was keen on joining the European Union and was thus 'intent on showing its European credentials'.[189] Moreover, by 1966 the British Empire had drastically reduced in size.[190]

In its decisions, the European Court of Human Rights consistently gives priority to the principle of state sovereignty, the 'well-established principle of international law' according to which states can control the entry and residence of 'aliens'.[191] Because the court's authority to adjudicate rests on the principle of state sovereignty, it cannot question the legitimacy of immigration law as an expression of state sovereignty. It is precisely the habitual exclusion from courts' consideration of the legitimacy or otherwise of the state's power to grant or refuse legal status that means that recognition-based arguments for migrant justice, including those based on human rights, are ultimately limited. The European Court of Human Rights has refused to comment on the human rights implications of citizen revocation decisions,[192] or to prevent the regular deportation of people categorised as 'foreign criminals'.[193] As Marie-Bénédicte Dembour writes, the court

> tends to regard migrant applicants as solely responsible for the problematic situation they are in. For example, they should not have had children when their status was insecure; they should have accessed nationality status when the opportunity was there; they should not have assumed that they would be able to settle and work outside their country of origin.[194]

In this way the European Court of Human Rights legitimises, reproduces and reinforces states' 'interference' with, or disproportionate violence against, racialised people.

The period covered in this chapter demonstrates how immigration and asylum laws worked in combination with a discourse around spontaneity and abuse of the asylum system peddled by officials to erase the colonial context in which contemporary migratory movements take place. The cases discussed show how the human rights framework fails, often with fatal consequences, to protect people who have been found to have no legal right of entry or stay. Courts cannot ultimately challenge state sovereignty without questioning their own power of adjudication. Their starting point will always be to accept the legitimacy of Britain's post-colonial articulation of its borders and their dispossessory effect. In the following chapter, we will see how many of the exclusionary elements in Britain's first asylum legislation were devised in the course of informal cooperation between European interior ministers, in which British governments played an agenda-setting role. Rather than pose a challenge to Britain's post-colonial articulation of its borders, European integration has served to accommodate and reinforce its border control regime.

Chapter 5

European citizens and third country nationals: Europe's colonial embrace

The mythological mainstream narrative on European integration is that it heralded a new dawn of peace, democracy and human rights. The reality is that the European Union's foundations lie in the colonial histories of its founding Member States, an origin story with which it has never grappled. European integration, rather than marking a turning point or rupture in relation to a violent past, is instead on a continuum of European colonialism.[1] Just as Britain passed immigration and nationality legislation designed to exclude racialised colony and Commonwealth citizens in the face of the defeat of its empire, European colonial powers came together in the post-war era to create a protectionist bloc to ensure that the spoils of European colonialism remained the domain of white Europeans. In view of this history, it is little surprise that Britain's European partners have been accommodating of its imperial identity and have not offered a challenge to its exclusion of its former colonial subjects.

In spite of this, a common misconception that gained traction in the run-up to the 2016 EU referendum was that Britain's control over its borders is hampered by its EU membership.[2] The reality is that Britain has always exploited its EU membership to enhance its capacity for

WORD CHOICE

SUPPORTED BY OTHER POWERS

control. It played the role of agenda setter in the context of early European intergovernmental cooperation on asylum and immigration policy, successfully pushing for the adoption of exclusionary policies across Europe. It retained its freedom to choose when to participate in measures on immigration and asylum after securing a flexible opt-out in 1997.[3] Britain has consistently used its opt-out to participate in restrictive measures that strengthen its capacity to exclude, while rejecting those aimed at enhancing protection standards for people seeking refuge in the EU.[4] Although it grudgingly accepted the principle of free movement of EU citizens, it did not join the Schengen Area and thus continues to exercise border controls in relation to the nationals of other EU Member States. In spite of this, the Leave campaign argued that exiting the EU would allow Britain to 'take back control' of its borders. Perhaps the most striking moment in this regard was when the UKIP leader Nigel Farage unveiled a poster depicting racialised refugees crossing the Croatia–Slovenia border in 2015 along with the slogan 'Breaking Point',[5] despite the fact that these individuals would have had no legal right to enter Britain.

LOOK THIS
POSTER UP

The EEC: substituting for the British Empire

A popular claim made by British politicians who supported a Leave vote in the run-up to the 2016 referendum on Britain's EU membership was that remaining in the EU hampers Britain's potential to be a global political and economic power.[6] Then Conservative MP Boris Johnson stated in a speech before the vote that '[i]t is absurd that Britain – historically a great free-trading nation – has been unable for 42 years' to negotiate a 'free trade deal' with Australia, New Zealand and India.[7] Quite apart from the

euphemistic characterisation of colonialism as being about
'free trade', the stark reality is that Britain's two applications to join the European Economic Community (EEC)
followed decades of post-war decline and ensuing indeci-
siveness about whether to join and thus jettison economic
dependence on Commonwealth markets, and with it any
prospect of a lasting imperial role for Britain. Membership
was seen as a means through which Britain could continue
to assert power globally in the face of the defeat of the
British Empire. As colonial populations ousted the British
and won their independence, post-war British governments
began to see the potential for growth and global influence as
lying exclusively in EEC membership. Britain's navigation
away from Commonwealth markets was not therefore a
liberal decolonising move in line with anti-colonial resistance movements. Instead, it was the outcome of successful
independence struggles based on long and varied histories of
resistance to British colonial rule from its outset.

EEC membership was thus seen as a substitute for
colonialism, both in economic and political terms.[8] On
asking Parliament to approve the government's decision to
seek to join the EEC in 1961, the Prime Minister, Harold
Macmillan, stated that '[t]he underlying issues, European
unity, the future of the Commonwealth, the strength of the
free world, are all of <u>capital</u> importance, and ... we firmly
believe that the United Kingdom has a positive part to play
in their development – for they are all related'.[9] Macmillan
went on to state that '[i]n this country, of course, there is a
long tradition of isolation',[10] a line that would be comical
if it did not reflect a profound and dangerous level of self-
delusion among British politicians, who continue to behave
as though Britain never had an empire spanning the greater
part of the globe. Macmillan even contradicted himself,

[margin notes, handwritten:]
EEC AS POWER ASSERTIVE
PRO COLONIALISM
★ QUESTION ABOUT CONSCIOUSNESS MAYBE

speaking of Britain's long-standing 'world-wide ties',[11] and insisting that 'entry into Europe' would not 'injure our relations with and influence in the Commonwealth, or be against the true interest of the Commonwealth'.[12]

Britain applied to join the EEC out of a wish to assume the position of 'the leading European power'.[13] Macmillan declared that 'our right place is in the vanguard of the movement towards the greater unity of the free world, and that we can lead better from within than outside'.[14] He considered that the EEC was a success, and believed that whichever nation emerged as the strongest within the bloc would come to lead western Europe.[15] Failure to join would result in 'the relative shrinking' of Britain's 'political and economic power compared with the massive grouping of the modern world'.[16] The Commonwealth was beginning to be regarded as having 'served its purpose admirably during the 1940s and early 1950s, when Britain was short of food and dollars, but, by the early 1960s ... seemed more of a burden than an asset'.[17] A strong economy was deemed crucial to Britain's capacity to advance a global political agenda. Macmillan thus considered that Commonwealth trade, while having 'been of great advantage', had 'reduced' in 'impact' over 'recent years'.[18]

In the face of the defeat of the British Empire, EEC membership was thus presented as a new avenue through which Britain could assert global power and influence. Arguments made by British politicians in favour of joining the EEC turned on the idea that membership would allow Britain to 'assert an independent role on the international stage', secure Britain's influence in the United States and guarantee 'an alternative locus of power' as Britain's colonial projects dwindled.[19] In 1967, the year Britain applied to join the EEC for the second time, the government also made the decision to withdraw entirely from east of Suez by the middle of the 1970s.[20] The idea that Britain should remain a global economic and political power was an unquestioned position in Whitehall. Helen Parr writes that while it would have been 'technically possible to remain apart', the government considered that 'to do so would be to limit Britain's international reach'.[21]

The decision to apply to join the EEC in 1961 carried with it an acceptance of the prospect of free movement of EEC populations.[22] This move coincided with the 1962 Commonwealth Immigrants Act, which was the first in a series of legislative measures that operated to close Britain's borders to racialised colony and Commonwealth citizens, and was passed within a year of the then Conservative government's first (unsuccessful) application to join the EEC. Ian Macleod, Secretary of State for the Colonies, raised concerns about what the relationship would be between 'the proposed control' and the European principle of the free movement of persons.[23] There was a desire among some in government that legislation preventing the arrival of racialised colony and Commonwealth citizens be enacted before Britain joined the EEC.[24]

[handwritten margin note: 1962 COMMONWEALTH IMMIGRANTS ACT]

Britain's application caused 'umbrage' among Old Dominion governments. It was seen as undermining the established principle of imperial preference, which guaranteed them advantageous trade arrangements with Britain.[25] The British government went to great lengths to make the Dominions' case to the EEC.[26] Before applying for EEC membership, British officials carried out diplomatic missions to the Dominions, going so far as to promise New Zealand that it would not sign the Treaty of Rome in the absence of its satisfaction with the terms.[27] However, it soon became clear that the EEC Member States were not willing to make any concessions to Britain in relation to the economic interests of Commonwealth countries. Any preferential treatment offered to New Zealand, for instance, was deemed to be in direct opposition to the interests of the EEC's Common Agricultural Policy, which was designed to provide economic security exclusively for European farmers.[28] Charles de Gaulle, President of France, made it clear that Britain was required to jettison the Commonwealth if it wished to join the EEC.[29] In 1961 he stated, '[w]e are willing to have the United Kingdom in the Common Market, but not the Commonwealth'.[30] 'I want her naked!' he declared, suggesting that Britain's EEC membership would only be considered once Britain's economic ties with the Commonwealth had been abandoned.[31]

The Commonwealth had been presented as the principal block to EEC membership in 1961, but by 1966 the Labour government was prepared to consider the matter as consisting of a small number of 'negotiable problems'.[32] Labour was responsive to the demand for manufactured goods, such as refrigerators, which had become 'more politically important than cheap bread', and these goods were purchased primarily from countries with equivalent income levels. The Prime Minister Harold Wilson's eventual decision to devalue the pound in 1967 was hotly resisted by sterling area countries. In a televised and radio broadcast address, Wilson blamed deficits exacerbated by costs incurred through recent British colonial interventions and the closure of the Suez Canal.[33]

Britain began to refuse to import goods such as textiles from racialised Commonwealth countries.[34] In spite of this the British government continued to exert influence on former colonies such as Nigeria, which was seeking to grow its national market, including by forging trade relationships with the EEC, to Whitehall's irritation.[35] Wilson lamented Commonwealth countries' refusal to do Britain's bidding in international fora. Despite centuries of British colonial exploitation, Wilson had the gall to tell the Commonwealth Secretary General in 1966 that '[t]he Commonwealth showed little disposition to help Britain or to play a constructive part, for example, at the UN'.[36] The British government was growing increasingly uncomfortable at what it arrogantly perceived as inappropriate expressions of independence and divergent interests by Commonwealth governments. A paper presented by the Commonwealth Secretary Herbert Bowden in 1967 insisted that 'the Commonwealth was a wasting asset. Commonwealth countries were diversifying their trade, were bargaining away Britain's preference in their markets and tended to exert pressure on Britain in global trading forums.'[37] Britain evidently overvalued its worth to Commonwealth economies, which were using their independence to grow their economies and demand equal trade structures, conditions that had been impossible under British rule.[38] India sought and received external post-war investment funds 'on a scale that Britain could not match'.[39] Britain had 'bled' India's economy 'of anything between 5 to 10%' of its GDP every year for almost two centuries prior to independence.[40] India's growth statistics only began to show improvement post-independence.[41]

Writing in 1970, Frederick Northedge questioned whether, with the end of its imperial role, Britain would be able to make 'the necessary mental adjustments' so as 'to maintain successfully the position of a Power of the second or perhaps third rank'.[42] He identified 'political nostalgia' as occupying 'a primary position' in the 'catalogue' of Britain's 'collective neuroses'.[43] The answer to Northedge's question must be that Britain did not make the necessary mental

SUN NEVER SETS ON THE BRITISH EMPIRE

adjustments. Britain has never known humility in the face of the loss of its empire, let alone the impulse to account for colonial terror. Instead, set deep within the British mindset is a delusion of ongoing imperial grandeur. Northedge's diagnosis of Britain's imperial nostalgia rested on the idea that its island status and colonial history meant that it suffered from a hubris complex. He wrote,

> [t]he British, because of their ancient security from foreign invasion, their remoteness, in mind if not in distance, from the complexities of European politics, their long-assured supremacy at the apex of the international pyramid of power, are peculiarly prone to assume that in all essentials the world is still much as it always was, and that Britain, despite all the evidence to the contrary, will still manage to come out on top, almost without effort.[44]

Northedge criticised the assumption among British politicians that, 'whatever the state of the British armed forces, no matter how weak the national economy and despite the reduction of the Commonwealth to an almost meaningless consultative association, British "influence" will somehow still continue to penetrate the Cabinets and Foreign Offices of the world'.[45]

The 2016 referendum on EU membership demonstrated that Britain still clings to such notions of imperial grandeur.[46] Skipping over the history of its bid to join the EU, politicians pushing for a Leave vote harboured fantasies of a Britain freed from the shackles of the EU and dominating the world stage.[47] The disastrous effects of Britain's misplaced imperial nostalgia and its refusal to recognise that the end of the British Empire was via defeat not decline continue to reverberate in Britain and beyond.[48] Paul Gilroy has shown how the 'postimperial hungering for renewed greatness' was key to Margaret Thatcher's leadership, 'particularly after

claim

her [triumph in the Falklands]'.[49] It has since 'mutated and emerged again as one significant element that propelled a largely reluctant country to war against Iraq in 2003',[50] the catastrophic results of which were the violent and premature deaths of two million Iraqis, and the destabilisation of the region, for which its inhabitants continue to pay the price.[51]

The above notwithstanding, it is important to recall that when Britain joined the EEC it was a colonial power with several overseas territories.[52] Its accession treaty with the EEC acknowledges this and lists the 'countries and territories' of Britain at the time it joined,[53] just as arrangements were made for the accommodation of overseas territories of the original members of the Community.[54] Britain's colonial identity on entry to the EEC is rarely noted in literature on EU integration, but it is crucial to understanding how it has been able to continue to harbour destructive notions of imperial grandeur. Its EEC membership did not serve as a rupture with Britain's colonial past. Rather, despite de Gaulle's rhetoric, the project of European integration has always accommodated Britain's and other Member States' colonial identities and ambitions in so far these have been compatible with its own.

European empires into European Union

> Leave this Europe where they are never done talking of Man, yet murder men everywhere they find them, at the corner of every one of their own streets, in all the corners of the globe.[55]

The European Union's idealised self-image is as a bastion of liberal civilisation, a defender of democracy and human rights. The mainstream narrative on the history of European integration is that its architects sought to build on what are assumed to be quintessentially European ideals of democracy, freedom and rights to build a future of peace and security for Europe.[56] The colonial origins and identity of the EU are rarely acknowledged in the many accounts of its history. Indeed, some widely cited texts dismiss altogether the importance of geopolitics in general and colonialism in particular, focusing instead on economic rationales in explaining the formation of the Union[57] While Europe's history includes the Reformation and the Enlightenment and a number of revolutions, each of which apparently inscribed in European identity progressive and universalist goals, coterminous with this history is one of colonial violence and theft. Europe's appeal to notions of *liberté, égalité, fraternité* has always coexisted with imperial wars and dispossession. Its founders drew on traditions that were undemocratic, militaristic, imperialistic, white and Christian-supremacist. At the core of the European project was the fortification of a space of white European supremacy in an era in which European colonialism was facing defeat. The idea that European integration was a desperate attempt by European colonial powers to regroup in the face of threats to their global supremacy was captured by the former Belgian Prime Minister Paul-Henri Spaak, speaking on the occasion of the establishment of the Council of Europe in 1948. 'A hundred and fifty million Europeans', he declared, 'have not the right to feel inferior to anyone, do you hear! There is no great country in this world that can look down on a hundred and fifty million Europeans who close their ranks in order to save themselves.'[58] Similar to Britain's seizure of colonial spoils via the passing of immigration and nationality legislation in the course of the 1960s, 1970s and 1980s, the origins of the European Union lie in a turn towards protectionism in an effort to seal off Europe's stolen riches in the face of victories over European colonialism worldwide.

Étienne Balibar has argued that the European Union never transcended its colonial past, hinting at 'European apartheid'.[59] For Balibar,

> [t]he colonial castes of the various nationalities (British, French, Dutch, Portuguese and so on) *worked together* to forge the idea of 'White' superiority, of civilisation as an interest that has to be defended against the savages. This representation – 'the White man's burden' – has contributed in a decisive way to moulding the modern notion of a supranational European or Western identity.[60]

Thus, the colonial garrison was where European identity was first forged. As Gerard Delanty has shown, in its confrontation with non-Christian civilisations, Europe sought to construct a hegemonic identity as one 'representing Freedom, Progress, Civilization and Christian Humanism'.[61] By portraying the Orient as despotic and morally backward, the 'Christian West was able to justify its imperialist drive'.[62] Racism, whether anti-black, anti-Muslim or antisemitic, is thus not recent or incidental to contemporary Europe, but has long been the means through which European powers have installed white supremacy at home and abroad. As Alana Lentin explains, 'the modern European project of constructing a "general idea of man" necessitates including a reference point: the non-human'[63]

It is estimated that the arrival of Europeans in the Americas in 1492 had led to 56 million deaths by 1600, and impacted the Earth's climate in the two centuries prior to the Industrial Revolution.[64] Despite the well-rehearsed account of the history of European integration, both in official and scholarly terms – that it was embarked upon in the interests of lasting peace and security in the wake of the Second World War[65] – European militaristic imperialism remained unabated. The Algerian War (1954–62), which killed more than a million people, is not cited as a breach of the peace promised by European integration, even though 'Algeria was just as much a part of France as ... Brittany'.[66] Despite the French government's assertion in 1954 that Algeria was part of France, its status as a colony with a majority Muslim and racialised population meant that it was not included in the white, Christian supremacist European integration project. Peace in Algeria was not prioritised, nor was Algeria deemed to qualify as a recipient of the benefits of EEC membership. Although Algeria was recognised as being part of France and Algerians were French citizens, negotiations yielded the outcome that the EEC principle of free movement of workers would not extend to Algerian workers.[67] Member States continue to take military action against non-EU Member States, and the EU has no inbuilt 'structural component' that is capable of preventing this.[68] The invasion of Iraq in 2003 by a handful of European governments in collaboration with the US, the death toll of which is estimated at two million,[69] along with France's periodic interventions in Mali,[70] demonstrate that the peace at the heart of the European project is promised only to the predominantly white European citizens living within the borders of Member States, while murderous imperialism continues elsewhere. Indeed, as Terese Jonsson has argued, the cost of stability within Europe is instability beyond its borders.[71]

Colonialism was firmly in situ at the time of the EEC's formation. The Paris agreement of 1957 saw EEC Member States include in the draft Treaty of Rome a set of special measures related to colonial investment concerning half the African continent and parts of the West Indies and Oceana.[72] The Rome Treaty's accommodation of colonialism meant that three-quarters of the EEC's landmass was located beyond the borders of continental Europe.[73] Despite the omission of the colonial in mainstream accounts of European integration, the European press at the time of the agreement of the 1957 Rome Treaty highlighted as one of its most important aspects the EEC's creation of 'Eurafrica', a colonial policy that would see the African continent exploited for its labour and resources in the interests of growing European economies.[74] The European integrationist Richard Coudenhove-Kalergi advocated for the project of Eurafrica on the basis that 'Africa could provide Europe with raw materials for its industry, nutrition for its population, land for its overpopulation, labor for its unemployed, and markets for its products'.[75]

Yet the emphasis in mainstream historical narratives of European integration is often on its economic drivers as these pertain to the creation of the European single market, while neglecting its racial capitalist dimensions.[76] It is no coincidence that racial capitalism emerged in western Europe and now finds its expression in European integration. Cedric Robinson argued that capitalism developed within a context of feudalism in a Europe that was already racially stratified.[77] Robin Kelley has written that '[t]he first European proletarians were racial subjects (Irish, Jews, Roma or Gypsies, Slavs, etc.)'.[78] Rather than being a break from feudalism, capitalism and racism 'evolved from it to produce a modern world system of "racial capitalism" dependent on slavery, violence, imperialism, and genocide'.[79] As Kelley explains, capitalism's role has not been to 'homogenize but to differentiate – to exaggerate regional, subcultural, and dialectical differences into

187

"racial" ones'.[80] Thus, as Gargi Bhattacharyya argues, 'capitalism as we have known it has had only this [racialised] trajectory of global development, in coincidence with the period of racialised demarcation of the world'.[81] The operation of racial capitalism has always depended upon particular institutions, such as markets and law. Law, in its claim to embody norms of universalism, equality, neutrality and rationality, serves to legitimise the global system of racial capitalism. ?.

Peo Hansen and Stefan Jonsson have argued that the 1957 Treaty's incorporation of the colonial project of Eurafrica had the effect of ensuring 'a continuation of old relations of dominance even under the new system'.[82] They describe Eurafrica as an institution of a 'transitory character', a '"vanishing mediator"'.[83] It functioned as 'a historical catalyst', which facilitated 'a smooth passage' from empire to European integration.[84] Once it had served its purpose of sustaining 'existing relations of dominance ... Eurafrica "vanishes", thus creating the impression of a historical break or discontinuity – between colonial and postcolonial; pre- and post-European integration; white supremacy and partnership; colonial exploitation and development; civilizing mission and third-world aid'.[85] Yet the EU was then, as it is now, an imperial entity. The fact that many Member States still have overseas colonial territories is something of an open secret. The geographical reach of contemporary colonial Europe[86] is neither depicted on maps that claim to show EU territory, nor in the European imaginary. Statistical information provided by the European Commission frequently lacks acknowledgement of the populations of overseas territories, despite their European status.[87] The transition from empires to union fostered a climate in which Member States neither had to reflect on nor account for colonialism

RICH DISCUSSION
QUESTION

and its legacies. Over the course of European integration a profound colonial amnesia has set in, reflected in dominant accounts of the EU's formation. The vacuum in recollection has in turn facilitated colonial nostalgia and ambition, sentiments that have long been allowed to fester in a Union that refuses to acknowledge its violent origins.[88]

European Union citizens: whiteness as free movement

Taken together, Articles 18, 20 and 21 of the Treaty on the Functioning of the European Union (TFEU) comprise EU citizenship and establish the rights that stem from it. Article 20(1) of the TFEU sets out European Union citizenship as follows: 'Citizenship of the Union is hereby established. Every person holding the nationality of a Member State shall be a citizen of the Union. Citizenship of the Union shall be additional to and not replace national citizenship.' EU citizenship is thus derivative of Member State nationality. This is important because it means that EU citizenship does not pose a challenge to Member State articulations of nationality law. Britain's exclusive post-colonial national boundaries are accommodated within the framework of EU law.

The legal benefits that stem from European citizenship include first and foremost that of free movement and non-discrimination. Article 21 of the TFEU states that 'Every citizen of the Union shall have the right to move and reside freely within the territory of the Member States, subject to the limitations and conditions laid down in the Treaties and by the measures adopted to give them effect.' Article 2(5) of the Schengen Borders Code defines 'persons enjoying the right of free movement under Union law' as follows:

LAW MAKERS MAKING HISTORY

Union citizens within the meaning of Article 20(1) TFEU, and third-country nationals who are members of the family of a Union citizen exercising his or her right to free movement to whom Directive 2004/38/EC of the European Parliament and of the Council applies; third country nationals and their family members, whatever their nationality, who, under agreements between the Union and its Member States, on the one hand, and those third countries, on the other hand, enjoy rights of free movement equivalent to those of Union citizens.

Those who enjoy the right of free movement are thus first and foremost EU citizens, on whose rights non-EU nationals who are family members can piggyback under certain conditions, as well as nationals of select states with which the EU has negotiated agreements. EU citizens are predominantly white, and the vast majority of those who take up their right to free movement are white.[89] Adam Weiss has argued that white skin facilitates the movement of white Europeans within the EU, allowing them 'to fit in wherever they go, inside or outside their country of nationality'.[90] European citizenship thus 'has a close affinity with whiteness'.[91] Vilna Bashi has argued that the clear preference among European states for white migration constructs white people as occupying a 'position at the top of two intersecting hierarchical systems: one a racial system, and the other a hierarchy of nations'.[92]

The protectionist European project thus necessitates the exclusion of non-members and the prioritisation of the interests of Member States. This is reflected in the principle of mutual recognition under EU law, which dictates that Member States are to permit the entry of workers trained and products sold in other Member States to circulate freely on their territories. Underpinning the principle is the assumption that goods are of a high quality simply by virtue of the fact that they originate in the EU, and similarly, that workers trained in the EU are necessarily better qualified than those trained elsewhere. The implication is that the same assumption cannot be made for persons and goods from outside the EU, which are presented as being potentially threatening to service users or hazardous to consumers. By contrast, discrimination by Member States against the citizens of other Member States is taken seriously under EU law. Article 18 of the TFEU declares that 'Within the scope of application of the Treaties, and without prejudice to any special provisions contained therein, any discrimination on grounds of nationality shall be prohibited.' In the 2001 case of *Grzelczyk* the Court of Justice of the European Union (CJEU) declared that 'Union citizenship is destined to be the fundamental status of nationals of the Member States, enabling those who find themselves in the same situation to enjoy the same treatment in law irrespective of their nationality, subject to such exceptions as are expressly provided for.'[93]

Patricia Tuitt has argued that the principle of free movement of persons has allowed the European Union to expand territorially, and thus locates the project of European integration on a continuum of imperialism.[94] 'Far from witnessing the birth of a political community without historical precedent', she writes, 'the origins of the European Union are distressingly familiar.'[95] The Rome Treaty generated 'the beginnings of a political force that gestures toward the age of discovery'.[96] For Tuitt the centrality of the principle of free movement to European unity, along with the doctrine of direct effect, which allows European citizens to invoke their rights under EU law in national courts, means that the success of the European project depends on its being taken up by EU citizens. Thus, the 'appropriation of Europe to

[handwritten margin notes: "NATIONALISM OR/AGIN PREJUDICE", "IS THIS TRUE THOUGH?"]

the exigencies of the European Union has occurred in the time-honoured fashion of encouraging the most courageous (most often too the economically advantaged) to test the new spaces to discover to what extent its seeming dissolution can yield hidden riches'.[97] For those who qualify as EU citizens, movement to another EU Member State may provide opportunities for the betterment of their lives. When considered alongside the position of those without a legal status under EU law, including those who must travel in an irregularised manner, making dangerous journeys in an attempt to reach European shores, EU citizenship emerges as a hyper-privileged category.

Article 19 of the TFEU empowers the Union to take action against racial discrimination, and a Directive exists prohibiting race discrimination.[98] However, it is rarely enforced. Article 10 of the Treaty on European Union (TEU) states, 'In defining and implementing its policies and activities, the Union shall aim to combat discrimination based on sex, racial or ethnic origin, religion or belief, disability, age or sexual orientation.' Thus, while the Treaties prohibit nationality discrimination, they only 'aim to' combat race discrimination. Cases before the CJEU on race discrimination are limited in number, 'unlike the extensive case law under Articles 18, 20, and 21 TFEU and the crush of cases arising under EU secondary law on the free movement of citizens within the Union'.[99] Drawing on Sara Ahmed, Adam Weiss describes the prohibition on nationality discrimination within the EU as 'performative', and the prohibition on race discrimination as 'non-performative'.[100] A 'performative' provision in the context of EU law would be one that has direct effect, which means it would create directly enforceable legal obligations. He writes, '[i]f the words "aim to" [in Article 10 of the TEU] were struck out,

Handwritten margin notes:
CLASSISM

LAW AS PERFORMATIVE
WHAT IS THE POINT OF
THE LAW IF IT IS NOT
BEING ENFORCED?

the provision would be performative', in the sense that it would have legal effects.[101] As it stands, the inclusion of the words 'aim to' mean that the provision is too vague to give it direct effect, because it does not fulfil the criteria of being clear and precise which are necessary for a provision to be directly effective.[102] In a context in which EU Member State nationals and those exercising free movement are predominantly white, it is significant that discrimination on the basis of nationality is enforced, while that against race is not. The elevation of nationality in the ordinance of the EU's anti-discrimination law framework means that it is predominantly white Europeans who benefit from legal protection under EU law.

The racially exclusive dimensions of the principle of free movement are well illustrated with reference to the story of Britain's entry into the EEC. Faced with the prospect of British membership, Member States were concerned about colony and Commonwealth citizens entering the Union.[103] The British government made sure to clarify that in so far as the EEC was concerned, and particularly regarding the right of free movement of persons, its nationals were those with a right of abode in Britain. It attached a declaration on the definition of the term 'nationals' to its accession treaty with the EU.[104] Fellow EEC Member States were willing to accept the declaration on the meaning of a British national on condition that it excluded Commonwealth citizens outside Britain.[105] The declaration states that the term 'nationals of Member States' is understood to refer to 'persons who are citizens of the United Kingdom and Colonies or British subjects not possessing that citizenship or the citizenship of any other Commonwealth country or territory, who, in either case, have the right of abode in the United Kingdom, and are therefore exempt from United Kingdom

[handwritten margin note: WHAT DO WHITE EUROPEANS NOT BENEFIT FROM?]

[handwritten margin note: HOW DO WE DEFINE NATIONALS?]

immigration control', and 'persons who are citizens of the United Kingdom and Colonies by birth or by registration or naturalization in Gibraltar, or whose father was so born, registered or naturalized'.[106] Thus, the definition of a British national for the purposes of EEC law was the same as that set out in the Immigration Act 1971, which came into force on 1 January 1973, the same date as the entry into force of Britain's Accession Treaty with the EEC. The definition excluded many Commonwealth citizens living in Britain at the time.[107] One commentator captured the influence of the colonial mindset in Britain on the determination of the scope of the declaration in 1973:

> it would certainly not please the anti-immigration lobby [in Britain] to have economic, social, and legal rights extended to the Black British which would put them on a par with white British, nor would it please the racialist element in Community countries to see Black British grasping the opportunity to work on the Continent.[108]

The fact that the British government made the declaration on acceding to the EEC is indicative of the EEC's consternation about colony and Commonwealth subjects' potential claims to Europeanness as a result of the existence of a multitude of contested claims to Britishness stemming from its colonial status and history.

I'M NOT QUITE SURE ABOUT WHAT THIS MEANS...

The derivative nature of the concept of EU citizenship means that it has not posed a challenge to Britain's postcolonial articulation of its borders and nationality. The 2001 CJEU case of *Kaur* concerned Manjit Kaur, who was born in Kenya in 1949 and was a citizen of the United Kingdom and Colonies at the time that the 1968 Commonwealth Immigrants Act and the 1971 Immigration Act were passed. Under this legislation she lost her right of abode in Britain because she was not a 'patrial'. She thus fell outside the

ANECDOTAL UNDERSTANDING

definition of a Member State national for the purposes of EEC law as set out in the declaration attached to Britain's Accession Treaty. Following the passing of the British Nationality Act 1981 Ms Kaur became an Overseas British citizen, still with no right of abode. After the 1981 Act was passed, the British government substituted the 1972 declaration with one in 1982 stating that Member State nationals for the purposes of EEC law were British citizens, British subjects with a right of abode pursuant to the 1981 Act and British Dependent Territory citizens who acquire British citizenship via a connection with Gibraltar. The Member States issued a collective declaration that was annexed to the Treaty on European Union clarifying that, 'wherever in the Treaty establishing the European Community reference is made to nationals of the Member States, the question whether an individual possesses the nationality of a Member State shall be settled solely by reference to the national law of the Member State concerned'.[109] In 1996 Ms Kaur applied for leave to remain in Britain, which was refused the following year. The High Court, to which she applied for judicial review of this decision, referred a question to the CJEU on the matter relating to the application of EEC law. Ms Kaur argued that she wanted to travel and work in other Member States.[110] Her position was that although a Member State can define a concept of nationality, it can do so only in observance of fundamental rights that form part of EEC law. She asserted that British nationality law infringed fundamental rights by depriving Overseas British citizens of the right to enter the territory of which they are nationals and rendered them effectively stateless.[111] The British government defended its decision to refuse Ms Kaur leave to remain on the basis that she had 'no close connection' with Britain, and was one of many people who, as a result of its imperial history, retained 'some form of link' with Britain despite never having lived there or visited.[112]

The CJEU, ruling on the matter, accepted the British government's argument that 'it is for each Member State, having due regard to Community law, to lay down the conditions for the acquisition and loss of nationality'.[113] It considered that Britain had, on the basis of customary international law and 'in the light of its imperial and colonial past, defined several categories of British citizens whom it has recognised as having rights which differ according to the nature of the ties connecting them' to Britain.[114] The court thus accepted that the 1971 Immigration Act's rationale was to 'reserve the right of abode ... to those citizens who had the closest connections' to Britain.[115] In doing so, the court accepted patriality, that is, a connection to whiteness, as being the legitimate basis for belonging in Britain, and by implication, in the EEC. The CJEU's wholly deferential attitude towards British immigration and nationality laws serves to legitimise their colonially appropriative effects. EU law thus not only fails to challenge ongoing colonial violence in the form of Britain's immigration and nationality laws, it also reinforces and reproduces that violence within the EU, creating it as a racially exclusive space.

Third country nationals in a European colonial order

Rather than transcending the excesses of Europe's past, the project of European integration has bolstered the structures of global inequality left in place by colonialism. Intrinsic to the making and maintaining of itself as a space of white European supremacy has been the EU's abolition of internal frontiers and the fortification of its external borders. The Schengen Agreement of 1985 set some European countries on the path to the abolition of all internal borders, culminating in the 1986 Single European Act which carved out a commitment among Member States to invent a borderless Europe in which capital, goods and persons could move freely. The riches that this extravagant, top-down scheme promised to deliver were argued to necessitate the construction of the greatest of all frontiers at the outer borders of the Union. Since the EU's inception its borders have extended further, gradually encompassing in its exclusive folds southern, central and eastern European countries.[116] Membership has always demanded exclusion of non-members and their nationals. The well-rehearsed justification for the heightened policing of Europe's external borders is based on a perceived need for flanking measures designed to provide increased security for Europeans.[117] The official narrative is that European Member States, in opening themselves up from the inside, are vulnerable to all manner of transnational ills from the outside, not least criminals, drugs, terrorists and migrants.[118] Yet the borders of the EU are not pre-ordained. With its colonial past in mind, the EU must be understood as an appropriated continent. Its borders 'lie wherever those with power choose to put them and cast them in concrete and barbed wire'.[119] Meanwhile, overseas colonial territories are made invisible through selective and inaccurate cartography and scholarly accounts, processes which feed a pervasive amnesia in relation to the EU's origins.

Third country nationals are defined in EU law as 'Any person who is not a citizen of the Union within the meaning of Art. 20(1) of the TFEU and who is not a person enjoying the European Union right to free movement.'[120] Essentially, third country nationals are non-Member State nationals to whom Member State immigration laws apply. Since EU citizenship derives from Member State nationality, people denied legal status in Member States are also excluded from the European polity. Intensified border and immigration control measures significantly affect the means and routes that irregularised people use to travel to the EU. Such measures, which have proliferated over recent decades, include the imposition of visa requirements, carrier sanctions, the use of 'safe country' concepts, juxtaposed border controls, bilateral and European return agreements,[121] and the activities of Frontex, the EU Borders Agency. Consular officials are instructed to be 'particularly vigilant when dealing with … unemployed persons or those with irregular income'.[122] Thomas Spijkerboer has found that the impact of intensified border control is an increase in the number of deaths.[123] Between 1993 and 2006, 7,182 deaths at the European border were documented by the NGO UNITED. By 2019 the number had leapt to 36,570.[124] Following the intensification of border controls at departure points, people travelling to Europe have shifted their departure points further south, to Libya, Tunisia, Guinea-Bissau, Ivory Coast, Mauritania and Senegal. Thus, while the number of people entering at particular points of the Union can be reduced, this merely has a displacement effect whereby people move their departure points further away, making more dangerous and often fatal journeys.

The EU has made concerted efforts to contain people in regions of origin and has sought to facilitate the removal of people found to have no legal right to be in the EU, both through EU law in the form of the Return Directive,[125] as well as through the conclusion of readmission agreements, action plans and mobility partnerships with non-European countries.[126] As Jon Gubbay notes, '[t]he process of repatriation is eased administratively … where member states have agreements that, in return for cash (euphemistically referred to as aid), non-EU countries will readmit their citizens'.[127] Gargi Bhattacharyya has argued that the move to control and contain displaced populations has been exploited by European countries seeking to outsource border control tasks. She writes, 'adjacency to the nations most committed to bordering' can facilitate trade agreements and political recognition.[128] The effect of the EU–Turkey deal, agreed on 18 March 2016, which limits access to Greek islands from Turkey, has been the 'choice of the deadlier route from Libya to Italy'.[129] The result has been a spike in deaths among those attempting the journey to the EU. At least three boats sank in the Mediterranean in the summer of 2016, killing more than 700 people in a week.[130] In 2017 the death toll of people crossing the Mediterranean via the dangerous passage between Libya and Italy passed a record 1,000.[131]

The EU–Turkey deal has also resulted in the imprisonment on islands of people arriving in Greece. Long-term and even permanent camps are a product of agreements negotiated with states bordering the EU.[132] As Bhattacharyya writes, 'we witness a remapping of the world where new concentrations of population arise as the by-product of prevented journeys'.[133] People trapped in Greece and Turkey are in limbo and living in harrowing conditions. Camps are overcrowded and under-resourced. Médecins Sans Frontières has described the Moria detention centre on the Greek island of Lesbos, which was built to hold 3,500 people but has held up to 11,000, 3,000 of whom are children, as a giant open-air mental asylum.[134] In January 2017 three refugees died in the space of a week in the Moria centre.[135] At least thirteen refugees have died in Greece, five of them in Moria.[136] Children trapped in the camp have attempted suicide.[137] The Moria

DEATH + IMPRISONMENT

refugees are subject to removal because the EU–Turkey deal commits Turkey to accepting the return of people who travel to Greece irregularly. In return, the EU agreed to resettle one Syrian refugee from Turkey for every person returned. As part of the deal Turkey received €6 billion and Turkish nationals were granted visa-free travel to the EU. The justificatory premise underlying the deal is that Turkey is a safe country for refugees. Despite Turkey having committed to protecting Syrian refugees, it is not a signatory of the 1967 Protocol. This means it does not generally recognise non-Europeans as refugees. The result is that refugees in Turkey are denied access to protection, permanent residency and citizenship rights.[138]

The CJEU has refused to scrutinise the terms of the EU–Turkey deal.[139] In 2017 it rejected arguments from claimants seeking asylum trapped in Greece that the deal is an international agreement which the European Council, as an institution acting in the name of the EU, concluded with Turkey, and that the agreement infringes the rules of the TFEU relating to the conclusion of international agreements by the EU. The EU General Court decided that it did not have jurisdiction to hear the cases because the deal was agreed by the Member States intergovernmentally and not by the EU. The reasoning is unconvincing considering the existence of the EU–Turkey readmission agreement, and the fact that the European Council placed a press release on its website at the time of the agreement claiming that the EU had agreed a deal with Turkey.[140]

European cooperation on asylum and immigration

In 1976 the Parliamentary Assembly of the Council of Europe encouraged European signatories to the 1951 Refugee

Convention to establish a formal procedure to examine asylum applications.[141] A particular concern was 'de facto refugees', persons not falling within the 1951 Convention definition of a refugee but who were fleeing conflict. The Assembly recommended the introduction of harmonised measures to deal with this group of persons.[142] The UNHCR representative in Britain supported the Assembly's recommendation, noting that 'the period between the arrival of the refugee and his recognition and acceptance for asylum, is a problem area' due to Britain's failure to implement the Refugee Convention.[143] In his submission to the House of Commons Select Committee on Race Relations and Immigration in 1978, the UNHCR representative noted that apart from a few discretionary rules on asylum,

> there is no provision for the treatment of refugees in UK law; no legislation as to how the provisions of the [Convention and the Protocol] should be applied; and no mechanism to determine to whom they should be applied; and the protection of these instruments cannot be invoked by refugees before immigration appeal authorities or before courts.[144]

In his view, a specific asylum procedure was required. Two legal developments were considered to be essential. The first was for the Refugee Convention to be incorporated into domestic law, and the second was the introduction of a formal procedure for the determination of refugee status by an independent body.[145]

Despite the views expressed by the Parliamentary Assembly of the Council of Europe, the harmonisation of European asylum procedures neither took place within the framework of the Council of Europe, nor under the auspices of the then European Community (EC), which lacked the relevant legal powers at the time. Instead, cooperation began informally between a number of EC states.[146]

(margin note: FLYING UNDERNEATH THE RADAR)

Although formal asylum legislation was eventually introduced in Britain in 1993, as discussed in the previous chapter, the interim period saw a high level of informal intergovernmental cooperation on asylum and immigration between European interior ministers, in which Britain was an enthusiastic participant. Didier Bigo has described this form of policy making as being characterised by 'a labyrinth of administrative interactions, the lack of a clear sense of direction, and a curious mixture of cooperation and competition'.[147] Trevi, an ad hoc group set up to enable informal cooperation in 1976, said to be an acronym for terrorism, radicalism, extremism and international violence,[148] comprised the then 12 EC Member States. Its task was to develop counter-terrorism policies and coordinate policing within the EC. The EU institutions, the European Commission and the Parliament, were excluded from its work.[149] Operating outside the treaty framework and the auspices of the supranational EC institutions, political and judicial scrutiny of Trevi's work was almost entirely absent at the national and European level.[150] Civil servants were made responsible for presenting the work of Trevi to the interior ministers, who then reported to their governments. There was no guarantee that national parliaments would be informed of Trevi's work, and practice differed in individual EC states.[151] Trevi's meetings were held twice a year and were chaired by the interior minister of the country holding the EC presidency. It had a number of working groups, staffed by national officials, dealing with topics such as terrorism, public order, drugs and serious crime. Andrew Geddes notes that Trevi established 'a "wining and dining" culture of co-operation among interior ministry officials' and lacked 'democracy and accountability' mechanisms.[152] When in 1987 proposals were put forward for a slightly more

(margin note: HOW IS THIS ALLOWED)

(margin note: FEELS LIKE A GAME)

formal and administrative structure in which the ministers could operate more efficiently, the group was hesitant.[153]

According to Bigo, traditionally Britain has attempted to 'paralyse certain groups at the European Community level'.[154] Notwithstanding the existence of de facto hierarchies between EU Member States, Britain has long been uncomfortable with its position as a formally equal partner in European cooperation as compared with its historical position at the helm of an empire and then as 'first among equals' in the Commonwealth. However, the British government was a keen participant in the work of Trevi.[155] According to evidence submitted to the Home Affairs Select Committee, the government saw Trevi's particular strength as lying in the informal, spontaneous and practical character of its negotiations.[156] The first recorded parliamentary written answer on Trevi was given in 1981 and consisted of a short outline in very general terms.[157] Trevi's work was hidden from view until 1989 when the first communiqué for public purposes was made available in Britain. Following this, every six months there was a written answer to a 'planted' parliamentary question after every meeting of the interior ministers. When prompted as to whether there were adequate democratic controls and safeguards in the work of Trevi, the Conservative Home Secretary commented that

> [i]t does not need any safeguards. You have to remember what Trevi is. Trevi is merely a gathering together of the Ministers of the Interior of the EC countries to find, hopefully, political impetus to various plans or closer police co-operation. That is all it is. It is not an executive body. Therefore, accountability is from the individual Ministers of the Interior to their own governments, and there is no need for the body as a whole to be thought of as responsible to any other organisation.[158]

[handwritten margin note: WHY WOULD THIS BE A STRENGTH?]

[handwritten margin note: SHAMY]

The Trevi group's most significant legacy in the field of asylum is the Dublin Regulation.[159] It incorporated into EU law the Dublin Convention, the blueprint of which was agreed at a June 1990 meeting of the Trevi group, and which is the central binding EU instrument for determining the Member State responsible for assessing an asylum claim.[160] Dublin, a legal instrument with its origins in a most undemocratic forum, has had calamitous consequences for people seeking asylum in the EU. Dublin is founded on the notion that responsibility for a claim lies with the first Member State with which an asylum applicant establishes contact, whether by the issue of a transit visa, the legal presence of a close family member, or in the absence of these, the first physical contact with territory.[161] The instrument essentially limits the number of countries in the EU in which an individual can legitimately lodge an asylum claim to one. Member States are required to readmit individuals transferred on the basis of the Dublin regime, while respecting the principle of mutual recognition with regard to the application of its rules. European cooperation on asylum is thus founded on 'the assumption of common standards of refugee protection that would justify the loosening of the exclusive responsibility of sovereign States under international law'.[162] However, Dublin ignores the reality that asylum claimants have vastly different chances of having their protection needs recognised depending on which Member State assesses their claim.[163] Britain, for instance, has a low recognition rate of claims originating from its former colonies and places that it has recently invaded (such as Afghanistan, Iraq and Somalia), as compared with other EU Member States.[164] Further, the Convention does not regard as relevant Europe's colonial history, which drives claimants from former colonies towards former colonial powers.

[handwritten margin note, left: LITERALLY WHAT DOES THIS MEAN?]

[handwritten margin note, left: SMITH BETRAY!]

Dublin has led to the confinement in southern Member States of persons seeking asylum in Europe, where they have been exposed to extreme socio-economic deprivation and are at risk of being sent back to harm.[165]

Britain is a strong supporter of the Dublin regime because of its deflection of asylum applicants from its shores. In defence of the Convention, the 2010 Conservative–Liberal Democrat coalition government declared that '[g]enuine refugees ... should be offered protection in the Member State where they first arrive ... Decisions about who gets asylum in the UK ... should stay in the UK.'[166] Yet the Dublin system in no way forces on Britain a determination of an asylum claim. It merely allocates responsibility for deciding a claim. It does not stipulate its outcome. Thus, contrary to the British government's rhetoric, which habitually presents the EU as a threat to its sovereignty and borders, the power to decide the merits of an asylum claim remains the exclusive purview of Member States, albeit with national and European judicial oversight in relation to procedural matters.

EU immigration and asylum law à la carte

Despite the rhetoric of 'taking back control', which took hold in the course of the 2016 EU referendum debate, EU law has reinforced rather than limited Britain's capacity to control its borders. Britain, Ireland and Denmark each secured opt-outs from EU treaty provisions on immigration and asylum law via protocols to the 1999 Amsterdam Treaty.[167] Unlike Denmark, which does not have the option of opting in, Britain and Ireland can choose whether to participate in legislation on immigration and asylum. These opt-outs were secured following the European Council's agreement in 1999 to work towards building a Common European Asylum System in accordance with the Refugee Convention.[168] The system was to be part of an Area of Freedom, Security and Justice (AFSJ) described in Article 67 of the TFEU as a place defined by 'respect for fundamental rights and the different legal systems and traditions of the Member States'[169] and 'the absence of internal border controls for persons'.[170] People categorised as 'persons' are only those who qualify for free movement, since the provision differentiates between 'persons' and 'third-country nationals'.[171] It is clear that the AFSJ is in effect a set of policies designed to make the European space safe and navigable for its predominantly white European citizens and designated free movers. The EU's web summary is telling in this regard in its description of the AFSJ as having been 'created to ensure the free movement of persons and to offer a high level of protection to citizens'.[172]

[margin note: BREXIT]

[margin note: RACISM!]

The Common European Asylum System is based on the idea that the same minimum standards of protection apply in participating Member States across the Union. The first round of European asylum laws (directives) were highly discretionary, leaving Member States a wide scope for differentiation in implementation.[173] The most recent round of directives[174] has not sufficiently ameliorated this situation, nor has the European Commission adopted as vigilant an enforcement approach in relation to asylum law as it has in other legal fields, such as free movement of goods, or environmental or competition law.[175] The Commission's light-touch enforcement approach further underlines the way in which EU law produces the European space as a racially exclusive one that exists to serve the interests of white Europeans.

[margin note: WHY DO THESE SECTORS GET MORE ATTENTION?]

While previous British governments were willing to opt

into the highly discretionary asylum directives, the decision was taken to opt out of the latest EU asylum legislation on the grounds that it overly impinged on Member State discretion in implementation.[176] The decision went against the advice of the House of Lords European Union Committee and the UNHCR.[177] It has been criticised by lawyers, NGOs and scholars on the basis that the new directives contain, however limited, provisions that are designed to marginally improve protection standards for asylum seekers.[178] The opt-out thus allows Britain to participate in a deflective measure such as Dublin while rejecting potentially rights-enhancing legislation.

Maria Fletcher has argued that Britain has 'exploited' its flexible opt-out 'to the greatest extent'.[179] The 1998 Labour White Paper, *Fairer, Faster, Firmer – A Modern Approach to Immigration and Asylum*, proudly declared that Britain was 'the first country to ratify the Europol Convention and supported the decision to give Europol a role in combating illegal immigration'.[180] The British government was described as having 'played an active part in work to develop the Eurodac Convention to create a computerised central database of fingerprints of asylum seekers across the EU', and 'supported its extension to certain illegal migrants'. The White Paper also expressed the government's intention to 'continue to strengthen cooperation of this kind'.[181] It further emphasised that '[t]he main focus of UK immigration control has traditionally been at the point of entry … different from the practice in mainland Europe where, because of the difficulty of policing long land frontiers, there is much greater dependence on internal controls such as identity checks'.[182] Three influencing factors were set out as the basis on which the government would exercise its opt-out: the need to ensure effective co-operation within

Europe in tackling organised crime ... the need to preserve the UK system of frontier controls ... and the maintenance of UK control of policy on immigration and asylum'.[183] Tony Blair, the Prime Minister, in an interview in 2004 described Britain's position as securing 'the absolute right to opt in to any of the asylum and immigration provisions we wanted to in Europe. Unless we opt in, we are not affected by it. And what this actually gives us is the best of both worlds.'[184]

In practice, with regard to asylum, Britain has opted out of nearly all proposals concerning visa and migration facilitation, and has opted into (until recently) all proposals concerning asylum and civil law and nearly all proposals concerning irregularised migration.[185] The British government has sought to take part in EU-level measures that help to reinforce its border controls,[186] for instance opting into a 2001 directive giving effect to the provision on carrier sanctions in the Schengen Implementing Convention.[187] It has chosen to participate in all readmission agreements concluded with non-EU states. Since the 2002 Seville Council, cooperation with these countries has increased rapidly due to its prioritisation of controlling irregularised migration.[188] Though not covered by the opt-out, Britain has been involved in schemes such as IMMPACT I and II with Bosnia and Herzegovina, Serbia and Montenegro, Project MARRI (the Migration, Asylum, Refugees Regional Initiative), a part of the Stability Pact for south-east Europe, Operation Ulysses in June 2003 (to prevent migration from Africa towards the Canary Islands) and Project Deniz on detecting irregularised sea migration.[189] Britain has opted out of measures designed to be protective, such as the Directive on Victims of Trafficking,[190] and into the 2001 Council Directive on the Mutual Recognition of Decisions on the

Expulsion of Third Country Nationals, aimed at preventing irregularised migration.[191] This has been complemented by various soft law measures such as the Comprehensive Plan to Combat Illegal Immigration and Trafficking in Human Beings and the Plan for the External Management of the Borders of the EU.[192] The British government described its opt-in decisions as being 'in line with our predisposition to opt in to the adoption of measures to combat illegal immigration'.[193] According to Geddes, Britain 'has been most active in those areas where EU integration is seen as a potential solution to domestic political issues'; thus it has opted into measures that promise to reduce the number of asylum applications.[194] In this way, 'the means' through which people are deflected 'have become European'.[195] Thus, in spite of the call to 'take back control' of Britain's borders from the EU, it is precisely, paradoxically, EU law and policies that have allowed Britain unprecedented control over its borders.

[handwritten margin note: WHAT IS SOFT LAW?]

[handwritten margin note: ★ IMPORTANT]

Practical cooperation with former colonies

On rejecting the possibility of further EU legislative cooperation on asylum, the British government declared itself an active supporter of informal 'practical cooperation'.[196] Alongside informal cooperation with EU Member States, Britain has embarked on bilateral projects designed to curb immigration with governments of its former colonies. Just as the British government sought to persuade colony and Commonwealth governments to prevent racialised subjects from travelling to Britain in the 1950s and 1960s, it continues to draw on residual pseudo-colonial relations to exert similar political pressure. In a joint document published in 2010 by the Home Office and the Foreign and

[handwritten margin note: WHAT DOES THIS LOOK LIKE?]

Commonwealth Office, these departments celebrated having worked with the producers of a popular Kenyan soap opera called *Makutano Junction*, which attracts millions of viewers across East Africa, to convey ideas about immigration to the Kenyan population. According to the report,

> [t]he main story involves one of the most popular characters in the soap, the aptly named Dodgy. Having sold all of his belongings, Dodgy and his friend Toni hand over large sums of money – intended to buy a UK visa – to a man in a car with blacked out windows. Inevitably the man speeds off, leaving Dodgy and Toni standing in a cloud of dust. The story continues in the next series, showing the effect this has on one of their families ... The soap opera ... has proven to be a highly effective way of delivering the main message, which is 'The only way is the legal way' – or to put that in character, 'Don't be like Dodgy'.[197]

The high number of viewers combined with the significant cultural role played by soap operas more generally is indicative of the scale of the British government's imperial intervention in Kenya in the service of immigration control. The recent meddling with soap opera storylines must be placed in the context of Britain's colonial history in Kenya.

The British government's sense of entitlement to Kenyan culture and its willingness to exert influence over the country's population is reminiscent of British colonial rule. British rule in Kenya extended from 1888 until 1963, during which it stole and settled fertile land, exploited labour and systematically tortured and abused the Kenyan population.[198] Kenyans collectively rebelled against the British authorities. In the course of an armed rebellion by the anti-colonial organisation, the Mau Mau, the British army was deployed. It rounded up hundreds of thousands of Mau Mau suspects, many of whom were detained, murdered and

CULTURAL ROLE OF SOAP OPERAS

tortured at the behest of the Colonial Office. One and a half million Kenyans were forced to live in detention camps under a system of terror entailing rape, murder and forced labour, and where they had no access to sustenance.[199] Before the British government withdrew from Kenya it destroyed and removed swathes of documents relating to its atrocities, thereby seeking to erase from history the horrific modalities of its colonial rule.[200] The British government has since sought to deny its responsibility for the brutal actions of its predecessors in the course of legal challenges brought by surviving victims.[201] Meanwhile, it draws on its imperial connections with Kenya to culturally manipulate Kenyans in a bid to dissuade them from seeking to travel to Britain.

The British government has also cooperated with the British High Commission in Accra, Ghana, another former British colony, and the Ghanaian authorities to curb the movement of Ghanaians to Britain.[202] Projects established include an arrest programme whereby 'individuals applying for visas with false or forged supporting documentation, or in multiple identities, are now routinely referred to the Ghanaian police'.[203] A joint Home Office and Foreign and Commonwealth Office report proudly claims that '[i]n the five years since [its] introduction, there have been over 3,000 arrests with numerous prosecutions'.[204] There is no mention of the widespread brutality and corruption in the Ghanaian police force. In a 2007 report published by the Commonwealth Human Rights Initiative, the Ghanaian police force is stated as being 'marred by widespread corruption, illegal arrest and detention, excessive use of force and a failure to respond to complaints. These are all hallmarks of a regime-style police force that is not held accountable for its actions.'[205] Ironically, the report into abuses by the

Ghanaian police force was funded by the British Foreign and Commonwealth Office, the very same government department that produced the joint report with the Home Office on the success of the British government's interference in Kenyan popular culture and on the instigation of the arrest programme in Ghana. These instances of bilateral practical cooperation indicate that Britain remains a state embedded in colonial relations that are widely considered to be historical, or not known to have existed at all. It mobilises these relations in order to deflect its former subjects from its shores, thereby reinforcing its post-colonial borders.

Brexit as nostalgia for empire

> You will forget your part in the whole setup, that bureaucracy is one of your inventions, that Gross National Product is one of your inventions, and all the laws that you know mysteriously favour you.[206]

The 2016 referendum on Britain's EU membership should be understood as another in a long line of assertions of white entitlement to the spoils of colonialism. The Leave vote should not be exceptionalised as an object of study, or collapsed into the meaningless hashtag that is 'Brexit', but instead understood in the context of Britain's colonial history and ongoing colonial configuration. Exceptionalising the referendum result distracts from the structural forces underlying it. The terms on which the referendum debate took place are symptomatic of a Britain struggling to conceive of its place in the world post-Empire.[207] Present in the discourse of some of those arguing for a Leave vote was a tendency to romanticise the days of the British Empire, despite widespread amnesia about the details of Britain's imperial history.[208] A poll conducted six months prior to the referendum found that 44 per cent of the British public were proud of Britain's colonial history and 43 per cent considered the British Empire to have been a good thing.[209] In 2011 David Cameron, the Conservative Prime Minister, stated that 'Britannia didn't rule the waves with armbands on'.[210] Before him, the Labour Prime Minister, Tony Blair, stated in 1997 that he valued and honoured British history enormously and considered that the British Empire should neither elicit 'apology nor hand-wringing' and that it should be deployed to enhance Britain's global influence.[211]

The hankering after the halcyon days of empire was expressed in a tabloid headline following the referendum, which read, 'Now Let's Make Britain Great Again'.[212] The slogan, a version of which was made popular in the course of Donald Trump's presidential election campaign, has since been adopted by some of those who backed a Leave vote.[213] The idea of 'making Britain great again' captures a yearning for a time when 'Britannia ruled the waves' and was defined by its racial and cultural superiority. The vote to leave the EU is not only an expression of nostalgia for empire, it is also the fruit of empire. The legacies of British colonialism have never been addressed, including that of racism.[214] British colonial rule saw the exploitation of peoples, the theft of their land and their subjugation on the basis of a white supremacist racial hierarchy, a system that was maintained through the brutal and systematic violence of colonial authorities.[215]

The British Empire was vehemently resisted by local populations in colonised territories. As Richard Gott writes, there was always 'resistance to conquest, and rebellion against occupation, often followed by mutiny and revolt – by individuals, groups, armies and entire peoples. At one

SATIA

time or another, the British seizure of distant lands was hindered, halted and even derailed by the vehemence of local opposition.'[216] Priyamvada Gopal has challenged the discourse prevalent in Britain that credits anti-imperial resistance to the liberal imperialist project.[217] This project presents freedom from slavery and imperialism as having flowed from the 'benevolence of the rulers' and having been granted to colonies 'when they were deemed ready for it'.[218] Gopal's counter-history destroys this narrative, demonstrating instead how enslaved and colonised peoples were the agents of their own resistance and freedom.[219] They also shaped the British discourse on liberation, not only through scholarship but also in the form of struggle and insurgency, thereby 'interrogating the tenacious assumption that the most significant conceptions of "freedom" are fundamentally "Western" in provenance'.[220]

Paul Gilroy has argued that imperial nostalgia is sometimes combined with 'a reluctance to see contemporary British racism as a product of imperial and colonial power'.[221] The prevalence of structural and institutional racism in Britain today made it fertile ground for the effectiveness of the Leave campaign's rhetoric of 'taking back control' and reaching 'breaking point'. The Leave victory on 23 June 2016 resulted in a renewed level of legitimisation of racism and white supremacy. In Britain, a week prior to the referendum, the pro-immigration Labour MP Jo Cox was brutally murdered by a man who shouted 'Britain first' as he killed her, and who gave his name in court on being charged with her murder as 'Death to traitors. Freedom for Britain'.[222] In the months following the referendum, racist hate crime increased by 16 per cent across Britain, and peaked at a 58 per cent rise in the week following the vote.[223] Weeks after the referendum, Arkadiusz Jóźwik was beaten to death in

Essex, having reportedly been attacked for speaking Polish in the street.[224]

In an article that has proven remarkably prophetic, Vron Ware argued in 2008 that 'societies where whiteness has historically conferred some sort of guarantee of belonging and entitlement present an opportunity for political mobilisation in the name of white supremacy'.[225] The vote to exit the EU signified a shoring-up of white entitlement to territory, resources, and to identification as British. Despite the frequent refrain that the 2016 vote to leave the European Union was the result of a disenfranchised 'white working-class' revolt, Gurminder Bhambra has observed that the vote was disproportionately carried by 'the propertied, pensioned, well-off, white *middle class* based in southern England'.[226] According to Danny Dorling, 52 per cent of Leave voters lived in southern England and 59 per cent were middle class. The proportion of people who voted Leave in the lowest social classes was just 24 per cent.[227] The Leave campaign's violent rhetoric of 'taking back control' is thus symptomatic of an imagined victimhood on the part of white nationalists, in part a backlash against the gradual gains made in the realm of civil rights and non-discrimination on the part of minorities living in white hegemonic societies over the past decades.[228] James McDougall and Kim Wagner have pointed out that Enoch Powell's 'notorious line about the descendants of the enslaved and colonised gaining "the whip hand over the white man" was an early indication of the fantasy of victimhood that grips today's alt-right and feeds hostility to migration and multiculturalism'.[229]

In reality, colonial conquest historically benefited poor white Britons, as well as the ruling classes. Danny Dorling and Sally Tomlinson note, poor white Britons 'were encouraged to believe in their economic, political and racial superiority to the rest of the subjects of empire. This helped deflect attention from their own precarious position in the economic structure.'[230] Further, their wages could rise because there were colonial populations to exploit.[231] Aditya Mukherjee has shown how accumulation by colonial dispossession allowed for the betterment of economic conditions for the entirety of the metropole, including poor white people.

> The process of primitive accumulation in capitalism or the initial phase of industrialisation is a painful one as the initial capital for investment has to be raised on the backs of the working class or the peasantry. To the extent that Britain and other metropolitan countries were able to draw surplus from the colonial people, to that extent they did not have to draw it from their own working class and peasantry. That is one reason why colonialism is supra-class, it is not only the metropolitan bourgeoisie exploiting the colonial proletariat but the metropolitan society as a whole benefiting at the cost of the entire colonial people.[232]

Britain's impending departure from the EU now sees it turning once again to the Commonwealth.[233] It is no coincidence that Nigel Farage, MEP and former leader of the United Kingdom Independence Party (UKIP), expressed a preference for migrants from India and Australia as compared with east Europeans, and has advocated stronger ties with the Commonwealth.[234] Theresa May, in her speech on the government's plans for Britain's departure from the EU, referred to the Commonwealth as being indicative of Britain's 'unique and proud global relationships', and declared that it was 'time for Britain to get out into the world and rediscover its role as a great, global, trading nation'.[235] At the same time, paradoxically, spokespersons for the Leave campaign adopted the language of 'national liberation', resulting in the reframing of Britain's voluntary

[handwritten margin note: DISCONNECT FROM BEGINNING OF CHAPTER]

decision to leave the EU, an organisation it willingly chose to join, as 'an existential struggle between oppressor and oppressed'.[236] In reality, since the Leave vote, Britain's appetite for imperial mythology and fantasy has grown.[237] Boris Johnson, former Conservative Foreign Secretary and current Prime Minister, claimed in his first major speech following the referendum that 'Brexit emphatically does not mean a Britain that turns in on herself'.[238] As he romanticised Britain's long history of intervention in Afghanistan, he euphemistically described British colonialism in terms of 'astonishing globalism, this wanderlust of aid workers and journalists and traders and diplomats and entrepreneurs'.[239] He wondered whether 'the next generation of Brits will be possessed of the same drive, the same curiosity, the same willingness to take risks for far flung peoples and places'.[240] Johnson dressed up Britain's colonial history as being that of a small island nation's attempt to do good in the world. He promised that a post-Brexit Britain will be 'more outward-looking and more engaged with the world than ever before'.[241] Yet, as I have argued above, the prospect of Britain retaining its status as the leading global power in the face of the defeat of its empire was presented by British politicians in 1961 as a major reason in favour of joining the EEC. Britain's profound colonial amnesia and imperial ambition now see it making a drastic manoeuvre away from the EU.

At the same time, in the absence of radical reformulation, the project of European integration cannot provide an adequate alternative to the excesses of the nation-state. As European nations turn further inward on themselves, the violent effects of their global exploits continue to be felt viscerally across the world. In a context in which Britain has seen reported hate crimes more than double since 2013,[242] no

DELUSIONAL

CONSCIOUSNESS

doubt catalysed by the EU referendum, we are in dire need of an unsettling of what Sivamohan Valluvan has called 'the clamour of nationalism'.[243] The long-term mainstreaming of nationalist ideas in popular and official discourse has caused a frightening global surge in right-wing populism and authoritarian government, a trend European integration has been unable to counter. If as critical scholars teachers and activists we can work to provide urgently needed counter-histories and narratives to those we are offered by the mainstream political and media discourse daily, we might be able to begin to work our way out of the violence and ensnarement of the nation-state and its dangerous ideological counterpart of nationalism. *NO SMALL FEAT*

Considering the Leave vote's embodiment of a rejection of anyone considered to be a migrant, a post-Brexit Britain promises to be a dangerous place for racialised people and those without a secure status. We urgently need new strategies for organising collectively in the service of anti-racist and migrant solidarity. In the Conclusion that follows I argue that as anti-racist scholars and activists we must begin by imbibing a counter-pedagogy to that of immigration law, one that rejects the violence of legal categorisation and paves the way for a more empowering, redistributive and radical politics of racial justice.

WE HAVE SEEN THIS IN THE U.S. AS WELL

IMPLICATIONS

LOOKING AHEAD

WHAT IS ACADEMIC ACTIVISM?

Conclusion: 'Go home' as an invitation to stay

Do you believe this is YOUR country to welcome me to?[1]

Racialised people in Britain, whether categorised as citizens, migrants, refugees, asylum seekers or third country nationals, are habitually understood as having come from somewhere else. Britain's post-colonial articulation of its borders and national identity has driven the assumption that anyone who is not white could not be *from* Britain. Manifestations of this assumption are heard daily across Britain whether in the form of the subtly disguised racist question, 'Where do you come from, *originally?*' or the avowed racist slur, 'Go back to where you came from'. In 2013 Theresa May's Home Office plastered the decree, 'GO HOME or face arrest' on vans commissioned to drive around London in areas where racialised people live.[2] 'Leave', which became the designation for the campaign for Britain's withdrawal from the EU, began to take on a double meaning, embodying the 'go home' dictum as a rejection of anyone deemed to be a migrant. Meanwhile, people considered not to have a legal right to remain in Britain are expelled to places that are not home. The legal system thus enacts the 'go home' decree, the deportation flights carried forward by the justification that people without legal status do not belong in Britain.

While racism drives these utterances and enactments, they are also propelled by something else: the idea that Britain is somewhere and not everywhere. The 1960s–1980s was an era in which British officials were forced to come to terms with the defeat of the British Empire. As colonial populations overthrew British rulers and won their independence, British governments jettisoned the lie of imperial unity and equality and introduced racially exclusive immigration controls. Although Britain retained overseas colonies, a series of immigration and nationality laws passed in the 1960s, 1970s and 1980s effectively announced Britain as post-colonial. Racialised colony and Commonwealth subjects were treated as 'aliens' for the purpose of immigration control. In determining those who legally belonged in Britain on the basis of an ancestral link with the British mainland, Britain made itself, for all intents and purposes, an exclusionary white space. The inscription in law of a link between Britishness and whiteness created Britain as a domestic space of colonialism in which the presence of racialised people is constantly called into question. This manifests in their disproportionately being the targets of police harassment, street violence, detention, deportation and death. Meanwhile colonial processes of dispossession and inequality have carried over in the context of a global system of racial capitalism.[3]

People categorised as migrants are continually scapegoated for societal ills and painted in official and media discourse as taking what is not theirs. In reality, immigration and nationality laws of the 1960, 1970s and 1980s operated so as to extinguish the claims of colonised populations to material and temporal colonial resources appropriated by

Britain. Similar to the way in which indigenous people in Canada and Australia must submit to the rules and evidentiary standards of those colonial legal systems in order to be recognised as having enforceable rights to land,[4] those with ancestral, geographical and personal histories of British colonialism who wish to access stolen colonial wealth and resources in Britain must submit to the rules and evidentiary standards of British immigration law. Illegible to the law is the claim that the Commonwealth Immigrants Acts of 1962 and 1968, the Immigration Act 1971 and the British Nationality Act 1981 are part of the colonial infrastructure that continues to dispossess former British subjects. The injustice of requiring indigenous people to submit to colonial legal processes when seeking repossession of their land has been the subject of academic study.[5] A similarly unjust process is at work when former British subjects are required to meet the criteria of British immigration laws in order to have their rights to access Britain recognised.

The widespread acceptance of legal categories of people moving as defined in international, European and domestic law normalises the racial violence in which the legal system is implicated. Precluded is an understanding of law *as* racial violence. Ideas and practices of racial ordering which date back to the colonial era are embedded in contemporary articulations of immigration, asylum and nationality law. In operating to target racialised people, allocating chances at life and death on the basis of rights of entry and stay, and by preventing those deemed not to qualify for a legal status from accessing Britain, law is central to ongoing processes of colonial dispossession.

With this in mind, when seeking to formulate long-term strategies for racial justice of a reparative and redistributive kind, we must be wary of relying on a legal system that serves to legitimise Britain's colonial order. As Glen Coulthard has warned, we must not submit to the 'assimilative lure of the statist politics of recognition'.[6] Recognition-based approaches to migrant solidarity that focus on the inclusion of racialised people in and on the terms of the colonial state result in the construction of instances of state racial terror, such as the hostile environment, as aberrations rather than the norm. Such racial terror cannot be corrected through the doling out of legal status to a select few. The hostile environment is on the same continuum of colonial violence as legal status recognition processes such as immigration and citizenship laws.

The insistence on the Windrush generation being British citizens elides the colonial context in which the 1948 British Nationality Act was passed and feeds the lie that the Windrush generation were welcomed in post-war Britain. The appeal to British citizenship as a protective category skips over the reality that the bestowal of legal status by the British government is always a colonial act, one that legitimises and reinforces its sovereign and imperial power. Further, the pre-eminence of the principle of national state sovereignty means that seeking judicial scrutiny of refusals to recognise legal status will always be of limited effect. Despite ongoing questions as to where British legal jurisdiction begins and ends, courts cannot adequately respond to the claims of colonially dispossessed people without calling into question Britain's existence as a legitimately bordered sovereign nation-state, and by implication their own power of adjudication.

Appealing to citizenship rights as a means of challenging racial state violence thus works to preclude the adoption of broader anti-racist strategies and inadvertently legitimises the violence faced by those who do not meet the criteria for legal status recognition. Recognition processes force apart what might otherwise be collective claims for racial justice. While law-abiding members of the Windrush generation might be saved from racial exclusion, those with criminal convictions have been constructed as fair game for extreme forms of racial state violence. It is the idea that legal status recognition processes definitively determine entitlement to be in Britain that allowed former Home Secretary Sajid Javid to defend a chartered deportation flight to Jamaica on the basis that '[e]very single person ... on that flight ... is a foreign national offender'.[7] Appeals to the recognition of legal status thus have as their by-product the legitimisation of racial exclusion of people deemed to be present in Britain illegally, whether as a result of having been denied a legal status or having had a status withdrawn.

Similarly, appeals to Britain to show generosity towards refugees, which refer to a supposed long and strong tradition of refugee protection, elide the colonial impetus for refugee movements. They also inadvertently feed the convenient discourse of humanitarianism that successive governments use to shroud their reparative obligations towards former colonial subjects. While accepting the narrow confines of refugee law is necessary for legal practitioners, as critical scholars and activists we must be wary of the role of legal recognition processes in reinforcing rather than challenging the legitimacy of the colonial state. The movement of poor, racialised people, however legally categorised, takes place in a context in which colonial structures remain firmly in place in the form of unequal trade and debt arrangements. When contemporary migratory movements are placed in their proper historical context, one of British and wider European colonialism and their lasting legacies of conflict, instability and poverty, coupled with the formation of protectionist geopolitical structures such as the European Union, people seeking protection in Britain are also seeking refuge *from* Britain. Looked at in this way, people seeking political and economic security in Britain do so out of necessity, as an essential response to having been politically and economically persecuted *by* Britain. The impetus for movement, rather than being flight from a 'barbarous uncivilised third world country' is revealed as being flight from the legacies of colonialism. Such movement is about having basic needs fulfilled, such as access to food, water and breath – needs that in a world structured by colonialism are deemed to be the exclusive privilege of white people.

Leah Wise and Gerald Lenoir have argued that there is an insufficiency of migrant justice approaches, scholarly and activist, which address 'the system of policies and institutions' at the root of the racial terror experienced by migrants. Instead migrant justice activism tends to be 'locked into piecemeal strategies'.[8] I have pointed to some of the pitfalls of migrant solidarity campaigns framed around the recognition of legal status which work to reinforce rather than challenge the idea that wealth and resources within Britain belong first and foremost to white Britons. One way of reorienting the migration studies field towards anti-colonial and racial justice ends is to insist on a discourse that refuses terms such as 'host states', 'citizens', 'third country nationals', 'refugees' and 'migrants'. A significant drawback of much of the refugee literature is that it is driven by an agenda concerned with how Anglo-European countries can become more ethical or generous in their approach, rather than being grounded in an internationalist politics of anti-racism and anti-imperialism. Racialised people, far from being less deserving of access to welfare, or in a position to request assistance and be grateful for it, as media, official and much scholarly discourse would suggest, are in fact entitled to resources located in Britain. State-facilitated inclusion is an ever-elusive position for racialised people who, as I have shown, are acutely vulnerable to having their legal status revoked. In what follows I suggest how migrant justice discourse might be reframed so as to avoid falling into a liberal politics of recognition that fails to challenge the law's embodiment of colonial violence. I argue that irregularised presence in, and migration of racialised people to, Britain is more accurately conceptualised as anti-colonial resistance.

Irregularised migration as anti-colonial resistance

Postcolonial critique offers the possibility for a counter-pedagogy to that of law. Immigration law's lesson is one of exclusive white entitlement to colonial spoils and the crystallisation of racial hierarchies through legal categorisation. For the colonial British state to function, it has always depended on Britons, 87 per cent of whom are white, to imbibe a sense of entitlement and superiority over racialised people. Immigration, refugee and citizenship law regimes, in their legitimisation of differentiated access to resources according to immigration status, convey the lesson that the British national project is one of white ownership of colonial spoils, a project that is under constant threat from people who do not belong in Britain. Immigration controls are argued to be necessary to keep out people who are not entitled to access, and do not belong in, Britain. A postcolonial critique of immigration law, which understands it as ongoing colonial violence, disrupts law's pedagogical role, forcing an analysis of contemporary movement that accounts for colonial histories and legacies. As Stuart Hall argued, the postcolonial 'marks a critical interruption' of Eurocentric narratives of global histories.[9] For Doreen Massey, postcolonial retellings of history serve to 'rework modernity away from being the unfolding, internal story of Europe alone'.[10] Revisiting the story of modernity from a postcolonial perspective allows for the exposure of 'modernity's preconditions in and effects of violence, racism and oppression'.[11] It enables a shift away from the 'imagination of space as a continuous surface that the coloniser, as the only active agent, crosses to find the to-be-colonised simply "there"'.[12] The story of immigration law that I have retold in *(B)ordering Britain*, by placing it in the context of Britain's colonial history, has both enabled a reappraisal of contemporary legal and political discourses around immigration and demonstrated some of the pitfalls of seemingly progressive strategies for migrant solidarity and racial justice that centre on legal status recognition.

By calling for a reconceptualisation of irregularised migration as anti-colonial resistance, I am not arguing for a reformist strategy that would rely on nation-states or international organisations to introduce measures that might facilitate a more redistributive migration regime.[13] Although limited redistribution occurs as a result of immigration, for instance via the practice of sending remittances and the physical redirection of resources towards migrants present in Britain, the facilitation of migration in and of itself does little to contest broader ongoing colonial structures. Remittances, for instance, do little in the way of building the autonomy or infrastructure of former colonies. Nor am I proposing irregularised migration as a practical strategy for resisting ongoing colonial violence in the form of immigration and border controls. This is not to deny that irregularised migration can be seen as embodying a practice of resistance in contesting the border and forcing a redistributive element into the relationship between Britain and its former colonies, an element otherwise refused formal acknowledgement. It is precisely the irregularity, the illegality of the relationship that gives irregularised migration its radical, anti-colonial, reparative and redistributive dimension. In being illegal it amounts to a forcible return of something that was stolen in a context in which the laws being breached, immigration and border controls, are designed specifically to obstruct such an outcome. Nevertheless, irregularised people are made vulnerable to extreme conditions of racial terror, both in their journeys and attempts to cross borders as well as in their efforts to navigate legal status recognition processes and hostile environments pre- and post-arrival.

Rather, the reconceptualisation I offer of irregularised migration as anti-colonial resistance is primarily intended as a counter-pedagogy to that of law. Rather than being seen as rightfully at the mercy of legal status recognition processes, racialised people must both be understood, and understand themselves, as being collectively entitled to the reclamation of wealth accumulated via colonial dispossession. I am thus responding to the urgent need for a politics of migrant solidarity and racial justice in colonial contexts which resists that of state recognition. Such a politics, in the words of bell hooks, would 'require that we stop being so preoccupied with looking "to that Other for recognition"; instead we should be "recognizing ourselves and [then seeking to] make contact with all who would engage us in a constructive manner"'.[14] As scholars and activists we must acknowledge the connections between historical and ongoing racial projects of capitalist accumulation and contemporary migratory movements, and question former colonial powers' claims to legitimate and defensible sovereign borders policed and reproduced through immigration, asylum and nationality law. Much legal scholarship is implicated in propagating an ahistorical discourse that fails to address the role of immigration and refugee law concepts in sustaining the structures and concurrent discourse that enable and legitimise conditions of racial violence. We must work towards a language that refuses terms such as 'host states', 'refugee-producing states', 'irregular' or 'illegal/economic migrants'.[15] Some scholars in fields other than law are already doing this by talking, for instance, of irregularised rather than irregular migration,[16] thus placing the emphasis on the reason people find themselves without a legal status or a legal right to move.

Understanding how Britain came to be one of the wealthiest places in the world and how immigration law is deployed to exclude from its national project those at whose expense Britain was built is an important step towards formulating internationalist, anti-imperialist, racial justice strategies. Colonial subjects dispossessed of resources and then of access to Britain were intrinsic to its making. As George Orwell wrote in 1939, 'the overwhelming bulk of the British proletariat does not live in Britain, but in Asia and Africa'.[17] He described the British Empire as 'nothing but [a] mechanism for exploiting cheap coloured labour'.[18] Aditya Mukherjee has shown how 'at the heart of colonialism lay surplus appropriation from the colony to the metropolis'.[19] In the case of India, 'unrequited transfers', whereby the colony paid for the export of its own products to Britain, served as a massive and protracted drain on the Indian economy while simultaneously contributing to Britain's economic sustenance and growth.[20] Mukherjee writes that 'in 1801, at a crucial stage of Britain's industrial revolution, drain or unrequited transfers to Britain from

India represented about 9% of the GNP of the British territories in India, which was equal to about 30% of British domestic savings available for capital formation in Britain'.[21] Altogether in 1801, 'unrequited transfer from Asia and the West Indies amounted to 84.06% of British capital formation out of domestic savings'.[22] Transfers from the colonies were thus crucial to the process of capital accumulation in Britain. Mukherjee shows how 'direct seizure of surplus', which took many forms over different stages of colonisation, worked to 'sustain the development of capitalism in Britain and the standard of living of its people'.[23] The British also raised land revenues from their territories in India, which were 'estimated to have increased by 70% to 88% in the first half of the 19th century'.[24] Such extractive and exploitative methods were replicated across Britain's colonies.[25]

The fact that colonised populations grew and sustained the British economy is juxtaposed with the habitual official denial that Britain owes anything to those it enslaved and colonised. This erasure manifests in part through the refusal to engage in processes that would see Britain pay reparations to colonised nations.[26] In 2015 then Prime Minister David Cameron, on a visit to Jamaica, refused to apologise or engage with the question of payment of reparations for Britain's role in transatlantic slavery, preferring instead to 'move on from this painful legacy and continue to build for the future'.[27] The future building that Cameron was particularly interested in was the £25 million British 'aid'-funded prison to which people with Jamaican nationality convicted of criminal offences in Britain could be sent to serve out their sentences.[28] Although this project was not implemented, Britain has contributed to such a prison-building project in Nigeria, another of its former colonies.[29]

The presence in Britain of racialised people from countries with histories of colonisation has the effect of challenging and troubling white supremacist structures. Sarah Keenan has noted the way in which significant political potential can come when 'particular bodies that do not belong according to dominant networks of belonging nonetheless *remain* in that place'.[30] This troubling occurs in part through the taking up of physical space, but also in serving as a defiant reminder of Britain's colonial identity and the origins of its wealth. The arrival of the historically dispossessed in what was the heart of the British Empire has the effect of troubling racialised depictions of colonised populations as backward and uncivilised. Migration thus poses a challenge to colonial assertions of the stunted development and progress of colonised places and their populations, assertions that served as justification for colonial rule. Colonialism meant that 'different "places" were interpreted as different stages in a single temporal development'.[31] As Massey wrote, in this schema, Europe is constructed as 'advanced', while other parts of the world are presented as 'some way behind', and 'yet others are "backward"'.[32] In this way, places come to be denied their 'coeval existence'.[33] Massey thus argued that the arrival in Britain of people constructed as being 'from *the past*' in British imperial narratives meant that 'distance was suddenly eradicated both spatially *and* temporally. Migration was thereby an assertion of coevals.'[34] In this sense coevalness is a powerful assertion of presence in the here and now by people whom colonial processes have relegated to the past. Coevalness, as expressed through the immigration of racialised people to Britain, is thus 'an imaginative space of engagement: it speaks of an attitude ... It is a political act.'[35]

The imperial vanishing act performed by changes to

immigration and nationality laws in the 1960s, 1970s and 1980s cast Britain's imperial history into the shadows. The British Empire, about which most Britons know little,[36] can be remembered fondly as a moment of past glory, as a gift once given to the world. The erasure has been so complete that Conservative MP Liam Fox could declare in 2016 that '[t]he United Kingdom is one of the few countries in the European Union that does not need to bury its 20th century history',[37] and in 2019 the British government could take umbrage at the EU's perfectly accurate description of Gibraltar in a legal document as a British colony.[38] In announcing itself as post-colonial, Britain cut itself off symbolically and physically from its colonies and the Commonwealth, taking with it what it had plundered. In this way, Britain *is* the spoils of empire. While Britain may appear to be an island, it in fact remains everywhere. The British Empire's legacies of racism, slavery, labour exploitation, land dispossession, bordering and plunder are to this day felt viscerally across the world.[39] It is only with the confinement of British colonialism to the past that its former subjects, whether categorised today as citizens, migrants, refugees or asylum seekers, can be understood to have come from somewhere else. If Britain is acknowledged as being everywhere, its colonial legacies still reaching like tentacles across the world, then Britain is where we are from. In this way, the dictum 'go home' becomes paradoxically, subversively, an invitation to stay.

Notes

1 William Blake, 'Jerusalem', 1808.

1 Amelia Hill, '"Hostile environment": the hardline Home Office policy tearing families apart', *The Guardian*, 28 November 2017, www.theguardian.com/uk-news/2017/nov/28/hostile-environment-the-hardline-home-office-policy-tearing-families-apart (accessed 26 September 2019).

2 James Kirkup and Robert Winnett, 'Theresa May interview: "We're going to give illegal migrants a really hostile reception"', *The Telegraph*, 25 May 2012, www.telegraph.co.uk/news/uknews/immigration/9291483/Theresa-May-interview-Were-going-to-give-illegal-migrants-a-really-hostile-reception.html (accessed 26 September 2019).

3 In acknowledgement of Britain as a white supremacist context, I use the term 'racialised' to refer to people who are non-white.

4 See Daron Acemoglu and James A. Robinson, 'The economic impact of colonialism', in Stelios Michalopoulos and Elias Papaioannou (eds), *The Long Economic and Political Shadow of History, Vol. 1: A Global View* (CEPR Press, Vox.org, 2017), 81–7, https://voxeu.org/content/long-economic-and-political-shadow-history-volume-1 (accessed 21 October 2019); Luis Angeles, 'Income inequality and colonialism', *European Economic Review* 51.5 (2007), 1155–76; E. H. P. Frankema, 'The colonial origins of inequality: the causes and consequences of land distribution', research paper, Groningen Growth and Development Centre, June 2006, http://siteresources.worldbank.org/INTDECINEQ/

Resources/1149208-1147789289867/IIIWB_Conference_Colonial Origins_of_InequalityREVISED.pdf (accessed 21 October 2019).

5 See Ruth Wilson Gilmore, *Golden Gulag: Prisons, Surplus, Crisis, and Opposition in Globalizing California* (Berkeley, CA: University of California Press, 2006), 28. I elaborate on my use of Ruth Wilson Gilmore's definition of racism at pp. 24–6 below.

6 See Eric Williams, *Capitalism and Slavery* (Chapel Hill, NC: University of North Carolina Press, 1944); Joseph E. Inikori, *Africans and the Industrial Revolution in England: A Study in International Trade and Economic Development* (Cambridge: Cambridge University Press, 2002); Nicholas Draper, 'The City of London and slavery: evidence from the first dock companies 1795–1800', *Economic History Review* 61.2 (2008), 432–66.

7 See Legacies of British Slave-ownership (Centre for the Study of the Legacies of British Slave-ownership), www.ucl.ac.uk/lbs/.

8 Ibid.

9 Draper, 'The City of London and slavery'.

10 See Legacies of British Slave-ownership (Centre for the Study of the Legacies of British Slave-ownership), www.ucl.ac.uk/lbs/.

11 See Danny Dorling and Sally Tomlinson, *Rule Britannia: Brexit and the End of Empire* (London: Biteback Publishing, 2019).

12 See Sherene Razack, 'Racial terror: torture and three teenagers in prison', *Borderlands* 13.1 (2014), 1–27.

13 Ibid., 4.

14 *N* v. *Secretary of State for the Home Department* [2005] UKHL 31.

15 *Rhuppiah* v. *Secretary of State for the Home Department* [2018] UKSC 58.

16 See, for example, Gurminder K. Bhambra, 'Turning citizens into migrants', *Red Pepper*, 19 April 2018, www.redpepper.org.uk/talking-about-migrants-is-a-dogwhistle-way-of-talking-about-race/ (accessed 26 September 2019); David Lammy, 'Don't let Rudd's departure distract from a toxic policy that needs to die', *The Guardian*, 30 April 2018, www.theguardian.com/commentisfree/2018/apr/30/amber-rudd-departure-toxic-policy-windrush-generation-home-secretary-david-lammy (accessed 26 September 2019).

17 See Rieko Karatani, *Defining British Citizenship: Empire, Commonwealth and Modern Britain* (Abingdon: Routledge, 2003); Randall Hansen, *Citizenship and Immigration in Postwar Britain* (Oxford: Oxford University Press, 2000).

18 Literature exists on the politics and governance of migration and its relationship to race and colonial history in fields other than law. See, for example, Bridget Anderson, *Us and Them?*

The Dangerous Politics of Immigration Control (Oxford: Oxford University Press, 2013); Hansen, *Citizenship and Immigration in Postwar Britain*; Lucy Mayblin, *Asylum after Empire: Colonial Legacies in the Politics of Asylum-Seeking* (Lanham, MD: Rowman and Littlefield International, 2017); Karatani, *Defining British Citizenship*.

19 Sara Ahmed, 'A phenomenology of whiteness', *Feminist Theory* 8.2 (2007), 149–68 (p. 154).

20 Gina Clayton, *Textbook on Immigration and Asylum Law* (Oxford: Oxford University Press, 2nd edn, 2010), 409–15.

21 Exceptions include Maria O'Sullivan and Dallal Stevens (eds), *States, the Law and Access to Refugee Protection: Fortresses and Fairness* (Oxford: Hart Publishing, 2017); Marie-Bénédicte Dembour and Tobias Kelly (eds), *Are Human Rights for Migrants? Critical Reflections on the Status of Irregular Migrants in Europe and the United States* (Abingdon: Routledge, 2011).

22 A number of studies have looked specifically at the impact of border control on migrants' ability to access territory, but there is a need to consider how immigration and asylum law are intricately connected and to study them as such. See, for example, Frances Webber, 'Border wars and asylum crimes', research paper, Statewatch, 2006, https://www.statewatch.org/analyses/border-wars-and-asylum-crimes.pdf (accessed 21 October 2019); Thomas Spijkerboer, 'The human cost of border control', *European Journal of Migration and Law* 9 (2007), 127–39; Thomas Gammeltoft-Hansen and H. Gammeltoft-Hansen, 'The right to seek – revisited. On the UN Human Rights Declaration Article 14 and access to asylum procedures in the EU', *European Journal of Migration and Law* 10.4 (2008), 439–59; T. Gammeltoft-Hansen, 'The refugee, the sovereign and the sea: EU interdiction policies in the Mediterranean', Danish Institute for International Studies Working Paper no. 2008/6, 1–32; Silja Klepp, 'A contested asylum system: the European Union between refugee protection and border control in the Mediterranean Sea', *European Journal of Migration and Law* 12.1 (2010), 1–21; Thomas Gammeltoft-Hansen, *Access to Asylum: International Refugee Law and the Globalisation of Migration Control* (Cambridge: Cambridge University Press, 2011); Stefanie Grant, 'Irregular migration and frontier deaths: acknowledging a right to identity', in Marie-Bénédicte Dembour and Tobias Kelly (eds), *Are Human Rights for Migrants? Critical Reflections on the Status of Irregular Migrants in Europe and the United States* (Abingdon: Routledge, 2011), 48–70; Stefanie Grant, 'Recording and identifying European frontier deaths', *European*

Journal of Migration and Law 13.2 (2011), 135–56. See also Wayne A. Cornelius, 'Controlling "unwanted" immigration: lessons from the United States, 1993–2004', *Journal of Ethnic and Migration Studies* 31.4 (2005), 775–94.

23 See Nadine El-Enany, 'Asylum in the context of immigration control: exclusion by default or design?', in Maria O'Sullivan and Dallal Stevens (eds), *States, the Law and Access to Refugee Protection: Fortresses and Fairness* (Oxford: Hart Publishing, 2017), 29–44.

24 See note 6 above.

25 See, for example, David A. Martin, 'The new asylum seekers', in David A. Martin, *The New Asylum Seekers: Refugee Law in the 1980s* (Dordrecht: Martinus Nijhoff, 1988), 1–20; Alexander Betts, 'Proliferation and the global refugee regime', *Perspectives on Politics* 7.1 (2009), 53–8; Erika Feller, 'Asylum, migration and refugee protection: realities, myths and the promise of things to come', *International Journal of Refugee Law* 8.3–4 (2006), 509–36.

26 *R v. Secretary of State for the Home Department ex parte Bugdaycay* [1987] AC 514.

CHAPTER 1

1 See Nadine El-Enany, 'On pragmatism and legal idolatry: Fortress Europe and the desertion of the European refugee', *International Journal of Minority and Group Rights* 22.1 (2015), 7–38.

2 Following Cherryl Harris, I adopt the definition of white supremacy as posited by Frances Lee Ansley: 'By "white supremacy" I do not mean to allude only to the self-conscious racism of white supremacist hate groups. I refer instead to a political, economic, and cultural system in which whites overwhelmingly control power and material resources, conscious and unconscious ideas of white superiority and entitlement are widespread, and relations of white dominance and non-white subordination are daily reenacted across a broad array of institutions and social settings.' Frances L. Ansley, 'Stirring the ashes: race, class and the future of civil rights scholarship', *Cornell Law Review* 74.6 (1989), cited in Cherryl I. Harris, 'Whiteness as property', *Harvard Law Review* 106.8 (1993), 1707–91 (p. 1714).

3 Edward W. Said, *Orientalism* (London: Routledge and Kegan Paul, 1978), xvi.

4 Bernard S. Cohn, *Colonialism and Its Forms of Knowledge: The British in India* (Princeton, NJ: Princeton University Press, 1996), 3.

5 E. Tendayi Achiume, 'Reimagining international law for global migration: migration as decolonization?', *American Journal of International Law* 142 (2017), 142–6 (p. 143).

6 Lauren Benton and Lisa Ford, *Rage for Order: The British Empire and the Origins of International Law, 1800–1850* (Cambridge, MA: Harvard University Press, 2016), 1.

7 Said, *Orientalism*, 323.

8 Étienne Balibar, 'Is there a "neo-racism"', in Étienne Balibar and Immanuel Wallerstein (eds), *Race, Nation, Class: Ambiguous Identities* (London: Verso, 1993), 19.

9 Denise Ferreira da Silva, *Towards a Global Idea of Race* (Minneapolis, MN: University of Minnesota Press, 2007), 82–3.

10 Ibid., 82.

11 Étienne Balibar, 'Racism and nationalism', in Étienne Balibar and Immanuel Wallerstein (eds), *Race, Nation, Class: Ambiguous Identities* (London: Verso, 1993), 89, cited in Anderson, *Us and Them*, 35.

12 Alana Lentin, 'Concepts and debates 2: race and the human', *Understanding Race*, 13 August 2018, www.alanalentin.net/2018/08/13/concepts-and-debates-2-race-and-the-human/ (accessed 26 September 2019).

13 Ibid.

14 Alana Lentin, 'Race', in W. Outhwaite and S. Turner (eds), *The Sage Handbook of Political Sociology* (London: Sage, 2018), 860–77 (p. 864).

15 See John Newsinger, *The Blood Never Dried: A People's History of the British Empire* (London: Bookmarks, 2006).

16 Balibar, 'Racism and nationalism', 42.

17 Said, *Orientalism*, 108.

18 Ibid., 119 (emphasis in original).

19 See Irene Watson, 'Buried alive', *Law and Critique* 13 (2002), 253–69; Glen Coulthard, *Red Skin, White Masks: Rejecting the Colonial Politics of Recognition* (Minneapolis, MN: University of Minnesota Press, 2014).

20 Said, *Orientalism*, 45.

21 See Jonah Raskin, *The Mythology of Imperialism* (New York: Random House, 1971), 40, cited in Said, *Orientalism*, 45.

22 Said, *Orientalism*, 46.

23 Ibid., 46.

24 Cecil Rhodes, *Confessions of Faith*, cited in Dorling and Tomlinson, *Rule Britannia*, 124.

25 Dorling and Tomlinson, *Rule Britannia*, 78.

26 Gargi Bhattacharyya, *Rethinking Racial Capitalism: Questions of*

Reproduction and Survival (Lanham, MD: Rowman and Littlefield International, 2018), 102.

27 Stuart Hall (and Sut Jhally), 'Race, the floating signifier: featuring Stuart Hall', transcript of a talk for the Media Education Foundation (1997), 2.

28 Ibid., 8.

29 Ibid.

30 W. E. B. Du Bois, *Dusk of Dawn. An Essay Toward an Autobiography of a Race Concept: With an introduction by Kwame Anthony Appiah* (Oxford: Oxford University Press, 2007 [1940]), 43, cited in Lentin, 'Race', 861.

31 Lentin, 'Race', 866.

32 Anderson, *Us and Them*, 36.

33 Georges Nzongola-Ntalaja, *The Congo from Leopold to Kabila: A People's History* (London: Zed Books, 2002), and Mahmood Mamdani, 'The invention of the indigène', *London Review of Books* 33.2 (20 January 2011), cited in Anderson, *Us and Them*, 36.

34 Radhika Viyas Mongia, 'Race, nationality, mobility: a history of the passport', *Public Culture* 11.3 (1999), 527–55 (p. 539). See also, Radhika Mongia, *Indian Migration and Empire: A Colonial Genealogy of the Modern State* (Durham, Duke University Press, 2018).

35 Bhattacharyya, *Rethinking Racial Capitalism*, 102.

36 Ibid., 127.

37 Ibid.

38 Ibid., 147.

39 Ibid.

40 Gilmore, *Golden Gulag*, 28.

41 Dean Spade, *Normal Life: Administrative Violence, Critical Trans Politics and the Limits of the Law* (New York: South End Press, 2011), 46.

42 Ibid.

43 Eduardo Bonilla-Silva, '"New racism," color-blind racism, and the future of whiteness in America', in Ashley W. Doane and Eduardo Bonilla-Silva (eds), *White Out: The Continuing Significance of Racism* (Abingdon: Routledge, 2004), 271–84 (p. 271) (emphasis in original).

44 See STOPWATCH, 'Schedule 7 stops under the Terrorism Act 2000', www.stop-watch.org/uploads/documents/Factsheet_-_Schedule_7.pdf (accessed 26 September 2019).

45 See UNITED, 'The fatal policies of Fortress Europe', Amsterdam, UNITED for Intercultural Action, 5 May 2018, www.unite

dagainstracism.org/campaigns/refugee-campaign/fortress-europe/ (accessed 26 September 2019).

46 See Nadine El-Enany, 'The violence of deportation and the exclusion of evidence of racism in the case of Jimmy Mubenga', in Nadine El-Enany and Eddie Bruce-Jones (eds), *Justice, Resistance and Solidarity: Race and Policing in England and Wales* (London: Runnymede Trust, 2015), 14–15. See 'No deportations: residence papers for all', 24 March 2016, www.no-deportations. org.uk/Media-6-4-2011/DeathInRemovalCentres.html (accessed 26 September 2019) for details of detention centre deaths and statistics of those on suicide watch.

47 Bridget Anderson, Nandita Sharma and Cynthia Wright, 'Editorial: why no borders?', *Refuge* 26.2 (2009), 6.

48 Nira Yuval-Davis, Georgie Wemyss and Kathryn Cassidy, 'Everyday bordering, belonging and the reorientation of British immigration legislation', *Sociology* 52.2 (2017), 228–44 (pp. 229–30).

49 Ibid.

50 Sarah Keenan, 'A prison around your ankle and a border in every street: theorising law, space and the subject', in Andreas Philippopoulos-Mihalopoulos (ed.), *Handbook of Law and Theory* (Abingdon: Routledge 2018), 71–90; Gilmore, *Golden Gulag*, 28.

51 Sarah Keenan, 'Smoke, curtains and mirrors: the production of race through time and title registration', *Law & Critique* 28.1 (2017), 87–108 (p. 103).

52 Said, *Orientalism*, 1.

53 Ahmed, 'A phenomenology of whiteness', 158.

54 Ibid., 153.

55 Ibid.

56 Ibid., 154.

57 Ibid., 163.

58 Ibid. 153.

59 Renisa Mawani, 'Law as temporality: colonial politics and Indian settlers', *UC Irvine Law Review* 4.65 (2014), 65–96 (p. 68).

60 Hall (and Jhally), 'Race, the floating signifier', 2.

61 Lentin, 'Race', 862.

62 P. Edmonds and J. Carey, 'A new beginning for settler colonial studies', *Settler Colonial Studies* 3.1 (2013), 2–5 (p. 2); A. Goldstein, 'Introduction: toward a genealogy of the US colonial present', in A. Goldstein (ed.), *Formations of United States Colonialism* (Durham, NC: Duke University Press, 2014), 1–36 (p. 9), cited in Renisa Mawani, 'Law, settler colonialism, and the forgotten space of maritime worlds', *Annual Review of Law and Social Science* 12 (2016), 107–31 (p. 110). See also Patrick Wolfe,

'Settler colonialism and the elimination of the native', *Journal of Genocide Research* 8.4 (2006), 387–409 (p. 388).

63 Mawani, 'Law, settler colonialism, and the forgotten space of maritime worlds', 110.

64 See Sarah Keenan, *Subversive Property: Law and the Production of Spaces of Belonging* (Abingdon: Routledge, 2014); see also Davina Cooper, *Everyday Utopias: The Conceptual Life of Promising Spaces* (Durham, NC: Duke University Press, 2013).

65 Frantz Fanon, *Black Skin, White Masks* (London: Pluto Press, 2008).

66 Coulthard, *Red Skin, White Masks*, 16.

67 Ibid.

68 Sara Ahmed, *The Promise of Happiness* (Durham, NC: Duke University Press, 2010), 106.

69 See, for example, Elizabeth A. Povinelli, *The Cunning of Recognition: Indigenous Alterities and the Making of Australian Multiculturalism* (Durham, NC: Duke University Press, 2002); Glen Coulthard, 'Subjects of empire: indigenous peoples and the "politics of recognition" in Canada', *Contemporary Political Theory* 6.4 (2007), 437–60; Coulthard, *Red Skin, White Masks*.

70 Keenan, 'A prison around your ankle and a border in every street', 76.

71 See, for example, Amelia Gentleman, '"My life is in ruins": wrongly deported Windrush people facing fresh indignity', *The Guardian*, 10 September 2018, www.theguardian.com/uk-ne ws/2018/sep/10/windrush-people-wrongly-deported-jamaica-crim inal-offence (accessed 16 September 2019).

72 Kevin Rawlinson, 'Windrush: 11 people wrongly deported from the UK have died – Javid', *The Guardian*, 12 November 2018, www.theguardian.com/uk-news/2018/nov/12/windrush-11-peop le-wrongly-deported-from-uk-have-died-sajid-javid (accessed 16 September 2019). See also www.theguardian.com/uk-news/2019/ may/09/revealed-five-men-killed-since-being-deported-uk-jamaica-home-office (accessed 16 September 2019).

73 Lammy, 'Don't let Rudd's departure distract from a toxic policy that needs to die'.

74 HC Deb 22 October 2013, vol. 569, c. 214.

75 Gilmore, *Golden Gulag*, 28.

76 Nadine El-Enany, 'The colonial logic of Grenfell', 3 July 2017, www.versobooks.com/blogs/3306-the-colonial-logic-of-grenfell (accessed 16 September 2019).

77 Nadine El-Enany, 'The Iraq War, Brexit and imperial blowback', Truthout, 6 July 2016, www.truth-out.org/opinion/item/36703-t

he-iraq-war-brexit-and-imperial-blowback (accessed 16 September 2019); Nadine El-Enany, 'The next British Empire', *IPPR Progressive Review* 25.1 (2018), 30–8.

78 Coulthard, 'Subjects of empire', 437.
79 Povinelli, *The Cunning of Recognition*.
80 Coulthard, 'Subjects of empire', 446.
81 Ibid., 456.

CHAPTER 2

1 Jamaica Kincaid, *A Small Place* (New York: Farrar, Straus and Giroux, 1988), 37.
2 Ann Dummett and Andrew G. L. Nicol, *Subjects, Citizens, Aliens and Others: Nationality and Immigration Law* (London: Weidenfeld and Nicolson, 1990), cited in Anderson, *Us and Them*, 29.
3 Gina Clayton et al., *Textbook on Immigration and Asylum Law* (Oxford: Oxford University Press, 7th edn, 2016), 5.
4 Calvin's Case, English Reports, vol. 77, 1608, 397, 399.
5 The Navigation Acts had also significantly weakened the Scottish shipping industry and were part of the siege campaign waged against the Scots, designed to force the country into a union with England. Scotland's capitulation followed its own failed colonial endeavour to establish a trading post and colony on the isthmus of Panama. See Helen Julia Paul, 'The Darien scheme and Anglophobia in Scotland', University of Southampton, Discussion Papers in Economics and Econometrics, No. 0925, 2009; W. Douglas Jones, '"The bold adventurers": a qualitative analysis of the Darien subscription list (1696)', *Journal of Scottish Historical Studies* 21.1 (2008), 22–42.
6 Renisa Mawani, *Across Oceans of Law: The Komagata Maru and Jurisdictions in the Time of Empire* (Durham, NC: Duke University Press, 2018), 137.
7 Ibid., 117.
8 See, for example, the decision of the Privy Council in *Cooper* v. *Stuart* (1889) 14 App Cas 286, and in *Advocate-General of Bengal* v. *Ranee Surnomoye Dossee* (1863) 15 ER 811.
9 John Chesterman, 'Natural-born subjects? Race and British subjecthood in Australia', *Australian Journal of Politics and History* 5.1 (2005), 30–9.
10 Geoffrey Sawer, 'Opinion by Geoffrey Sawer', 26 July 1961, Appendix III to the 'Report from the Select Committee on Voting Rights of Aborigines, part one', Commonwealth Parliamentary

Papers, 1961, vol. 2 37, cited in Chesterman, 'Natural-born subjects?'

11 Ibid.

12 *Mabo* v. *Queensland* (No 2) ('Mabo case') [1992] HCA 23; (1992) 175 CLR 1 (3 June 1992).

13 Ibid., para. 38.

14 See Australian Human Rights Commission, *Close The Gap – 10 Year Review* (Australian Human Rights Commission 2018), www.humanrights.gov.au/our-work/aboriginal-and-torr es-strait-islander-social-justice/publications/close-gap-10-year-re view (accessed 26 September 2019).

15 Trans-migrants were those migrants seeking only temporary stay while waiting to migrate to another country, most commonly the United States during the era covered in this chapter.

16 Home Affairs Committee, Fifth Report 2005–6, para. 8, cited in Clayton, *Textbook on Immigration and Asylum Law*, 7th edn, 5.

17 Anderson, *Us and Them*, 31.

18 Ibid.

19 Steve Cohen, 'The local state of immigration controls', *Critical Social Policy* 22.3 (2002), 518–43 (p. 520).

20 See, for example, Watson, 'Buried alive'; Aileen Moreton-Robinson, *The White Possessive: Property, Power and Indigenous Sovereignty* (Minneapolis, MN: University of Minnesota Press, 2015); Coulthard, *Red Skin, White Masks*; Daniel N. Paul, 'The hidden history of the Americas: the destruction and depopulation of the indigenous civilisations of the Americas by European invaders', *Settler Colonial Studies* 1.2 (2011), 167–81.

21 Anderson, *Us and Them*, 31.

22 Rainer Muenz, 'Demographic change in EU27 and in neighboring Mediterranean regions', paper presented at the 9th Mediterranean Research Meeting, Florence and Montecatini, 12–15 March 2008, 5.

23 Patricia Tuitt, 'Used up and misused: the national state, the European Union and the insistent presence of the colonial', *Columbia Journal of Race and Law* 1.3 (2012), 490–9 (p. 491), citing Catherine Hall, 'Introduction: thinking the postcolonial, thinking the empire', in Catherine Hall (ed.), *Cultures of Empire: A Reader: Colonisers in Britain and the Empire the Nineteenth and Twentieth Centuries* (Manchester: Manchester University Press, 2000), 1, 5.

24 Dummett and Nicol, *Subjects, Citizens, Aliens and Others*, cited in Anderson, *Us and Them*, 29. See also Polly Price, 'Natural law and birthright citizenship in Calvin's Case (1608)', *Yale Journal of Law & the Humanities* 9.1 (1997), 73–145.

25 Ibid., 29–31.

26 See Harris, 'Whiteness as property'; Anderson, *Us and Them*, 31.

27 See Catherine Hall, Nicholas Draper, Keith McCelland, Katie Donington and Rachel Lang, *Legacies of British Slave-ownership: Colonial Slavery and the Formation of Victorian Britain* (Cambridge: Cambridge University Press, 2014).

28 Vilna Bashi, 'Globalized anti-blackness: transnationalizing Western immigration law, policy, and practice', *Ethnic and Racial Studies* 27.4 (2004), 584–606 (p. 588).

29 Ron Ramdin, *Reimagining Britain: Five Hundred Years of Black and Asian History* (London: Pluto Press, 1999), 14, cited in Bashi, 'Globalized anti-blackness', 587–8.

30 Harris, 'Whiteness as property'.

31 See Gilmore, *Golden Gulag*, 28.

32 Anderson, *Us and Them*, 31.

33 See House of Commons, 'An Act for the Protection of Natives of Her Majesty's Territories in the East Indies Contracting for Labour to be performed without the Said Territories, and for Regulating their Passage by Sea', Parliamentary Papers 1837–38, vol. 3, cited in Mongia, 'Race, nationality, mobility', 529–30.

34 P. D'Epinay to Hollier Griffiths, 5 January 1836, *Papers Respecting the East India Labourers' Bill*, 56, cited in Mongia, 'Race, nationality, mobility', 530.

35 Mongia, 'Race, nationality, mobility', 530.

36 Ibid., 539.

37 Anderson, *Us and Them*, 33.

38 Ibid., 29–31.

39 See House of Commons, 'An Act for the Protection of Natives of Her Majesty's Territories in the East Indies Contracting for Labour to be Performed without the Said Territories, and for Regulating their Passage by Sea', Parliamentary Papers 1837–38, vol. 3, cited in Mongia, 'Race, nationality, mobility', 530.

40 Mongia, 'Race, nationality, mobility', 537.

41 Viceroy of India, Calcutta, to the Secretary of State for India, London, telegram received 22 January 1908, cited in Mongia, 'Race, nationality, mobility', 537.

42 Communication from British Indian subjects in Canada to Colonial Office, London, 24 April 1910, *Proceedings A*, October no. 47 ser. no. 8 encl. no. 1 annex 1, cited in Mongia, 'Race, nationality, mobility', 543.

43 Anderson, *Them and Us*, 35.

44 Mongia, 'Race, nationality, mobility', 553–4.

45 Ibid., 553.

46 Sir Charles Dilke, Liberal Party MP for Gloucestershire, Forest of Dean, HC Deb 29 March 1904, vol. 132, cc. 987–95, 993.

47 Mayblin, *Asylum after Empire*, 24.

48 Ibid.

49 Robin Cohen, *Migration and its Enemies: Global Capital, Migrant Labour and the Nation-State* (Aldershot: Ashgate, 2006), 70.

50 Ibid.

51 See Didi Herman, *An Unfortunate Coincidence: Jews, Jewishness, and English Law* (Oxford: Oxford University Press, 2011).

52 Helen Shooter, 'Dispersing the myths about asylum: review of "No One is Illegal", Steve Cohen (Trentham Books)', *Socialist Review*, 272 (2003), http://socialistreview.org.uk/272/dispersing-myths-about-asylum (accessed 26 September 2019).

53 Deborah Hayes, 'The role of welfare in the internal control of immigration', in Janet Batsleer and Beth Humphries (eds), *Welfare, Exclusion and Political Agency* (London: Routledge, 2000), 63–78 (p. 65).

54 Ibid.

55 See John Cooper, *The Unexpected Story of Nathaniel Rothschild* (London: Bloomsbury, 2015), ch. 5.

56 David Pannick QC, 'A century ago immigration control was an alien concept – how it has changed', *The Times*, 28 June 2005, www.thetimes.co.uk/article/a-century-ago-immigration-control-was-an-alien-concept-how-it-has-changed-phzh6cp3wtc (accessed 26 September 2019).

57 Ibid.

58 Royal Commission on Alien Immigration, Report, Cd. 1742, 1903, vol. 1, part 2, *Measures Adopted for the Restriction and Control of Alien Immigration in Foreign Countries and in British Colonies, Law of the United States*, cited in Alison Bashford and Catie Gilchrist, 'The colonial history of the 1905 Aliens Act', *The Journal of Imperial and Commonwealth History* 40.3 (2012), 409–37 (p. 421).

59 Ibid., 422.

60 Ibid., 426.

61 HC Deb 29 March 1904, vol. 132, cc. 987–95, 987.

62 Ibid., 988.

63 Ibid.

64 Ibid., 991–2.

65 Ibid., 992. See also HC Deb 21 March 1904, vol. 132, cc. 321–71.

66 HC Deb 21 March 1904, vol. 132, cc. 321–71, 331.

67 Ibid., 324.

68 HC Deb 29 March 1904, vol. 132, cc. 987–95, 994.

69 Ibid., 995.

70 Aliens Act 1905

71 *Musgrove* v. *Chun Teeong Toy* [1891] AC 272.

72 [1899] 1 F. (Ct. Sess.) 823, at 827–28. See Dallal Stevens, *UK Asylum Law and Policy: Historical and Contemporary Perspectives* (London: Sweet and Maxwell, 2004), 48.

73 [1906] AC 542. See Stevens, *UK Asylum Law and Policy*.

74 Pannick, 'A century ago immigration control was an alien concept'.

75 Jill Pellew, 'The Home Office and the Aliens Act, 1905', *The Historical Journal* 32.2 (1989), 369–85 (p. 373).

76 Minute by Chalmers, 15 February 1906, HO45 10326/131787/6, cited in Pellew, 'The Home Office and the Aliens Act, 1905', 378.

77 Section 1(3)(a) Aliens Act 1905.

78 Lisa Marie Jakubowski, *Immigration and the Legalization of Racism* (Black Point, Nova Scotia: Fernwood Publishing, 1997), 16, cited in Bashi, 'Globalized anti-blackness', 597.

79 Aliens Act 1905.

80 John A. Garrard, *The English and Immigration 1880–1910* (Oxford: Oxford University Press, 1971), 45.

81 Ibid., 46.

82 Kushner and Knox, *Refugees in an Age of Genocide*, 26.

83 Garrard, *The English and Immigration*, 46.

84 Gina Clayton, *Textbook on Immigration and Asylum Law* (Oxford: Oxford University Press, 2nd edn, 2006), 5.

85 HC Deb 2 May 1905, vol. 145, c699. See Stevens, *UK Asylum Law and Policy*, 38, 6–11.

86 Prakash A. Shah, *Refugees, Race and the Legal Concept of Asylum in Britain* (Sydney: Cavendish Publishing, 2000), 202.

87 Kushner and Knox, *Refugees in an Age of Genocide*, 28–9.

88 Pellew, 'The Home Office and the Aliens Act, 1905', 370.

89 Ibid., 373.

90 Hayes, 'The role of welfare in the internal control of immigration', 66.

91 HO Note, 1908, HO45 10392/173811, cited in Pellew, 'The Home Office and the Aliens Act, 1905', 380.

92 Ibid.

93 Aliens Act 1905.

94 Pellew, 'The Home Office and the Aliens Act, 1905', 375.

95 Minute by John Pedder, 26 June 1907, HO45 10515/135080/11, cited in ibid., 376.

96 See further, Robbie Shilliam, *Race and the Undeserving Poor* (Newcastle upon Tyne: Agenda, 2018); Satnam Virdee, *Racism, Class and the Racialized Outsider* (London: Red Globe Press, 2014).

97 Pellew, 'The Home Office and the Aliens Act, 1905', 376.

98 Ibid.

99 Ibid.

100 Ibid.

101 Aliens Act 1905, section 1(3)(a).

102 Pellew, 'The Home Office and the Aliens Act, 1905', 376–7.

103 Ibid., 377.

104 Minute by Chalmers, 15 February 1906, HO45 10326/131787/6, cited in ibid.

105 Pellew, 'The Home Office and the Aliens Act, 1905', 375.

106 Minutes by Gladstone, 28 February 1907 and 20 March 1907, HO45 10362/131787/91 and 97, cited in ibid., 375.

107 Pellew, 'The Home Office and the Aliens Act, 1905', 379.

108 Ibid., 385.

109 *Immigrant traffic and inspection, 1906–1913*, annual reports of Inspector of Aliens, cited in ibid., 383.

110 Pellew, 'The Home Office and the Aliens Act, 1905', 377.

111 Garrard, *The English and Immigration*, 16.

112 Chalmers to Gladstone, 6 March 1906, Visc. Gladstone papers, Add.MSS 45993, fos. 17–18, cited in Pellew, 'The Home Office and the Aliens Act, 1905'.

113 Gladstone papers, February to June 1906, HO45 10334/137764, cited in Pellew, 'The Home Office and the Aliens Act, 1905', 381.

114 Pellew, 'The Home Office and the Aliens Act, 1905', 377.

115 Ibid., 381.

116 An extract from the *Daily Telegraph*, 11 February 1909, reprinted in 'Correspondence between the secretary of state for the Home Department and His Honour Judge Rentoul, KC, on the subject of the expulsion of aliens', PP 1909 LXX 5, cited in Pellew, 'The Home Office and the Aliens Act, 1905', 381.

117 Fifth annual report of the Inspector of Aliens for 1910, PP 1911, x [Cd. 5789], 4, cited in Pellew, 'The Home Office and the Aliens Act, 1905', 381.

118 Pellew, 'The Home Office and the Aliens Act, 1905', 382.

119 Eric Hobsbawm, *The Age of Empire, 1875–1914* (New York: Pantheon Books, 1987), 303.

120 Ibid., 303; Eric Hobsbawm, *The Age of Extremes: The Short Twentieth Century, 1914–1991* (London: Abacus, 1994), 23.

121 Hobsbawm, *Age of Extremes*, 23.

122 Hobsbawm, *Age of Empire*, 309–27.

123 HC Deb 5 August 1914, vol. 65, cc. 1989–90.

124 See Patricia Tuitt, 'Transitions: refugees and natives', *International Journal of Minority and Group Rights* 20.2 (2013), 179–97. See commentary on *Rhuppiah* v. *Secretary of State for the Home Department* at pp. ... below.

125 Kushner and Knox, *Refugees in an Age of Genocide*, 44.

126 Aliens Restriction Act 1914, Section 1(1)(d).

127 Ibid.

128 Kushner and Knox, *Refugees in an Age of Genocide*, 45.

129 'German spy scare: Portsmouth shopkeeper's window smashed', *Hampshire Telegraph and Post*, 21 August 1914, cited in Kushner and Knox, *Refugees in an Age of Genocide*, 45.

130 Kushner and Knox, *Refugees in an Age of Genocide*, 45.

131 *Census of England and Wales, 1911: County of Hampshire* (London: HMSO, 1914), table 31, and *Census of England and Wales, 1921 Hampshire and the Isle of White* (London: HMSO, 1923), table 22, cited in ibid., 47.

132 Stevens, *UK Asylum Law and Policy*, 49.

133 *R* v. *Governor of Brixton Prison ex parte Sarno* [1916] 2 KB 742, cited in Stevens, *UK Asylum Law and Policy*, 49.

134 [1916] 2 KB 747, cited in Stevens, *UK Asylum Law and Policy*, 49.

135 in *obiter* – [1916] 2 KB 749, cited in Stevens, *UK Asylum Law and Policy*, 49.

136 [1916] 2 KB 750, cited in Stevens, *UK Asylum Law and Policy*, 49–50.

137 [1917] 1 KB 929, cited in Stevens, *UK Asylum Law and Policy*, 50.

138 Stevens, *UK Asylum Law and Policy*, 51, 52.

139 Tony Kushner and Katharine Knox, *Refugees in an Age of Genocide: Global, National and Local Perspectives during the Twentieth Century* (Abingdon: Routledge, 1999), 47.

140 Ibid.

141 Ibid.

142 Caroline Shaw, *Britannia's Embrace: Modern Humanitarianism and the Imperial Origins of Refugee Relief* (Oxford: Oxford University Press, 2015), 2.

143 Peter Cahalan, *Belgian Refugee Relief in England During the Great War* (New York: Garland, 1982), 18, cited in Kushner and Knox, *Refugees in an Age of Genocide*, 49.

144 Kushner and Knox, *Refugees in an Age of Genocide*, 49.

145 Ibid., 48.

146 Cahalan, *Belgian Refugee Relief in England During the Great War*, 18, cited in Kushner and Knox, *Refugees in an Age of Genocide*, 53.

147 Kushner and Knox, *Refugees in an Age of Genocide*, 61.

148 Cahalan, *Belgian Refugee Relief in England During the Great War*, 18, cited in Kushner and Knox, *Refugees in an Age of Genocide*, 61.

149 Kushner and Knox, *Refugees in an Age of Genocide*, 61.

150 Colin Holmes, *John Bull's Island: Immigration & British Society, 1871–1971* (Basingstoke: Macmillan, 1988), 102, cited in Kushner and Knox, *Refugees in an Age of Genocide*, 57.

151 See the handbook of 'suggestions and advice' issued by the Official Committee of Belgians in 1914, cited in Kushner and Knox, *Refugees in an Age of Genocide*, 60.

152 Cahalan, *Belgian Refugee Relief in England During the Great War*, 18, cited in Kushner and Knox, *Refugees in an Age of Genocide*, 60.

153 Kushner and Knox, *Refugees in an Age of Genocide*, 63.

154 Bashi, 'Globalized anti-blackness', 591.

155 Kathleen Paul, *Whitewashing Britain* (Ithaca, NY: Cornell University Press, 1997), 113, cited in Bashi, 'Globalized anti-blackness', 591.

156 Paul, *Whitewashing Britain*, 113.

157 Ibid.

158 Ibid.

159 It is beyond the scope of this book to address in detail the colonial dimensions of the First World War. See Santanu Das (ed.), *Race, Empire and First World War Writing* (Cambridge: Cambridge University Press, 2011); Christian Koller, 'The recruitment of colonial troops in Africa and Asia and their deployment in Europe during the First World War', *Immigrants and Minorities* 26.1–2 (2008), 111–13; Pankaj Mishra, 'How colonial violence came home: the ugly truth of the first world war', *The Guardian*, 10 November 2017, www.theguardian.com/news/2017/nov/10/how-colonial-violence-came-home-the-ugly-truth-of-the-first-world-war (accessed 26 September 2019).

160 Louise Holborn, *Refugees: A Problem of Our Time: The Work of The United Nations High Commissioner for Refugees, 1951–1972* (Metuchen, NJ: Scarecrow Press, 1975), 4.

161 Ibid., 5.

162 Kushner and Knox, *Refugees in an Age of Genocide*, 43.

163 Holborn, *Refugees*, 3.

164 Ibid., 15.

165 Convention of 28 October 1933 relating to the International Status of Refugees.

166 Holborn, *Refugees*, 16.

167 Frank Field, 'The welfare state – never ending reform', BBC, www.bbc.co.uk/history/british/modern/field_01.shtml (accessed 26 September 2019).

168 HC Deb 6 July 1908, vol. 191, c. 1360.

169 Steve Cohen, 'Anti-semitism, immigration controls and the welfare state', in David Taylor (ed.), *Critical Social Policy: A Reader* (London: Sage, 1996), 27–47 (p. 35).

170 Section 45.

171 Cohen, 'The local state of immigration controls', 522.

172 Cohen, 'Anti-semitism, immigration controls and the welfare state', 38.

173 HC Deb 23 November 1917, vol. 99, cc. 1549–608, 1563.

174 Cohen, 'Anti-semitism, immigration controls and the welfare state', 37–8.

175 Section 3.

176 Dr T. J. Macnamara, HC Deb 16 March 1922, vol. 151, cc. 2406–7W, 2407W.

177 See Aditya Mukherjee, 'Empire: how colonial India made modern Britain', *Economic and Political Weekly* 45.50 (2010), 73–82 (p. 76). See also Gurminder K. Bhambra and John Holmwood, 'Colonialism, postcolonialism and the liberal welfare state', *New Political Economy* 23.5 (2018), 574–87.

178 Matthew Lange, James Mahoney and Matthias Vom Hau, 'Colonialism and development: a comparative analysis of Spanish and British colonies', *American Journal of Sociology* 111.5 (2006), 1412–62, 1430.

179 Mukherjee, 'Empire', 76.

Chapter 3

1 Immigration Act 1971, Section 2(6).

2 See Keenan, *Subversive Property*. See also Cooper, *Everyday Utopias*.

3 See UNITED, 'The fatal policies of Fortress Europe'.

4 See Keenan, 'A prison around your ankle and a border in every street'. See also Anderson, Sharma and Wright, 'Editorial', 6.

5 Andrea Levy, *Small Island* (London: Headline Review, 2004), 142.

6 Section 27.

7 Altered to indefinite transmission in the British Nationality and Status of Aliens Act 1922.

8 British Nationality and Status of Aliens Act 1914, Section 26(1).

9 Section 1.

10 Section 1(c).

11 Randall Hansen, 'From subjects to citizens: immigration and nationality law in the United Kingdom', in Randall Hansen and Patrick Weil (eds), *Towards a European Nationality: Citizenship, Immigration and Nationality Law in the EU* (Basingstoke: Palgrave, 2001), 69–94 (p. 73).

12 Section 2.

13 Cohen, 'Anti-semitism, immigration controls and the welfare state', 42.

14 Section 2(3).

15 Section 2(3).

16 Section 10(1).

17 Section 10(2).

18 'The Report of the Select Committee on the Nationality of Married Women', Parliamentary Papers, 1923, vol. 7, p. 17, cited in M. Page Baldwin, 'Subject to empire: married women and the British Nationality and Status of Aliens Act', *Journal of British Studies* 40.4 (2014), 522–56.

19 Levy, *Small Island*, 139.

20 'UK and Colonies', Government Information 1972, https://assets. publishing.service.gov.uk/government/uploads/system/uploads/ attachment_data/file/258242/ukandcolonies.pdf (accessed 26 September 2019).

21 Lord Goldsmith QC, Citizenship Review, 'Citizenship: Our Common Bond' (2008), 15, http://image.guardian.co.uk/sys-files/Politics/documents/2008/03/11/citizenship-report-full.pdf (accessed 21 October 2019).

22 Anderson, *Us and Them*, 39.

23 See Sherene Razack, *Dying From Improvement: Inquests and Inquiries into Indigenous Deaths in Custody* (Toronto: University of Toronto Press, 2015).

24 HL Deb 11 May 1948, vol. 155, cc. 754–99, 756.

25 Randall Hansen, 'The politics of citizenship in 1940s Britain: the British Nationality Act', *Twentieth Century British History* 10.1 (1999), 67–95 (p. 73).

26 HL Deb 11 May 1948, vol. 155, cc. 754–99, 756.

27 Ibid., 76.

28 Ibid., 754.

29 PREM, 8/851, 'British Nationality Law: Memorandum by the Secretary of State for the Home Department', 30 August 1946, cited in Hansen, 'The politics of citizenship in 1940s Britain', 76. See also Chuter Ede (Home Secretary), HC Deb 7 July 1948, vol. 453, cc. 385–510, 388.

30 Hansen, 'The politics of citizenship in 1940s Britain', 77.
31 Ibid., 79.
32 Ibid., 76.
33 Hansen, *Citizenship and Immigration in Postwar Britain*, 17–18.
34 Hansen, 'The politics of citizenship in 1940s Britain', 76–7.
35 Ibid., 76–7.
36 HC Deb 7 July 1948 vol. 453 cc. 385–510, 397.
37 HC Deb 7 July 1948, vol. 453, cc. 385–510, 394.
38 See, for example, HL Deb 11 May 1948, vol. 155, cc. 754–99, 762 and 795.
39 Ibid., 755.
40 HL Deb 11 May 1948, vol. 155, cc. 754–99, 762.
41 HC Deb 27 February 1968, vol. 759, cc. 1241–368, 1262.
42 Dagmar Brunow, *Remediating Transcultural Memory: Documentary Filmmaking as Archival Intervention* (Berlin: De Gruyter, 2015), 151.
43 'WELCOME HOME! Evening Standard plane greets the 400 sons of Empire', *Evening Standard*, 22 June 1948.
44 Richard Cavendish, 'Arrival of SS *Empire Windrush*', *History Today* 48.6 (1998), www.historytoday.com/richard-cavendish/ arrival-ss-empire-windrush (accessed 26 September 2019).
45 Ikuko Asaka, *Tropical Freedom: Climate, Settler Colonialism, and Black Exclusion in the Age of Emancipation* (Durham, NC: Duke University Press, 2017), 3.
46 Ibid., 7.
47 See, for example, Karia Adams, 'Postwar Britain welcomed these workers. Brexit Britain wants proof they belong', *The Washington Post*, 17 April 2018, www.washingtonpost.com/wo rld/europe/postwar-britain-welcomed-these-workers-brexit-brita in-wants-proof-they-belong/2018/04/17/ea153692–53a2–42c8-a7 29-d53d98adb5ba_story.html?noredirect=on&utm_term=.9b37e 739f96c (accessed 26 January 2018); 'The Empire Windrush and Tilbury Docks', www.thurrock.gov.uk/history-on-river-thames/ empire-windrush-and-tilbury-docks (accessed 26 January 2018); 'West Indians arrive in Britain on board the Empire Windrush – archive, 1948', *The Guardian*, 23 June 1948, www.theguardian. com/uk-news/2016/jun/23/immigration-windrush-west-indians-jamaica-britain (accessed 26 September 2019).
48 Gallup poll, September 1958, in *Attitudes Towards Coloured People in Great Britain, 1958–1982* (London, 1982), cited in Hansen, 'The politics of citizenship in 1940s Britain', 68. Hansen writes, '[a]lmost two-thirds of respondents supported restrictions on immigration'.

49 See John Solomos, *Race and Racism in Britain* (Basingstoke: Macmillan, 1993).

50 Memorandum by the Secretary of State for the Colonies, 'Arrival in the United Kingdom of Jamaican Unemployed', C.P. (48) 154 18 June 1948.

51 Ibid.

52 Hansen, *Citizenship and Immigration in Postwar Britain*, 18.

53 Memorandum by the Secretary of State for the Colonies, 'Arrival in the United Kingdom of Jamaican Unemployed', C.P. (48) 154 18 June 1948.

54 Caryl Phillips, *A New World Order* (New York: Vintage, 2001), 264; Anthony Payne, 'The Rodney Riots in Jamaica: the background and significance of the events of October 1968', *The Journal Commonwealth & Comparative Politics* 21.2 (1983), 158–74; T. A. Simone Patrice Wint, '"Once you go you know": tourism, colonial nostalgia and national lies in Jamaica', report to the Faculty of the Graduate School of the University of Texas at Austin, 2012, 6, https://repositories.lib.utexas.edu/bitstream/ha ndle/2152/ETD-UT-2012-05-5846/WINT-MASTERS-REPORT.p df?sequence=1&isAllowed=y (accessed 26 September 2019).

55 Catherine Hall, 'Histories, empires and the post-colonial moment', in I. Chambers and L. Curti (eds), *The Postcolonial Question: Common Skies, Divided Horizons* (London: Routledge, 2002), 65–77 (pp. 67–8).

56 Dennis Dean, 'The Conservative government and the 1961 Commonwealth Immigrants Act: the inside story', *Race and Class* 35.2 (1993), 57–74 (p. 58).

57 See Robert Miles and Diana Kay, *Refugees or Migrant Workers? European Volunteer Workers in Britain 1946–1951* (London: Routledge, 1992); Solomos, *Race and Racism in Britain*, 54.

58 Gurminder K. Bhambra, 'Brexit, the Commonwealth, and exclusionary citizenship', Open Democracy, 8 December 2016, www.opendemocracy.net/gurminder-k-bhambra/brexit-common wealth-and-exclusionary-citizenship (accessed 26 September 2019), citing Hywel Gordon Maslen, 'British Government and the European Voluntary Worker Programmes: The Post-war Refugee Crisis, Contract Labour and Political Asylum 1945–1965', PhD thesis, University of Edinburgh, 2011, 'When the war was over: European refugees after 1945', Briefing Paper 6, Coming to Britain, University of Manchester and University of Nottingham, 2012, www.nottingham.ac.uk/postwar-refugees/ documents/briefing-paper-6-coming-to-britain.pdf (accessed 26 September 2019), and Diana Kay and Robert Miles, 'Refugees or

migrant? The case of the European volunteer workers in Britain (1946–1951)', *Journal of Refugee Studies* 1.3–4 (1988), 214–36.

59 Dean, 'The Conservative government and the 1961 Commonwealth Immigrants Act'.

60 Paul, *Whitewashing Britain*, 67.

61 Dean, 'The Conservative government and the 1961 Commonwealth Immigrants Act', 68.

62 Bashi, 'Globalized anti-blackness', 593.

63 PRO, CAB 129/40, CP (5) 113, 'Coloured people from the British colonial territories', 20 March 1950. See Hansen, 'The politics of citizenship in 1940s Britain', 91.

64 Dean, 'The Conservative government and the 1961 Commonwealth Immigrants Act', 57–8.

65 PRO, CAB 129/44, CP (51), 'Immigration of British Subjects into the United Kingdom: Note by the Home Secretary', 12 February 1951. See Hansen, 'The politics of citizenship in 1940s Britain', 92.

66 Hansen, 'The politics of citizenship in 1940s Britain', 92–3.

67 PRO, CAB 129/44, CP (51) 51, 'Immigration of British Subjects into the United Kingdom: Note by the Home Secretary', 12 February 1951. See Hansen, 'The politics of citizenship in 1940s Britain', 93.

68 Dean, 'The Conservative government and the 1961 Commonwealth Immigrants Act', 58.

69 Hansen, 'The politics of citizenship in 1940s Britain', 92.

70 PRO, CO 1031/3938, Letter from M. Z. Terry, 28 November 1960, cited in Hansen, *Citizenship and Immigration in Postwar Britain*, 97.

71 Zig Layton-Henry, *The Politics of Immigration: Immigration, 'Race' and 'Race' Relations in Post-war Britain* (Oxford: Blackwell, 1992), 75, cited in Hansen, *Citizenship and Immigration in Postwar Britain*, 97.

72 Hansen, *Citizenship and Immigration in Postwar Britain*, 92.

73 PRO, CO 1031/2456, Letter from E. J. Toogood (Ministry of Labour) to M. Z. Terry (Colonial Office), 14 December 1959, cited in Hansen, *Citizenship and Immigration in Postwar Britain*, 92.

74 William Jowitt, Labour Lord Chancellor, HL Deb 11 May 1948, vol. 155, cc. 754–99, 759.

75 See, for example, Gentleman, 'My life is in ruins'.

76 See, for example, Bhambra, 'Turning citizens into migrants'; Lammy, 'Don't let Rudd's departure distract from a toxic policy that needs to die'.

77 Hansen, *Citizenship and Immigration in Postwar Britain*,

94; Anderson, *Us and Them*, 39; Bhambra, 'Brexit, the Commonwealth, and exclusionary citizenship'.

78 HL Deb 11 May 1948, vol. 155, cc. 754–99, 756–7.

79 Ibid., 787.

80 HC Deb 7 July 1948, vol. 453, cc. 385–510, 386.

81 Karatani, *Defining British Citizenship*, 16.

82 Ibid., 1.

83 HC Deb 7 July 1948, vol. 453, cc. 385–510, 393.

84 Ibid., 392.

85 Ibid., 397 and 398.

86 S. L. Polak, 'The Dominions and India', *Living Age*, 17 March 1917, 293, cited in Mawani, *Across Oceans of Law*, 138.

87 Mawani, *Across Oceans of Law*, 138.

88 HL Deb 11 May 1948, vol. 155, cc. 754–99, 757.

89 Ibid., 762–3.

90 British Nationality Act 1948 Section 6(2).

91 HL Deb 11 May 1948, vol. 155, cc. 754–99, 760.

92 Mahmoud Mamdani, *Citizen and Subject: Contemporary Africa and the Legacy of Late Colonialism* (Princeton, NJ: Princeton University Press, 1996), 17, cited in Mawani, *Across Oceans of Law*, 138.

93 Mawani, *Across Oceans of Law*, 140.

94 See Nisha Kapoor and Kasia Narkowicz, 'Characterising citizenship: race, criminalisation and the extension of internal borders', *Sociology* 53.4 (2019), 652–70.

95 See Section 32 of the UK Borders Act 2007. See also Luke de Noronha, 'The "Windrush generation" and "illegal immigrants" are both our kin', Open Democracy, 1 May 2018, www.opende mocracy.net/uk/luke-de-noronha/windrush-generation-and-illeg al-immigrants-are-both-our-kin (accessed 26 September 2019); Luke de Noronha, *Deporting Black Britons: Portraits of Deportation to Jamaica* (Manchester: Manchester University Press, forthcoming).

96 Rieko Karatani consistently refers to the British Empire and Commonwealth as 'the global institution' of which mainland Britain was the 'dynamic hub'. See *Defining British Citizenship*, 4, 5.

97 Mawani, *Across Oceans of Law*, 117.

98 Robert Miles, 'The riots of 1958: notes on the ideological construction of "race relations" as a political issue in Britain', *Immigrants & Minorities* 3.3 (1984), 270.

99 See Coulthard, 'Subjects of empire', 437, 439.

100 HC Deb 16 November 1961, vol. 649, cc. 687–819, 687.

101 Ibid., 689.

102 Ibid., 689.

103 Ibid., 689.

104 Ibid., 695.

105 Ibid.

106 Ibid., 694.

107 Ibid.

108 Commonwealth Immigrants Act 1962, Section 1.

109 Section 1(2)(a) and (b). See Lord Goldsmith QC, Citizenship Review, 'Citizenship: Our Common Bond' (2008), 15.

110 HC Deb 16 November 1961, vol. 649, cc. 687–819, 695.

111 Section 2(3)(a).

112 Section 2(4)(a).

113 Section 2(4)(b).

114 Section 2(4)(c).

115 Section 7(1).

116 Dean, 'The Conservative government and the 1961 Commonwealth Immigrants Act', 58.

117 PRO, CAB 134/1466, 22 July 1959. See Dean, 'The Conservative government and the 1961 Commonwealth Immigrants Act', 59.

118 Dean, 'The Conservative government and the 1961 Commonwealth Immigrants Act', 58.

119 Ibid., 67.

120 Ibid.

121 Miles, 'The riots of 1958', 266.

122 Ibid., 272.

123 Ibid., 265.

124 Ibid., 262.

125 *The Times*, 28 August 1958, cited inMiles, 'The riots of 1958', 262.

126 Miles, 'The riots of 1958'.

127 Ibid., 263.

128 Ibid.

129 Ibid., 268.

130 Ibid., 268.

131 See John Campbell, *Pistols at Dawn: Two Hundred Years of Political Rivalry from Pitt and Fox to Blair and Brown* (London: Vintage, 2010).

132 Dean, 'The Conservative government and the 1961 Commonwealth Immigrants Act', 71.

133 Ibid., 71.

134 HC Deb 16 November 1961, vol. 649, cc. 687–819, 691.

135 Hansen, *Citizenship and Immigration in Postwar Britain*, 116–17.

136 Ibid.

137 Mongia, 'Race, nationality, mobility', 545.

138 G. C. K. Peach, *West Indian Migration to Britain: A Sociological Geography* (London: Institute of Race Relations. Oxford University Press, 1968), 10, cited in Catherine Jones, *Immigration and Social Policy in Britain* (Cambridge: Tavistock Publications, 1977), 122.

139 Home Office estimates summarised in Jim Rose, *Colour and Citizenship: A Report on British Race Relations* (London: Institute of Race Relations, Oxford University Press, 1969), cited in Jones, *Immigration and Social Policy in Britain*, 123.

140 The numbers are likely to have been higher in the year preceding the Act's coming into force as people sought to enter before it came into effect. Jones, *Immigration and Social Policy in Britain*, 124.

141 Census 1971, Commonwealth Immigrant Tables, summarised in ibid., 125.

142 Labour MP Charles Pannell, HC Deb 27 February 1968, vol. 759, cc. 1241–368, 1281.

143 In the year preceding the introduction of the Commonwealth Immigrants Act 1968, around 1,000 Kenyan Asians were entering Britain each month. By February 1968 the number had increased to 750 daily. See Home Office statistics cited in *The Times*, 'Citizens from Kenya', 16 February 1968, cited in Randall Hansen, 'The Kenyan Asians, British politics, and the Commonwealth Immigrants Act, 1968', *The Historical Journal* 42.3 (1999), 817.

144 See Okwudiba Nnoli, *Ethnic Politics in Nigeria* (Enugu, Nigeria: Fourth Dimension Publishers, 1978), ch. 1.

145 Hansen, 'The Kenyan Asians, British politics, and the Commonwealth Immigrants Act, 1968', 814.

146 Ibid., 828.

147 Ibid., 829.

148 HC Deb 27 February 1968, vol. 759, cc. 1241–368, 1268.

149 Ibid., 1276.

150 See www.alamy.com/stock-photo-1968-east-african-asian-crisis-kenyan-asians-demonstrate-at-nairobi-84180007.html (accessed 26 September 2019).

151 HC Deb 27 February 1968, vol. 759, cc. 1241–368, 1279.

152 Ibid., 1281.

153 Anthony Lester, 'Thirty years on: the East African Asians case revisited', *Public Law* (spring 2002), 60–1, cited in

Marie-Bénédicte Dembour, *When Humans Become Migrants: Study of the European Court of Human Rights with an Inter-American Counterpoint* (Oxford: Oxford University Press, 2015), 84.

154 Stevens, *UK Asylum Law and Policy*, 76.

155 HC Deb 27 February 1968, vol. 759, cc. 1241–368, 1251.

156 Ibid., 1247.

157 Ibid., 1271.

158 NOP quoted in LPA, Study Group on Immigration, 'Public opinion and immigration, by Dr. Mark Adams', January 1969, cited in Hansen, 'The Kenyan Asians, British politics, and the Commonwealth Immigrants Act, 1968', 812, 818.

159 Richard Crossman, *The Diaries of a Cabinet Minister, II* (London, 1976), 679, cited in Hansen, 'The Kenyan Asians, British politics, and the Commonwealth Immigrants Act, 1968', 819.

160 PRO, CAB 129/135, Home Secretary's memorandum C(68) 34, 12 February 1968, cited in Hansen, 'The Kenyan Asians, British politics, and the Commonwealth Immigrants Act, 1968', 819.

161 Paul Gilroy, *After Empire: Melancholia or Convivial Culture* (London: Routledge, 2004), 103.

162 See Hansen, *Citizenship and Immigration in Postwar Britain*, 138, 140.

163 HC Deb 23 March 1965, vol. 709, cc. 378–453, 443–4, cited in Hansen, *Citizenship and Immigration in Postwar Britain*, 138, 141.

164 Fanon, *Black Skin, White Masks*, 157.

165 Ibid.

166 HC Deb 27 February 1968, vol. 759, cc. 1241–368, 1267.

167 Ibid., 1293.

168 Stuart Hall et al., *Policing the Crisis* (London: Pan Macmillan, 1978), 59.

169 Ibid.

170 Ibid., 29.

171 Hansen, *Citizenship and Immigration in Postwar Britain*, 123.

172 Yumiko Hamai, '"Imperial burden" or "Jews of Africa"? An analysis of political and media discourse in the Ugandan Asian crisis (1972)', *Twentieth Century British History* 22.3 (2011), 415–36 (p. 418).

173 Hansen, 'The Kenyan Asians, British politics, and the Commonwealth Immigrants Act, 1968', 810.

174 HL Deb 16 July 1969, vol. 304, cc. 421–59, 423.

175 The Commonwealth Immigrants Act 1968, Section 1.

176 Hansen, 'The Kenyan Asians, British politics, and the Commonwealth Immigrants Act, 1968', 825.

177 B. A. Hepple, 'Commonwealth Immigrants Act 1968', *Modern Law Review* 31 (1968), 424–8 (p. 425).

178 Dembour, *When Humans Become Migrants*, 84.

179 James Callaghan, HC Deb 27 February 1968, vol. 759, cc. 1241–368, 1246.

180 Hansen, 'The Kenyan Asians, British politics, and the Commonwealth Immigrants Act, 1968', 810. Hansen notes that this was the position of Iain Macleod, Sir Edward Boyle, Nigel Fisher and Ian Gilmour in the Conservative Party, and Andrew Faulds, Michael Foot, Anthony Lester and Shirley Williams in the Labour Party.

181 HC Deb 27 February 1968, vol. 759, cc. 1241–368, 1272.

182 Ibid., 1278.

183 Ibid.

184 Ibid., 1264.

185 Ibid., 1266.

186 Ibid., 1267.

187 Speech to the Annual General Meeting of the West Midlands Area Conservative Political Centre, Birmingham, 20 April 1968, in Enoch Powell, *Reflections of a Statesman* (London: Bellew Publishing, 1991), 373–9.

188 See Hall et al., *Legacies of British Slave-ownership*.

189 Mukherjee, 'Empire', 76.

190 Avery F. Gordon, 'On "lived theory": an interview with A. Sivanandan', *Race & Class* 55.4 (2014), 1–7 (p. 2).

191 Dembour, *When Humans Become Migrants*, 62.

192 Ibid., 62–3.

193 *East African Asians* v. *the United Kingdom*, appl. 4403/70 and thirty others, Report (EComHR), 14 December 1973, para. 196.

194 *East African Asians* v. *the United Kingdom*, cited in Dembour, *When Humans Become Migrants*, 63, 88.

195 Ibid., 63.

196 *East African Asians* v. *the United Kingdom*, para. 199.

197 Dembour, *When Humans Become Migrants*, 63.

198 British Protected Persons were not granted British subjecthood and were treated as aliens by the British Nationality Act 1948. According to Randall Hansen, 'British Protected Persons' was a miscellaneous category comprising, for example, descendants of British subjects who no longer enjoyed that status under *jus sanguinis* and persons in territories where the British government

enjoyed executive power but not territorial sovereignty. See Hansen, 'The politics of citizenship in 1940s Britain', 78, 79.

199 Dembour, *When Humans Become Migrants*, 65.

200 *East African Asians* v. *the United Kingdom*, para. 213.

201 Dembour, *When Humans Become Migrants*, 66.

202 Ibid., 94.

203 Fred W. S. Craig (ed.), *British General Election Manifestos 1959–1987* (Aldershot: Dartmouth, 1990), 127, cited in Hansen, *Citizenship and Immigration in Postwar Britain*, 192.

204 HC Deb 8 March 1971, vol. 813, cc. 42–173, 42.

205 See Stuart Bentley, 'Merrick and the British Campaign to Stop Immigration: populist racism and political influence', *Race & Class* 33.3 (1995), 57–72.

206 See, for example, HC Deb 8 March 1971, vol. 813, cc. 42–173, 50 and 51.

207 Ibid., 45.

208 Ibid., 43–4.

209 Ibid., 44.

210 Ibid., 49.

211 Ibid., 44.

212 See, for example, Gentleman, 'My life is in ruins'.

213 Frances Webber, 'The "Windrush generation" retreat and the hostile environment', Institute of Race Relations, 19 April 2018, www.irr.org.uk/news/the-windrush-generation-retreat-and-the-hostile-environment/ (accessed 28 January 2019).

214 See Amelia Gentleman, 'Home Office destroyed Windrush landing cards, says ex-staffer', *The Guardian*, 17 April 2018, www.theguardian.com/uk-news/2018/apr/17/home-office-destroyed-windrush-landing-cards-says-ex-staffer (accessed 26 September 2019)

215 Section 3(8) (emphasis added).

216 Immigration Act 1971, Section 2.

217 Immigration Act 1971, Section 2(6).

218 The racialised population in Britain in 1971 is estimated to have been 1.3 million of a total population of 55 million. See David Owen, 'Ethnic minorities in Great Britain: patterns of population change, 1981–91', Centre for Research in Ethnic Relations, National Ethnic Minatory Data Archive, 1991 Census Statistical Paper No. 10, December 1995.

219 HC Deb 8 March 1971, vol. 813, cc. 42–173, 46.

220 Ibid., 65.

221 Hansen, *Citizenship and Immigration in Postwar Britain*, 195.

222 Paul, *Whitewashing Britain*, 181.

223 Immigration Act 1971, Section 2(1)(c).

224 Hansen, *Citizenship and Immigration in Postwar Britain*, 193.

225 *The Times*, 'Britons to need visas for India', 14 July 1970, cited in Hansen, *Citizenship and Immigration in Postwar Britain*, 194.

226 See Evan Smith and Marinella Marmo, *Race, Gender and the Body in British Immigration Control: Subject to Examination* (Basingstoke: Palgrave, 2014).

227 Hansen, *Citizenship and Immigration in Postwar Britain*, 202.

228 HC Deb 25 January 1973, vol. 849, cc. 653–64

229 Ibid.

230 Hansen, *Citizenship and Immigration in Postwar Britain*, 197.

231 Big Bill Broonzy, 'Black, Brown and White', 1951.

232 Hamai, '"Imperial burden" or "Jews of Africa"', 417.

233 D. Tilbe, *The Ugandan Asian Crisis* (London, 1972), 8–9, cited in Hamai, '"Imperial burden" or "Jews of Africa"', 416.

234 *Sunday Telegraph*, 13 August 1972, cited in Hamai, '"Imperial burden" or "Jews of Africa"', 433.

235 See, for example, Anthony Lester, 'East African Asians versus the United Kingdom: the inside story', lecture delivered to the Odysseus Trust, London, 23 October 2003, 7.

236 Hamai, '"Imperial burden" or "Jews of Africa"', 418.

237 Ibid., 433.

238 Ibid., 433–4.

239 Ibid., 434.

240 Layton-Henry, *The Politics of Immigration*, 86–7, cited in Hamai, '"Imperial burden" or "Jews of Africa"', 419.

241 Hamai, '"Imperial burden" or "Jews of Africa"'.

242 D. Kohler, 'Public opinion and the Ugandan Asians', *New Community* 2 (1973), 194–7, cited in Hamai, '"Imperial burden" or "Jews of Africa"', 419, 425.

243 Hamai, '"Imperial burden" or "Jews of Africa"', 421.

244 Lester, 'East African Asians versus the United Kingdom', 7.

245 Hamai, '"Imperial burden" or "Jews of Africa"', 421.

246 M. L. Pirouet, 'Welcoming the Ugandan Asians 1972?', Institute of Commonwealth Studies and Education, University of London Seminar Paper (London, 1998), 5, cited in Hamai, '"Imperial burden" or "Jews of Africa"', 421.

247 Kushner and Knox, *Refugees in an Age of Genocide*, 270, 273.

248 HC Deb 18 October 1972, vol. 843 cc. 261–75, 269.

249 Hamai, '"Imperial burden" or "Jews of Africa"', 421, 430.

250 TNA, FCO 31/1380, Expulsion of holders of British passports

of Asian origin from Uganda. A Letter from T. Fitzgerald of the Home Office to C. P. Scott in the Foreign and Commonwealth Office on 17 August 1972, cited in Hamai, '"Imperial burden" or "Jews of Africa"', 429.

251 See El-Enany, 'On pragmatism and legal idolatry', 7–38.

252 Bhambra and Holmwood, 'Colonialism, postcolonialism and the liberal welfare state', 582.

253 TNA, CAB 130/614, UKPHs in Uganda: Meeting Minutes, Contingency Planning for the Evacuation of UK 'Belongers', cited in Hamai, '"Imperial burden" or "Jews of Africa"', 424.

254 Hamai, '"Imperial burden" or "Jews of Africa"', 424.

255 William Whitelaw MP, HC Deb 28 January 1981, vol. 997, cc. 935–1047, 997.

256 HC Deb 28 January 1981, vol. 997, cc. 935–1047, 935.

257 *British Nationality Law: Outline of Proposed Legislation*, Cmnd 7987 (HMSO, July 1980), 7, cited in Karatani, *Defining British Citizenship*, 17.

258 Karatani, *Defining British Citizenship*, 185.

259 HC Deb 28 January 1981, vol. 997, cc. 935–1047, 935.

260 Ibid., 182.

261 Ibid., 184.

262 British Nationality Act 1981, Section 7.

263 Conservative Party General Election Manifesto 1979.

264 See Hansen, *Citizenship and Immigration in Postwar Britain*, 213.

265 Ibid., 214.

266 Dora Kostakopoulou and Robert Thomas, 'Unweaving the threads: territoriality, national ownership of land and asylum policy', *European Journal of Migration and Law* 6 (2004), 5–26 (p. 5).

267 See Hansen, *Citizenship and Immigration in Postwar Britain*, 220.

268 Karen Wells and Sophie Watson, 'A politics of resentment: shop-keepers in a London neighbourhood', *Ethnic and Racial Studies* 28.2 (2005), 261–77 (p. 275), cited in Vron Ware, 'Towards a sociology of resentment: a debate on class and whiteness', *Sociological Research Online* 13.5 (2008), 5.2, www.socres online.org.uk/13/5/9.html (accessed 21 October 2019).

269 Cited by Roy Hattersley, HC Deb 28 January 1981, vol. 997, cc. 935–1047, 946.

270 British Nationality Act 1981, Section 1(a) and (b).

271 HC Deb 28 January 1981, vol. 997, cc. 935–1047, 936.

272 Ibid., 948.

273 Kapoor and Narkowicz, 'Characterising citizenship', 2.

274 Hansen, *Citizenship and Immigration in Postwar Britain*, 217.

275 Ibid., 213.

276 HC Deb 28 January 1981, vol. 997, cc. 935–1047, 954.

277 Ibid.

278 Ibid., 964, 965.

279 Ian Patel, 'Enoch Powell's altered world', *London Review of Books Blogs*, 20 April 2018, www.lrb.co.uk/blog/2018/april/enoch-powell-s-altered-world (accessed 26 September 2019).

280 Amnesty International, 'Submission to the Windrush Lessons Learned Review' (October 2018), section 9, www.amnesty.org.uk/files/Resources/AIUK%20to%20Home%20Office%20Windrush%20Lessons%20Learned%20Review.pdf (accessed 26 September 2019).

281 Ibid.

282 The author is grateful to Colin Yeo for this point.

283 Speech at Southall, 4 November 1971, cited in Paul Gilroy, *There Ain't No Black in the Union Jack* (London: Routledge, 1987), 45.

284 Bhambra, 'Brexit, the Commonwealth, and exclusionary citizenship'.

285 Gilroy, *There Ain't No Black in the Union Jack*, 44.

286 Ibid., 44–5.

287 Bhambra and Holmwood, 'Colonialism, postcolonialism and the liberal welfare state', 582.

288 Gilroy, *There Ain't No Black in the Union Jack*, 46.

289 Church of England, cited in Rachel Robinson, 'A border in every street', Liberty, 3 April 2014, www.libertyhumanrights.org.uk/news/blog/border-every-street (accessed 28 January 2019).

CHAPTER 4

1 See, for example, Shah, *Refugees, Race and the Legal Concept of Asylum in Britain*; Stevens, *UK Asylum Law and Policy*; Kushner and Knox, *Refugees in an Age of Genocide*.

2 TV interview for Granada with Margaret Thatcher, *World in Action* (January 1978), www.youtube.com/watch?v=sHhKI5ijnxQ (accessed 26 September 2019). Transcript available at www.margaretthatcher.org/document/103485 (accessed 26 September 2019).

3 Natasha Carver, 'The silent backdrop: colonial anxiety at the border', *Journal of Historical Sociology* 32.2 (2019), 154–72 (p. 162).

4 Dembour, *When Humans Become Migrants*, 65.

5 Ibid.
6 Ibid.
7 TV interview with Margaret Thatcher.
8 Ibid. See interview transcript www.margaretthatcher.org/document/103485 (accessed 26 September 2019).
9 Immigration Act 1971, Schedule 2, para 21.
10 Eric Neumayer, 'Bogus refugees? The determinants of asylum migration to Western Europe', *International Studies Quarterly* 49.3 (2005), 389–410.
11 See, for example, Martin, 'The new asylum seekers'; Betts, 'Proliferation and the global refugee regime'; Feller, 'Asylum, migration and refugee protection'.
12 Teresa Hayter, *Open Borders: The Case Against Immigration Control* (London: Pluto Press, 2000), 5.
13 Parts of this section appeared in El-Enany, 'On pragmatism and legal idolatry'.
14 It is beyond the scope of this book to address in detail the colonial dimensions of the Second World War. See Alexander Weheliye, *Habeas Viscus: Racializing Assemblages, Biopolitics, and Black Feminist Theories of the Human* (Durham, NC: Duke University Press, 2014). Mukherjee notes the way in which Britain heavily exploited its colonies in order to fund the war, noting that 'Britain took massive forced loans from India (popularly called the sterling balance) of about Rs 17,000 million (estimated at 17 times the annual revenue of the Government of India and one-fifth of Britain's gross national product in 1947) at a time when over three million Indians died of famine!' See Mukherjee, 'Empire', 80.
15 Holborn, *Refugees*, 31.
16 Mayblin, *Asylum after Empire*, 135.
17 Ian Talbot and Gurharpal Singh, *The Partition of India* (Cambridge: Cambridge University Press, 2009), cited in Mayblin, *Asylum after Empire*, 35.
18 Article 1(B).
19 Guy Goodwin-Gill and Jane McAdam, *The Refugee in International Law* (Oxford: Oxford University Press, 2007), 36.
20 Refugee Convention, Preamble, paragraph 2.
21 Talbot and Singh, *The Partition of India*, cited in Mayblin, *Asylum after Empire*, 35.
22 Mayblin, *Asylum after Empire*, 36.
23 Patricia Tuitt, *False Images: The Law's Construction of the Refugee* (London: Pluto Press, 1996), 42.

24 John H. Simpson, *Refugees – A Preliminary Report of a Survey* (Royal Institute of International Affairs, 1938), 1.

25 Refugee Convention, Article 1(A)(2).

26 Deborah E. Anker, 'Refugee law, gender, and the human rights paradigm', *Harvard Human Rights Journal* 15 (2002), 133–54 (p. 134).

27 Goodwin-Gill and McAdam, *The Refugee in International Law*, 15.

28 Jodi A. Byrd, Alyosha Goldstein, Jodi Melamed and Chandan Reddy, 'Predatory value: economies of dispossession and disturbed relationalities', *Social Text* 135.36.2 (2008), 1–16.

29 Tuitt, *False Images*, 43.

30 Ibid., 47.

31 Ibid., 42.

32 Congo, Madagascar, Monaco and Turkey. See 'States Parties to the 1951 Convention relating to the Status of Refugees and the 1967 Protocol' (United Nations High Commissioner for Refugees), www.unhcr.org/uk/protection/basic/3b73bod63/stat es-parties-1951-convention-its-1967-protocol.html (accessed 26 September 2019).

33 Holborn, *Refugees*, 182.

34 Mayblin, *Asylum after Empire*, 157.

35 Prakash Shah, 'From legal centralism to official lawlessness', in Prakash Shah (ed.), *The Challenge of Asylum to Legal Systems* (London: Cavendish Publishing, 2005), 1–12 (p. 2).

36 See El-Enany, 'On pragmatism and legal idolatry'. See also Simon Behrman, *Law and Asylum: Space, Subject, Resistance* (Abingdon: Routledge, 2018).

37 Patricia Tuitt, 'Refugees, nations, laws and the territorialisation of violence', in P. Fitzpatrick and P. Tuitt (eds), *Critical Beings: Law, Nation and the Global Subject* (Aldershot: Ashgate, 2004), cited in Keenan, *Subversive Property*, 133.

38 Keenan, *Subversive Property*, 147.

39 Ibid., 148.

40 Ibid., 147.

41 V. Bevan, *The Development of British Immigration Law* (London: Croom Helm, 1986), 223, cited in Robert Thomas, 'The impact of judicial review on asylum', *Public Law* (June 2003), 481.

42 Stevens, *UK Asylum Law and Policy*, 78.

43 (Cmd. 9171), Statement of Immigration Rules for Control of Entry of Commonwealth Citizens, HC 79, 25 January 1973, para. 54.

44 Home Affairs Committee Race Relations and Immigration

Sub-Committee, Session 1984–85, 'Refugees', Minutes of Evidence, 17 December 1984, paras. 5 and 9, 68

45 Stevens, *UK Asylum Law and Policy*, 81.

46 Thomas, 'The impact of judicial review on asylum', 483.

47 Martin, 'The new asylum seekers', 91.

48 *Home Office Statistical Bulletin, Asylum Statistics UK 1992*, Issue 19/93, 15 July 1993, table 1.3 and 2.1. These figures do not include dependants.

49 Thomas, 'The impact of judicial review on asylum', 483.

50 Liz Fekete, 'Blackening the economy: the path to convergence', *Race and Class* 39.1 (1997), 1–17.

51 Thomas, 'The impact of judicial review on asylum', 483.

52 Clayton et al., *Textbook on Immigration and Asylum Law*, 7th edn, 196.

53 Tuitt, *False Images*, 73.

54 Stevens, *UK Asylum Law and Policy*, 97.

55 Turkey in 1989, Uganda in 1991, the former Yugoslavia in 1992, Sierra Leone and the Ivory Coast in 1994, Kenya in 1996, Slovakia in 1998 and Zimbabwe and Algeria in 2003. See Stevens, *UK Asylum Law and Policy*, 97.

56 Clayton et al., *Textbook on Immigration and Asylum Law*, 7th edn, 196.

57 Declaration of suspension contained in a letter from the Permanent Representative of the United Kingdom, 7 February 2003, cited in ibid., 197.

58 Anderson, *Us and Them*, 41.

59 HC Deb 16 March 1987, vol. 16, c. 706.

60 See Ruben Andersson, *Illegality Inc.* (Berkeley, CA: University of California Press, 2014).

61 Kostakopoulou and Thomas, 'Unweaving the threads', 12.

62 HC Deb 2 November 1992, vol. 213, cc. 21–120, 21.

63 Ibid.

64 Ibid.

65 Ibid., 22.

66 Ibid., 51.

67 Ibid., 23, 56.

68 Section 2.

69 Clayton, *Textbook on Immigration and Asylum Law*, 4th edn, 446.

70 Stevens, *UK Asylum Law and Policy*, 166. Sections 4 and 5 of the 1993 Act.

71 Ibid., 80.

72 Council of the European Communities, Conclusions of the

Ministers Responsible for Immigration (London, 30 November–1 December 1992), *Conclusions on Countries in which there is generally no risk of persecution.*

73 Letter to Amnesty International, 16 September 1993, from the Home Office minister, Charles Wardle MP, cited in Richard Dunstan, 'Playing human pinball: the Amnesty International United Kingdom Section Report on UK Home Office "safe third country" practice', *International Journal of Refugee Law* 7.4 (1995), 606–52 (p. 613).

74 Immigration Rules, Paragraph 345.

75 HC Deb 20 November 1995, vol 267, cc. 335–48, 335.

76 Rosemary Sales, 'The deserving and the undeserving? Refugees, asylum seekers and welfare in Britain', *Critical Social Policy* 22.3 (2002), 456–78 (p. 457).

77 Sections 4–7.

78 Section 6.

79 Section 7.

80 Section 8.

81 Immigration (Restriction on Employment) Order 1996, SI 1996/3225; Asylum and Immigration Appeals Act 1996, Section 8(2).

82 Refugee Council, 'Catch 22', *iNexile* 5 (1999), 4–5.

83 Colin Harvey, 'Restructuring asylum: recent trends in United Kingdom asylum law and policy', *International Journal of Refugee Law* 9.1 (1997), 60–73 (p. 68).

84 Schedule 2, para. 5, as amended.

85 Council of the European Communities, Conclusions of the Ministers Responsible for Immigration (London, 30 November–1 December 1992), *Conclusions on Countries in which there is generally no risk of persecution.*

86 Section 3.

87 From 1 July 1997 to 30 September 1997. See Stevens, *UK Asylum Law and Policy*, 173.

88 *R* v. *Secretary of State for the Home Department ex parte Bugdaycay* [1987] AC 514.

89 *Rhuppiah* v. *Secretary of State for the Home Department* [2018] UKSC 58.

90 *N* v. *Secretary of State for the Home Department* [2005] UKHL 31.

91 Thomas, 'The impact of judicial review on asylum', 484.

92 Maurice Sunkin, 'The judicial review case-load 1987–1989', *Public Law* (1991), 491–9 (p. 494).

93 Stephen H. Legomsky, *Immigration and the Judiciary: Law and*

Politics in Britain and America (New York: Oxford University Press, 1987), 242–6.

94 C. Vincenzi, 'Aliens and the judicial review of immigration law', *Public Law* 93 (1985), cited in Thomas, 'The impact of judicial review on asylum', 480.

95 [1987] Imm AR 250, 263.

96 *Bugdaycay* [1987] AC 514.

97 [1987] Imm AR 250.

98 Anthony Lester and Jeffrey Jowell, 'Beyond Wednesbury: substantive principles of administrative law', *Public Law* (1987), 368–82 (p. 369).

99 *Bugdaycay* [1987] AC 514.

100 Human Rights Act 1998, Section 6(1), which incorporated the ECHR into domestic law.

101 *Niemitz* v. *Germany* (Application No. 13710/88, Judgement of 16 December 1992), para. 29.

102 Section 117B(1).

103 Section 117B(1)(a) and (b).

104 Section 117B(3)(a) and (b).

105 *Rhuppiah* [2018] UKSC 58, para. 44.

106 Home Office, 'Nationality policy guidance and casework instruction Chapter 18, Annex D: The good character requirement. Version 4.0' (London: Home Office, 2003), cited in Kapoor and Narkowicz, 'Characterising citizenship', 1

107 See further Nisha Kapoor, *Deport, Deprive, Extradite* (London: Verso, 2018).

108 British Nationality Act 1981, Section 40(4A)(c).

109 Kapoor and Narkowicz, 'Characterising citizenship', 2, 8.

110 Ibid., 11.

111 Home Office, 'General grounds for refusal Section 4 of 5: Considering leave to remain' (London: Home Office, 2017), 3 cited in Kapoor and Narkowicz, 'Characterising citizenship', 2.

112 Kapoor and Narkowicz, 'Characterising citizenship', 2.

113 Home Office, 'Nationality: good character requirement' (London: Home Office, July 2017), 9–10.

114 These countries include Iraq, Afghanistan, Turkey, Vietnam, Kosovo, Angola, Jamaica, Rwanda, Congo, Tunisia, Algeria, Sudan, Sierra Leone, Iran, Palestine and Libya. See Kapoor and Narkowicz, 'Characterising citizenship', 8, 11.

115 Kapoor and Narkowicz, 'Characterising citizenship', 17.

116 See, for example, the decision of the Privy Council in *Cooper* v. *Stuart* (1889) 14 App Cas 286, and in *Advocate-General of Bengal* v. *Ranee Surnomoye Dossee* (1863) 15 ER 811.

117 *Mitchell* v. *The United Kingdom*, ECHR Application no. 40447/98.

118 *Bringing them Home: Report of the National Inquiry into the Separation of Aboriginal and Torres Strait Islander Children from Their Families* (Australian Human Rights Commission, April 1997).

119 See Leo Huberman, *Man's Worldly Goods: The Story of the Wealth of Nations* (Albany, NY: New York University Press, 2009), 7.

120 See Natasha Carver, 'Displaying genuineness: cultural translation in the drafting of marriage narratives for immigration applications and appeals', *Families, Relationships and Societies* 3.2 (2014), 271–86; Helena Wray, 'An ideal husband? Marriages of convenience, moral gate-keeping and immigration to the UK', *European Journal of Migration and Law* 8.3–4 (2006), 303–20.

121 Shamaan Freeman-Powell, 'Windrush row over criminal deportation flight to Jamaica', 6 February 2019, www.bbc.co.uk/news/uk-47123841 (accessed 26 September 2019).

122 See Melanie Griffiths, 'Seeking asylum and the politics of family', *Families, Relationships and Societies* 6.1 (2017), 153–6; Mark Townsend, '"I left my daughter at nursery. I didn't see her for a month": how UK splits migrant families', *The Guardian*, 5 August 2018, www.theguardian.com/uk-news/2018/aug/05/child-separation-migrant-parents-uk-hostile-environment-trump (accessed 26 September 2019).

123 'Safe but not settled: the impact of family separation on refugees in the UK', Refugee Council, Oxfam, January 2018, https://www.refugeecouncil.org.uk/wp-content/uploads/2019/03/Safe_but_not_settled.pdf (accessed 21 October 2019).

124 *The Lammy Review: An independent review into the treatment of, and outcomes for, Black, Asian and Minority Ethnic individuals in the Criminal Justice System* (September 2017), https://assets.publishing.service.gov.uk/government/uploads/system/uploads/attachment_data/file/643001/lammy-review-final-report.pdf (accessed 26 September 2019).

125 HC Deb 20 November 1995, vol. 267, cc. 335–48, 338.

126 Home Office Circular IMG/69 (1996), Home Office Circular to Local Authorities in GB, Exchange of Information with the Immigration and Nationality Directorate of the Home Office, Home Office: HMSO.

127 Sales, 'The deserving and the undeserving?', 463.

128 Ibid.

129 'Doctor accuses hospital of racism for refusing Kurds', *The*

Guardian, 21 February 1995, 11, cited in Hayes, 'The role of welfare in the internal control of immigration', 69.

130 IMG/96 1176/1193/23.

131 The Social Security (Persons from Abroad) Miscellaneous Amendment Regulations 1996. See Hayter, *Open Borders*, 106.

132 *R* v. *Secretary of State for Social Security, ex parte Joint Council for the Welfare of Immigrants* [1996] 4 All ER 385 (Eng. CA, June 21, 1996).

133 See Hayter, *Open Borders*, 107.

134 *R* v. *Westminster City Council ex parte M* (1997) 1 CCLR 85.

135 Hayter, *Open Borders*, 463.

136 Sales, 'The deserving and the undeserving?', 463, 464.

137 Alice Bloch and Lisa Schuster, 'Asylum policy under New Labour', *Benefits* 13.2 (2005), 116–18 (p. 116).

138 Home Office, 'Report of the Operational Reviews of the Voucher and Dispersal Schemes of the National Asylum Support Service' (October 2001).

139 UK Government White Paper, *Fairer, Faster, Firmer – A Modern Approach to Immigration and Asylum*, July 1998.

140 'Asylum seeker figures', BBC, 7 February 2001, http://news.bbc.co.uk/1/hi/uk/1157031.stm (accessed 21 October 2019).

141 Andrew Geddes, 'Getting the best of both worlds? Britain, the EU and migration policy', *International Affairs* 81.4 (2005), 723–40 (p. 727).

142 Preface by the Home Secretary, UK Government White Paper, *Fairer, Faster, Firmer*.

143 Ibid., chapter 3, 1.

144 Ibid.

145 Ibid.

146 Stevens, *UK Asylum Law and Policy*, 176.

147 Immigration and Asylum Act 1999, Section 2, inserting Section 24A(1) in Immigration Act 1971.

148 Sections 128–46.

149 Sales, 'The deserving and the undeserving?', 463.

150 Sections 94–127.

151 Section 97(2)(a).

152 *Report of the Operational Reviews of the Voucher and Dispersal Schemes of the National Asylum Support Service*, 29 October 2001, para. 3.2.2, cited in Stevens, *UK Asylum Law and Policy*, 191.

153 Kate Lyons and Pamela Duncan, '"It's a shambles": data shows most asylum seekers put in poorest parts of Britain', *The Guardian*, 9 April 2017, www.theguardian.com/world/2017/ap

r/09/its-a-shambles-data-shows-most-asylum-seekers-put-in-poo rest-parts-of-britain (accessed 26 September 2019).

154 Fiona Williams, 'Racism and the discipline of social policy: a critique of welfare theory', *Critical Social Policy* 7.2 (1987), 4–29 (pp. 26–7).

155 Bhambra and Holmwood, 'Colonialism, postcolonialism and the liberal welfare state', 574–87.

156 Ibid., 581.

157 Home Office, Asylum policy guidance, UK Visas and Immigration, 'Considering human rights claims' (2009), 19.

158 *D* v. *United Kingdom* (1997) 24 EHRR 425.

159 Home Office, Asylum policy guidance (2009), 19. In terms of the effect of the ECHR ruling in *Paposhvili* v. *Belgium* ECHR Application no. 41738/10, *N* v. *UK* is still to be treated as precedent in Article 3 medical cases.

160 *N* [2005] UKHL 31.

161 Ibid., para, 3.

162 Ibid., para 20.

163 Ibid., para. 3.

164 Ibid., para. 21.

165 Ibid., para. 53.

166 Ibid., para. 92.

167 Ibid., dissenting judgment, para 8.

168 See Inikori, *Africans and the Industrial Revolution in England*.

160 Verena Raschke and Birinder S. Cheema, 'Colonisation, the new world order, and the eradication of traditional food habits in East Africa: historical perspective on the nutrition transition', *Public Health Nutrition* 11.17 (2008), 662–74.

170 *N* [2005] UKHL 31, para. 53.

171 Cindy Patton, 'Inventing "African AIDS"', in Peter Aggleton and Richard Parker (eds), *Culture, Society and Sexuality: A Reader* (Abingdon: Routledge, 2002), 387–404 (p. 388).

172 In the Grand Chamber's judgment in *S.J.* v. *Belgium* ECHR Application no. 70055/10 (Judge Pinto's dissenting opinion refers to how '[u]nsurprisingly, N. died shortly after her removal to Uganda', para 2). In Marie-Bénédicte Dembour's *When Humans Become Migrants*, at 239, she writes, 'N's death followed, as predicted, within months of her return to Uganda', but there is no reference to a primary source. I am grateful to Nicolette Busuttil for these references.

173 *N* [2005] UKHL 31, para. 80 (emphasis added).

174 Ibid., para. 66.

175 *Soering* v. *United Kingdom* (1989) 11 EHRR 439.

176 *N* [2005] UKHL 31, para. 66, para 43.
177 See Sheldon Watts, *Epidemics and History: Disease, Power and Imperialism* (New Haven, CT: Yale University Press, 1997).
178 Dinyar Patel, 'Viewpoint: how British let one million Indians die in famine', 11 June 2016, www.bbc.co.uk/news/world-asia-india-36339524 (accessed 26 September 2019).
179 Ibid.
180 See further Dembour, *When Humans Become Migrants*. See also Dembour and Kelly (eds), *Are Human Rights for Migrants?*.
181 The others were Belgium, Denmark, France and the Netherlands. See Dembour, *When Humans Become Migrants*, 72.
182 Ibid., 65.
183 Geoffrey Marston, 'The United Kingdom's part in the preparation of the European Convention on Human Rights, 1950', *International and Comparative Law Quarterly* 42 (1993), 825, cited in Dembour, *When Humans Become Migrants*, 75.
184 Now Article 56 ECHR. See Dembour, *When Humans Become Migrants*, 70–1.
185 Now Article 56 ECHR. See ibid., 70–1.
186 Ibid., 70.
187 They were originally provided for in Articles 25 and 46. Dembour, *When Humans Become Migrants*, 71.
188 Isidore Bonabom, 'The Development of a Truth Regime on the "Human": Human Rights in the Gold Coast (1945–1957)', PhD thesis, University of Sussex, 2012, cited in Dembour, *When Humans Become Migrants*, 76, 77.
189 Dembour, *When Humans Become Migrants*, 74, 78.
190 Ibid.
191 Ibid., 187.
192 Ibid., 147.
193 See UK Borders Act 2007, Section 32. See Dembour, *When Humans Become Migrants*, ch. 6.
194 Dembour, *When Humans Become Migrants*, 504.

CHAPTER 5

1 See Tuitt, 'Used up and misused', 498.
2 See, for example, Boris Johnson, 'Ever more centralizing, interfering and anti-democratic' (2016), in Brian MacArthur (ed.), *The Penguin Book of Modern Speeches* (Harmondsworth: Penguin, 2017), available at www.conservativehome.com/parliament/2016/05/boris-johnsons-speech-on-the-eu-referendum

-full-text.html (accessed 21 October 2019); Heather Stewart and Rowena Mason, 'Nigel Farage's anti-migrant poster reported to police', *The Guardian*, 16 June 2016, www.theguardian.com/politics/2016/jun/16/nigel-farage-defends-ukip-breaking-point-poster-queue-of-migrants (accessed 26 September 2019).

3 See cases in which the Court of Justice of the EU has interpreted the limits on the scope of the opt-in. See Jorrit Rijpma, 'Case C-77/05, *United Kingdom* v. *Council*, Judgement of the Grand Chamber of 18 December 2007, not yet reported, and Case C-137/05, *United Kingdom* v. *Council*, Judgement of the Grand Chamber of 18 December 2007, not yet reported', *Common Market Law Review* 45 (2008), 836.

4 See Nadine El-Enany, 'EU migration and asylum law under the Area of Freedom, Security and Justice', in Anthony Arnull and Damian Chalmers (eds), *The Oxford Handbook of European Union Law* (Oxford: Oxford University Press, 2015), 867–86; Nadine El-Enany, 'The perils of differentiated integration in the field of asylum', in Andrea Ott and Bruno De Witte (eds), *Between Flexibility and Disintegration: The Trajectory of Differentiation in EU Law* (Cheltenham: Edward Elgar, 2017), 362–83.

5 Stewart and Mason, 'Nigel Farage's anti-migrant poster reported to police'.

6 See, for example, Johnson, 'Ever more centralizing, interfering and anti-democratic'.

7 Ibid.

8 Ronald Hyam, 'The primacy of geo-politics: the dynamics of British imperial policy, 1763–1963', *Journal of Imperial and Commonwealth History* 27 (1999), 27–52, cited in Jim Tomlinson, 'The decline of the Empire and the economic "decline" of Britain', *Twentieth Century British History* 14.3 (2003), 208.

9 HC Deb 2 August 1961, vol. 645, cc. 1480–606, 1480.

10 Ibid., 1482.

11 Ibid., 1483.

12 Ibid., 1493–4.

13 Kristian Stiennes, 'The European challenge: Britain's EEC application in 1961', *Contemporary European History* 7.1 (1998), 61–79 (p. 72).

14 Ibid.

15 Ibid.

16 HC Deb 2 August 1961, vol. 645, cc. 1480–606, 1484–5.

17 Paul Robertson and John Singleton, 'The old Commonwealth and Britain's first application to join the EEC, 1961–3', *Australian Economic History Review* 40.2 (2000), 153–77 (p. 175).

18 HC Deb 2 August 1961, vol. 645, cc. 1480–606, 1485.

19 Helen Parr, 'Britain, America, east of Suez and the EEC: finding a role in British foreign policy, 1964–67', *Contemporary British History* 20.3 (2006), 403–21 (p. 405).

20 Ibid., 409–10.

21 Ibid., 408.

22 Dean, 'The Conservative government and the 1961 Commonwealth Immigrants Act', 73.

23 PRO CAB 135/35 Pt1, 30 May 1961.

24 Dean, 'The Conservative government and the 1961 Commonwealth Immigrants Act', 73.

25 Robertson and Singleton, 'The old Commonwealth', 173.

26 Ibid., 155.

27 Ibid., 158. See also HC Deb 2 August 1961, vol. 645, cc. 1480–606, 1480.

28 Robertson and Singleton, 'The old Commonwealth', 159.

29 Ibid., 175–6.

30 Ibid., 175–6.

31 Ibid., 175–6.

32 Tomlinson, 'The decline of the Empire', 219.

33 'Wilson defends "pound in your pocket"', BBC, 1967, http://news.bbc.co.uk/onthisday/hi/dates/stories/november/19/newsid_3208000/3208396.stm (accessed 26 September 2019). See also Alan Sked, 'Why Britain really joined the EEC (and why it had nothing to do with helping our economy)', *LSE Brexit Blog*, 26 November 2015, http://blogs.lse.ac.uk/brexit/2015/11/26/why-britain-really-joined-the-eec-and-why-it-had-nothing-to-do-with-helping-our-economy/ (accessed 26 September 2019).

34 Tomlinson, 'The decline of the Empire', 220.

35 Ibid., 216.

36 PRO, Prem 13/1367, 'Note of Meeting of PM with Secretary General of Commonwealth', 5 April 1967, cited in Tomlinson, 'The decline of the Empire', 217.

37 NA PRO CAB 129/129, C(67)59, The Value of the Commonwealth, Commonwealth Secretary, 24 April 1967, cited in Parr, 'Britain, America, east of Suez and the EEC', 410.

38 See Mukherjee, 'Empire'.

39 Tomlinson, 'The decline of the Empire', 220.

40 Mukherjee, 'Empire', 81.

41 According to Angus Maddison, '[a]fter independence, on the other hand, per capita income in India grew annually at 1.4% in the first couple of decades (about three times faster than the best phase, 1870–1913, under colonialism) and much faster,

at 3.01% in the next 30 years, 1973–2001 (a rate considerably higher than that achieved by west Europe'. Angus Maddison, *The World Economy: Vol. I, A Millennial Perspective, Vol. II, Historical Statistics* (OECD, 2006; New Delhi, 2007), 643, cited in Mukherjee, 'Empire', 75.

42 Frederick S. Northedge, 'Britain as a second-rank power', *International Affairs (Royal Institute of International Affairs 1944)* 46.1 (1970), 37–47 (pp. 37–8).

43 Ibid., 38.

44 Ibid.

45 Kenneth Waltz, *Foreign Policy and Democratic Politics* (London: Longman, 1968), 151, cited in Northedge, 'Britain as a second-rank power', 38.

46 Nadine El-Enany, 'Brexit as nostalgia for empire', *Critical Legal Thinking*, 19 June 2016, http://criticallegalthinking.co m/2016/06/19/brexit-nostalgia-empire/ (accessed 26 September 2019).

47 See Nadine El-Enany, 'Empire en vogue', *Red Pepper*, 24 June 2017, www.redpepper.org.uk/empire-en-vogue/ (accessed 26 September 2019).

48 See Priyamvada Gopal, *Insurgent Empire: Anti-colonial Resistance and British Dissent* (London: Verso, 2019). See also Gilroy, *After Empire*; El-Enany, 'The Iraq War, Brexit and imperial blowback'.

49 Gilroy, *After Empire*, 103–4.

50 Ibid.

51 Medea Benjamin and Nicolas J. S. Davies, 'The Iraq death toll 15 years after the US invasion', *Common Dreams*, 15 March 2018, www.commondreams.org/views/2018/03/15/iraq-death-toll-15-years-after-us-invasion (accessed 26 September 2019); Amnesty International, 'Iraq 2018', www.amnesty.org/en/coun tries/middle-east-and-north-africa/iraq/report-iraq/ (accessed 26 September 2019).

52 The British Overseas Territories are Anguilla, Bermuda, British Antarctic Territory, British Indian Ocean Territory, British Virgin Islands, Cayman Islands, Falkland Islands, Gibraltar, Montserrat, Pitcairn Island, Henderson, Ducie and Oeno Islands, St Helena, Ascension and Tristan da Cunha, South Georgia and South Sandwich Islands, Turks and Calcos Islands. Akrotiri and Dhekelia are Sovereign Base Areas on the island of Cyprus.

53 In Annex IV to the EEC Treaty, Britain's colonies are listed as the Anglo-French Condominium of the New Hebrides, the Bahamas, Bermuda, British Antarctic Territory, British Honduras, British

Indian Ocean Territory, British Solomon Islands, British Virgin Islands, Brunei, Associated States in the Caribbean (Antigua, Dominica, Grenada, St Lucia, St Vincent, St Kitts-Nevis-Anguilla), Cayman Islands, Central and Southern Line Islands, Falkland Islands and Dependencies, Gilbert and Ellice Islands, Montserrat, Pitcairn, St Helena and Dependencies, the Seychelles, Turks and Caicos Islands.

54 HC Deb 2 August 1961, vol. 645, cc. 1480–606, 1493.

55 Frantz Fanon, *The Wretched of the Earth* (New York: Grove Weidenfeld, 1963), 251.

56 See, for example, Derek W. Urwin, *The Community of Europe: A History of European Integration Since 1945* (London: Routledge, 1994); Martin J. Dedman, *The Origins and Development of the European Union 1945–95: A History of European Integration* (London: Routledge, 1996); Desmond Dinan, *Europe Recast: A History of European Union* (Boulder, CO: Lynne Rienner, 2014).

57 See, for example, Andrew Moravcsik, *The Choice for Europe: Social Purpose and State Power from Messina to Maastricht* (London: Routledge, 1998).

58 Peo Hansen, 'European integration, European identity and the colonial connection', *European Journal of Social Theory* 5.4 (2002), 483–98 (p. 491).

59 Étienne Balibar, *We, the People of Europe? Reflections on Transnational Citizenship* (Princeton, NJ: Princeton University Press, 2004), 45, cited in Tuitt, 'Used up and misused', 492.

60 Balibar, 'Racism and nationalism', 43.

61 Gerard Delanty, *Inventing Europe: Idea, Identity, Reality* (Basingstoke: Palgrave Macmillan, 1995), 96, 99, cited in Gareth Dale and Nadine El-Enany, 'The limits of social Europe: EU law and the ordoliberal agenda', *German Law Journal* 14.5 (2013), 613–49 (p. 642).

62 Ibid., 642.

63 Étienne Balibar, *Masses, Classes, Ideas: Studies on Politics and Philosophy Before and After Marx* (London: Routledge, 1994), 192, cited in Lentin, 'Concepts and debates 2'.

64 Alexander Koch, Chris Brierley, Mark M. Maslin and Simon L. Lewis, 'Earth system impacts of the European arrival and Great Dying in the Americas after 1492', *Quaternary Science Reviews* 207 (2019), 13–36.

65 The first 'goal' listed under the 'goals and values of the EU' on the 'EU in brief' page on its website is to 'promote peace, its values

and the well-being of its citizens', https://europa.eu/european-union/about-eu/eu-in-brief_en (accessed 26 September 2019).

66 Hansen, 'European integration, European identity and the colonial connection', 487.

67 Peo Hansen and Stefan Jonsson, 'Eurafrica incognita: the colonial origins of the European Union', *History of the Present* 1.1 (2017), 1–32 (p. 11).

68 Hansen, 'European integration, European identity and the colonial connection', 487.

69 Benjamin and Davies, 'The Iraq death toll 15 years after the US invasion'.

70 See Mark Levine, 'France in Mali: the longue durée of imperial blowback', *Al Jazeera*, 19 January 2013, www.aljazeera.com/indepth/opinion/2013/01/201311915355818585275.html (accessed 26 September 2019).

71 Terese Jonsson, 'Shattering the white supremacist myth of safety', *Wildcat Dispatches*, 4 June 2017, http://wildcatdispatches.org/2017/06/08/shattering-the-white-supremacist-myth-of-safety/ (accessed 26 September 2019).

72 Hansen and Jonsson, 'Eurafrica incognita', 10.

73 Ibid., 12.

74 Ibid., 11.

75 Richard Coudenhove-Kalergi, 'Afrika', *Paneuropa* 5.2 (1929), 3, cited in Hansen and Jonsson, 'Eurafrica incognita', 6.

76 See, for example, Moravcsik, *The Choice for Europe*.

77 Cedric J. Robinson, *Black Marxism: The Making of the Black Radical Tradition* (Chapel Hill, NC: University of North Carolina Press, 2000 [1983]).

78 Robin D. G. Kelley, 'What did Cedric Robinson mean by racial capitalism?', *Boston Review*, 12 January 2017, http://bostonreview.net/race/robin-d-g-kelley-what-did-cedric-robinson-mean-racial-capitalism (accessed 26 September 2019).

79 Ibid.

80 Ibid.

81 Bhattacharyya, *Rethinking Racial Capitalism*, 101–2.

82 Hansen and Jonsson, 'Eurafrica incognita', 16.

83 Hansen and Jonsson, 'Eurafrica incognita', 16, citing Fredric Jameson, 'The vanishing mediator; or, Max Weber as storyteller', in Fredric Jameson, *The Ideologies of Theory, Essays 1971–1986; Volume 2: The Syntax of History* (Minneapolis, MN: University of Minnesota Press, 1988), 3–34.

84 Ibid.

85 Hansen and Jonsson, 'Eurafrica incognita', 16.

86 Such as French Guyana, the Spanish enclaves of Melilla and Ceuta and the British Virgin Islands, Anguilla, Bermuda and the Falkland Islands, to name a few.

87 Hansen, 'European integration, European identity and the colonial connection', 489.

88 El-Enany, 'Brexit as nostalgia for empire'; El-Enany, 'The next British Empire'.

89 See Chantelle Lewis, '"No, where are you really from?": Being a UK citizen of colour living in the EU27', *LSE Brexit Blog*, http://blogs.lse.ac.uk/brexit/2018/05/11/no-where-are-you-really-from-being-a-uk-citizen-of-colour-living-in-the-eu27/ (accessed 26 September 2019); Chantelle Lewis, 'Who is allowed to be British (abroad)?', *Brexit Brits Abroad*, 1 March 2018, https://brexitbritsabroad.com/2018/03/01/who-is-allowed-to-be-british-abroad/ (accessed 26 September 2019).

90 Adam Weiss, 'Whiteness as international citizenship in European Union law', 2 March 2018, https://voelkerrechtsblog.org/whiteness-as-international-citizenship-in-european-union-law/ (accessed 26 September 2019).

91 Ibid. Weiss concludes his critique of European citizenship by oddly celebrating Brexit as heralding an age in which a system based on white privilege is rejected in favour of a more equitable migration regime, writing that '[t]o the extent that Brexit is about stopping citizens of other Member States from coming to the UK to enjoy equal treatment there, it represents the triumph of national over European identity ... and a rejection of the ideal of European citizenship and a related rejection of common feeling based on white skin'. I disagree strongly with Weiss's conclusion in that I consider Brexit to be a rejection of European citizenship and free movement as emblematic of migration and the fluidity of borders, and a means through which to reassert white identity and entitlement as against the inclusion of racialised people within the British polity. In the course of the referendum, the Leave campaign argued that Europe served to enhance the porousness of borders to the detriment of white British people. This was, for instance, suggested by UKIP's 'Breaking Point' poster depicting non-white refugees crossing the Croatia–Slovenia border.

92 Bashi, 'Globalized anti-blackness', 585.

93 Case C-184/99 Judgment of the Court of 20 September 2001. *Rudy Grzelczyk* v. *Centre public d'aide sociale d'Ottignies-Louvain-la-Neuve*.

94 Tuitt, 'Used up and misused', 498.

95 Ibid., 491–2.

96 Ibid., 494.

97 Ibid., 498.

98 Council Directive 2000/43/EC of 29 June 2000 implementing the principle of equal treatment between persons irrespective of racial or ethnic origin, Official Journal L 180, 19/07/2000 P. 0022–0026.

99 Weiss, 'Whiteness as international citizenship in European Union law'.

100 Sara Ahmed, 'Declarations of whiteness: the non-performativity of anti-racism', *Borderlands* 3.2 (2004), cited in Weiss, 'Whiteness as international citizenship in European Union law'.

101 Weiss, 'Whiteness as international citizenship in European Union law'.

102 Case 26–62 *NV Algemene Transport- en Expeditie Onderneming van Gend & Loos* v. *Netherlands Inland Revenue Administration* Judgment of the Court of 5 February 1963.

103 Karatani, *Defining British Citizenship*, 165–6.

104 Treaty between the Kingdom of Belgium, the Federal Republic of Germany, the French Republic, the Italian Republic, the Grand Duchy of Luxembourg, the Kingdom of the Netherlands, Member States of the European Communities, the Kingdom of Denmark, Ireland, the Kingdom of Norway, and the United Kingdom of Great Britain and Northern Ireland concerning the accession of the Kingdom of Denmark, Ireland, the Kingdom of Norway and the United Kingdom of Great Britain and Northern Ireland to the European Economic Community and to the European Atomic Energy Community OJ 27. 3. 72, https://eur-lex.europa.eu/legal-content/EN/TXT/PDF/?uri=CELEX:11972B/TXT&rid=5 (accessed 26 September 2019).

105 Karatani, *Defining British Citizenship*, 166.

106 Declaration by the Government of the United Kingdom of Great Britain and Northern Ireland on the definition of the term 'nationals', paras (a) and (b).

107 Prakash Shah, 'British nationals under Community law: the Kaur case', *European Journal of Migration and Law* 3 (2001), 271–8 (p. 273).

108 W. R. Böhning, *The Migration of Workers in the United Kingdom and the European Community* (Oxford: Oxford University Press for the Institute of Race Relations, London, 1973), 131–2, cited in Shah, 'British nationals under Community law', 273.

109 Declaration No. 2.

110 *R* v. *Secretary of State for the Home Department, ex parte Kaur (Manjit)* 11 December 1998 CO/985/97.
111 *Kaur* C-192/99 Judgment of the Court of 20 February 2001, para. 17.
112 Ibid., para. 18.
113 Ibid., para. 19.
114 Ibid., para. 20.
115 Ibid., para. 21.
116 This paragraph is adapted from Nadine El-Enany, 'The "new Europe" and the "new European refugee": the subversion of the European Union's refugee law by its migration policy', in Satvinder Juss (ed.), *The Ashgate Research Companion to Migration Theory and Policy* (Aldershot: Ashgate, 2011), 3–24.
117 See Article 67 TFEU.
118 The Trevi Group was an intergovernmental forum set up in 1976 and composed of European interior and justice ministers. Its task was to counter terrorism as well as to coordinate policing of and within the then European Community. See Tony Bunyan, 'Trevi, Europol and the European state', in Tony Bunyan (ed.), *Statewatching the New Europe: A Handbook on the European State* (London: Statewatch, 1993), 1–15 (p. 15).
119 Mike Haynes, 'Setting the limits to Europe as an "imagined community"', in Gareth Dale and Mike Cole (eds), *The European Union and Migrant Labour* (Oxford: Berg, 1999), 17–42 (p. 22).
120 Art. 2(6) of Regulation (EU) 2016/399 (Schengen Borders Code). See Art. 2(5) of Regulation (EU) 2016/399 (Schengen Borders Code) and Art. 3(1) of Directive 2008/115/EC (Return Directive).
121 Council Directive 2008/115/EC of 16 December 2008 on common standards and procedures in Member States for returning illegally staying third country nationals [2008] OJ L348/98.
122 Gammeltoft-Hansen, *Access to Asylum*, 133.
123 Spijkerboer, 'The human cost of border control', 127.
124 See UNITED, 'The fatal policies of Fortress Europe'; see also the Missing Migrants Project, https://missingmigrants.iom.int/ (accessed 26 September 2019).
125 Council Directive 2008/115/EC of 16 December 2008 on common standards and procedures in Member States for returning illegally staying third country nationals [2008] OJ L348/98.
126 Under the 1999 Treaty of Amsterdam, the EU has the authority to conclude readmission agreements with non-EU states. Although the first multilateral readmission agreement was the 1991 Readmission Agreement between Poland and the Schengen countries, the EU has concluded further accords with countries such

as Hong Kong, Sri Lanka, Macao, Albania, Russia and Ukraine. Member States may also conclude bilateral accords of their own. For esample, together with its constitutional reforms implementing the 'safe third country' concept, Germany negotiated agreements with both European and non-European states, including Romania, Poland, the Czech Republic, Bulgaria, Croatia, the Federal Republic of Yugoslavia, Bosnia, Vietnam, Pakistan and Algeria. The rapid increase in the use of readmission agreements can be seen in Poland's conclusion of similar instruments with the Czech Republic in 1993, four days after that with Germany, and with Slovakia, Ukraine, Romania and Bulgaria in the same year. See Sandra Lavenex, '"Passing the buck": European Union refugee policies towards Central and Eastern Europe', *Journal of International Law* 11.2 (1998), 126–45 (p. 139).

127 J. Gubbay, 'The European Union role in the formation, legitimation and implementation of migration policy', in Gareth Dale and Mike Cole (eds), *The European Union and Migrant Labour* (Oxford: Berg, 1999), 43–67 (p. 60).

128 Bhattacharyya, *Rethinking Racial Capitalism*, 147.

129 Kim Rygiel, Feyzi Baban and Suzan Ilcan, 'The Syrian refugee crisis: the EU-Turkey "deal" and temporary protection', *Global Social Policy* 16.3 (2016), 315–20 (p. 315).

130 Patrick Kingsley, 'More than 700 migrants feared dead in three Mediterranean sinkings', *The Guardian*, 29 May 2016, www.theguardian.com/world/2016/may/29/700-migrants-feared-dead-mediterranean-says-un-refugees (accessed 26 September 2016), cited in Rygiel, Baban and Ilcan, 'The Syrian refugee crisis', 315.

131 Lizzie Dearden, 'Refugee death toll passes 1000 in record 2017 as charities attacked for conducting Mediterranean rescues', *The Independent*, 22 April 2017, www.independent.co.uk/news/world/europe/refugee-crisis-migrants-asylum-seekers-mediterranean-see-libya-italy-ngos-smugglers-accusations-a7696976.html (accessed 26 September 2016).

132 Bhattacharyya, *Rethinking Racial Capitalism*, 147.

133 Ibid.

134 Lorenzo Tondo, '"We have found hell": trauma runs deep for children at dire Lesbos camp', *The Guardian*, 3 October 2018, www.theguardian.com/global-development/2018/oct/03/trauma-runs-deep-for-children-at-dire-lesbos-camp-moria (accessed 26 September 2016).

135 Al Jazeera, 'Concern over spate of deaths in Greek refugee camps', 30 January 2017, www.aljazeera.com/news/2017/01/

concern-spate-deaths-greek-refugee-camps-170130180746859.ht ml (accessed 21 October 2019).

136 Liz Fekete, 'No one accepts responsibility: thirteen refugees dead in Greece', Institute of Race Relations, 9 February 2017, www. irr.org.uk/news/no-one-accepts-responsibility-thirteen-refugees-dead-in-greece/ (accessed 21 October 2019).

137 Tondo, 'We have found hell'.

138 Rygiel, Baban and Ilcan, 'The Syrian refugee crisis', 317.

139 Cases T-192/16, T-193/16 and *NF, NG and NM* v. *European Council on EU-Turkey deal* 2017. An appeal was found to be inadmissible by the CJEU in 2018. See Joined Cases C-208/17 P to C-210/17 P 12 September 2018.

140 Ibid.

141 See Recommendation 787 (1976) of the Parliamentary Assembly of the Council of Europe on harmonisation of eligibility practice under the 1951 Geneva Convention on the Status of Refugees and the 1967 Protocol, paragraph 2. See also Committee of Ministers, *Declaration on Territorial Asylum* of 28 November 1977.

142 Recommendation 1088 of the Parliamentary Assembly of the Council of Europe (1988).

143 Note on the Application of the 1951 Convention and the 1967 Protocol relating to the Status of Refugees in the United Kingdom (Submitted by the Representative in the United Kingdom of the United Nations High Commissioner for Refugees) (House of Commons Select Committee on Race Relations and Immigration, Session 1977–78 *The Effect of the United Kingdom's Membership of the EEC on Race Relations and Immigration* (Minutes of Evidence 6 July, 1978 (EEC Membership), Appendix IV, para 1.

144 Ibid.

145 Ibid., para 9.

146 Didier Bigo, 'The European internal security field: stakes and rivalries in a newly developing area of police intervention', in Malcolm Anderson and Monica den Boer (eds), *Policing Across National Boundaries* (London: Pinter, 1994), 161–73 (p. 169).

147 Monica den Boer, 'The quest for European policing: rhetoric and justification in a disorderly debate', in Malcolm Anderson and Monica den Boer (eds), *Policing Across National Boundaries* (London: Pinter, 1994), 174–96 (pp. 179–80).

148 Bunyan, 'Trevi, Europol and the European state', 15.

149 Andrew Geddes, *Immigration and European Integration: Towards Fortress Europe?* (Manchester: Manchester University Press, 2000), 74.

150 Bunyan, 'Trevi, Europol and the European state', 24.

151 Ibid.

152 Anderson and den Boer (eds), *Policing Across National Boundaries*, cited in Geddes, *Immigration and European Integration*, 74.

153 'Declaration of the Belgian Presidency: Meeting of Justice and Interior Ministers of the European Community' (Brussels, 28 April 1987) (Trevi Group – 'ad hoc' meeting on immigration) in Tony Bunyan (ed.), *Key Texts on Justice and Home Affairs in the European Union, Vol. 1: From Trevi to Maastricht* (London: Statewatch, 1997), 11.

154 Bigo, 'The European internal security field', 170.

155 Bunyan (ed.), *Key Texts on Justice and Home Affairs in the European Union*, 21; Bigo, 'The European internal security field', 170.

156 *Practical Police Cooperation in the European Community*, Home Affairs Select Committee, HC 363-I, 5 (London: HMSO, 1990).

157 Bunyan (ed.), *Key Texts on Justice and Home Affairs in the European Union*, 35.

158 *Practical Police Cooperation in the European Community*, Home Affairs Select Committee, 162–3.

159 Regulation (EU) No 604/2013 of the European Parliament and of the Council of 26 June 2013 establishing the criteria and mechanisms for determining the Member State responsible for examining an application for international protection lodged in one of the Member States by a third-country national or a stateless person (recast).

160 Convention determining the State responsible for examining applications for asylum lodged in one of the Member States of the European Communities 15 June 1990 [1997] OJ C254/1.

161 Articles 4–8, Dublin Convention and Articles 28–38, Convention implementing the Schengen Agreement of 14 June 1985 between the Governments of the States of the Benelux Economic Union, the Federal Republic of Germany and the French Republic on the gradual abolition of checks at their common borders 14 June 1985 [1985] OJ L 176. See Lavenex, '"Passing the buck"', 130.

162 Sandra Lavenex, *The Europeanisation of Refugee Policies: Between Human Rights and Internal Security* (Aldershot: Ashgate, 2001), 87.

163 See ECRE, 'Asylum statistics 2017: shifting patterns, persisting disparities', 19 January 2018, www.ecre.org/asylum-statistics-2017-shifting-patterns-persisting-disparities/ (accessed 26 September 2019).

164 Kristy Siegfried and Joe Dyke, 'Playing the EU asylum lottery',

IRR, 2005, www.irinnews.org/maps-and-graphics/2015/07/21/playing-eu-asylum-lottery (accessed 26 September 2019), cited in Carver, 'The silent backdrop', 162.

165 See cases *M.S.S.* v. *Belgium and Greece* ECHR [2011] Application no. 30696/09 and *NS and ME* and Joined Cases C-411/10 and C-493/10 *NS and Others* v. *SSHD* and *M.E. and Others* v. *Refugee*. See Dembour, *When Humans Become Migrants*, ch. 12; El-Enany, 'The perils of differentiated integration in the field of asylum'; Patricia Mallia, 'Case of *MSS* v. *Belgium and Greece*: a catalyst in the re-thinking of the Dublin II Regulation', *Refugee Survey Quarterly* 30.3 (2011), 107–28; Steve Peers, 'Court of Justice: the NS and ME opinions – the death of "mutual trust"?', Statewatch, 2011, https://www.statewatch.org/analyses/no-148-dublin-mutual-trust.pdf (accessed 21 October 2019).

166 Minutes of Evidence taken before the Select Committee on the European Union Sub-Committee (Home Affairs), Wednesday 13 October 2010, 3.

167 Protocol (No. 21) on the position of the United Kingdom and Ireland in respect of the area of freedom, security and justice OJ C 202/295; Protocol (No. 22) on the position of Denmark.

168 Tampere European Council Presidency Conclusions 1999, para 13.

169 Article 67(1) TFEU.

170 Article 67(2) TFEU.

171 Ibid.

172 See 'Justice, freedom and security', https://eur-lex.europa.eu/summary/chapter/justice_freedom_security.html?root_default=SUM_1_CODED%3D23 (accessed 26 September 2019).

173 See El-Enany, 'The perils of differentiated integration in the field of asylum'.

174 Directive 2011/95/EU of the European Parliament and of the Council of 13 December 2011 on standards for the qualification of third-country nationals or stateless persons as beneficiaries of international protection, for a uniform status for refugees or for persons eligible for subsidiary protection, and for the content of the protection granted (recast) OJ L 337/9 20.12.2011; Directive 2013/33/EU of the European Parliament and of the Council of 26 June 2013 laying down standards for the reception of applicants for international protection (recast) OJ L 180/96 26.6.2013; Directive 2013/32/EU of the European Parliament and of the Council of 26 June 2013 on common procedures for granting and withdrawing international protection (recast) OJ L 180/60 29.6.13.

175 See Jonas Tallberg, 'Making states comply: the European Commission, the European Court of Justice, and the enforcement of the internal market', thesis, Lund University, 1999, 109, https://lup.lub.lu.se/search/publication/19167 (accessed 21 October 2019).

176 Explanatory Memorandum 14863/09 on the Proposal for a Directive of the European Parliament and of the Council on minimum standards for the qualification and status of third country nationals or stateless persons as beneficiaries of international protection and the content of the protection granted (Home Office, 5 November 2009).

177 House of Lords European Union Committee, *Asylum directives: scrutiny of the opt-in decisions* (1st Report of Session 2009–10, HL Paper 6, 4 December 2009); UNHCR, 'Briefing to the House of Lords on the adoption and application of the proposed EU Asylum Procedures and Qualifications Directives' (UNHCR, London, January 2010).

178 See, for example, ILPA, 'Immigration Law Practitioners', Association briefing for House of Lords Debate 12 January 2010 on the UK opt-in to the draft EU Asylum Procedures Directive and Qualifications Directives.

179 Maria Fletcher, 'Schengen, the European Court of Justice and flexibility under the Lisbon Treaty: balancing the United Kingdom's "ins" and "outs"', *European Constitutional Law Review* 5 (2009), 71–98 (p. 74).

180 UK Government White Paper, *Fairer, Faster, Firmer*.

181 Ibid., ch. 2, 2.

182 Ibid., 2, 3–4.

183 Ibid., 4.

184 Nigel Morris and Stephen Castle, 'Government pledges to opt out of common EU asylum system', *The Independent*, 26 October 2004.

185 The Irish practice has been almost identical to that of Britain.

186 Geddes, 'Getting the best of both worlds?', 735.

187 Council Directive 2001/51/EC of 28 June 2001 supplementing the provisions of Article 26 of the Convention implementing the Schengen Agreement of 14 June 1985.

188 Geddes, 'Getting the best of both worlds?', 735.

189 Ibid.

190 Council Directive 2004/81/EC of 29 April 2004 on the residence permit issued to third-country nationals who are victims of trafficking in human beings or who have been the subject of an

action to facilitate illegal immigration, who cooperate with the competent authorities.

191 Council Directive 2001/40/EC of 28 May 2001 on the mutual recognition of decisions on the expulsion of third country nationals.

192 Council of the European Union, Proposal for a comprehensive plan to combat illegal immigration and trafficking of human beings in the European Union [Official Journal C 142 of 14.06.2002]; Council of the European Union, Status Report on the Follow-up on the Plan for the Management of the External Borders of the Member States of the European Union and the Comprehensive Plan to Combat Illegal Immigration, Document 12931/02, October 2002.

193 Letter from Barbara Roche, Home Office Minister, to House of Lords Select Committee on the EU, 11 May 2002, cited in Ryszard Chowlewinski, 'EU measures preventing irregular migration and UK participation', *Tolley's Immigration, Asylum and Nationality Law Journal* 18.2 (2004), 1–2, cited in Geddes, 'Getting the best of both worlds?', 736.

194 Geddes, 'Getting the best of both worlds?', 738.

195 Ibid.

196 See, for example, evidence given by James Brokenshire MP, then Parliamentary Under-Secretary of State and Minister for Crime Prevention, Home Office, to the House of Lords European Union Committee, House of Lords European Union Committee, *The Treaty of Lisbon: An Impact Assessment: Vol. I Report* (10th Report, Session 2007–2008), 125–6.

197 Home Office UK Border Agency and Foreign and Commonwealth Office, *International Challenges, International Solutions: Managing the Movement of People and Goods* (March 2010), 17.

198 See David Anderson, *Histories of the Hanged: The Dirty War in Kenya and the End of Empire* (New York: W. W. Norton, 2005).

199 See Caroline Elkins, *Britain's Gulag: The Brutal End of Empire in Kenya* (London: Random House, 2005).

200 Ibid.; Anderson, *Histories of the Hanged*.

201 *Ndiki Mutua & others* v. *The Foreign and Commonwealth Office* [2012] EWHC 2678 (QB).

202 Home Office UK Border Agency and Foreign and Commonwealth Office, *International Challenges, International Solutions: Managing the Movement of People and Goods* (March 2010), 17.

203 Ibid.

204 Ibid.

205 Commonwealth Human Rights Initiative, *The Police, The People, The Politics: Police Accountability in Ghana* (2007), 28,

www.humanrightsinitiative.org/publications/police/police_acco
untability_in_ghana.pdf (accessed 26 September 2019)..

206 Kincaid, *A Small Place*, 36.

207 El-Enany, 'The colonial logic of Grenfell'.

208 Kojo Koram and Kerem Nisancioglu, 'Britain: the empire that
never was', *Critical Legal Thinking*, 31 October 2017, http://
criticallegalthinking.com/2017/10/31/britain-empire-never/
(accessed 26 September 2019).

209 Jon Stone, 'British people are proud of colonialism and the British
Empire, poll finds', *The Independent*, 19 January 2016, www.
independent.co.uk/news/uk/politics/british-people-are-proud-of
-colonialism-and-the-british-empire-poll-finds-a6821206.html#c
ommentsDiv (accessed 26 September 2019).

210 Cited in Richard Gott, 'Let's end the myths of Britain's imperial
past', *The Guardian*, 19 October 2011, www.theguardian.com/
books/2011/oct/19/end-myths-britains-imperial-past (accessed
26 September 2019).

211 Ibid.

212 Jeff Farrell, 'Now let's make Britain great again', *Daily Star*, 25
June 2016, www.pressreader.com/uk/daily-star/20160625/2831
32838125934 (accessed 26 September 2019).

213 Georgia Diebelius, 'UKIP's youth wing sold "Make Britain Great
Again Hats" for price of £9.11', *Metro*, 10 November 2016,
http://metro.co.uk/2016/11/10/ukips-youth-wing-sold-make-brit
ain-great-again-hats-for-price-of-9-11-6250052/ (accessed 26
September 2019).

214 Catherine Hall, 'The racist ideas of slave owners are still with
us today', *The Guardian*, 26 September 2016, www.theguardian.
com/commentisfree/2016/sep/26/racist-ideas-slavery-slave-own
ers-hate-crime-brexit-vote (accessed 26 September 2019).

215 See Newsinger, *The Blood Never Dried*.

216 Gott, 'Let's end the myths of Britain's imperial past'. See Richard
Gott, *Britain's Empire: Resistance, Repression and Revolt*
(London: Verso, 2011).

217 Gopal, *Insurgent Empire*, 3.

218 Ibid., 3.

219 Ibid., 5–6.

220 Ibid., 7, 8.

221 Gilroy, *After Empire*, 103.

222 Robert Booth, Vikram Dodd, Kevin Rawlinson and Nicola
Slawson, 'Jo Cox murder suspect tells court his name is
"death to traitors, freedom for Britain"', *The Guardian*, 18
June 2016, www.theguardian.com/uk-news/2016/jun/18/tho

mas-mair-charged-with-of-mp-jo-cox (accessed 26 September 2019).

223 Alan Travis, 'Lasting rise in hate crime after EU referendum, figures show', *The Guardian*, 7 September 2016, www.theguard ian.com/society/2016/sep/07/hate-surged-after-eu-referendum-p olice-figures-show (accessed 26 September 2019).

224 Louie Smith, 'He was killed for speaking Polish: brother's claim as man murdered in UK street in suspected race-hate attack', *The Mirror*, 30 August 2016, www.mirror.co.uk/news/uk-news/he-killed-speaking-polish-brothers-8738218 (accessed 26 September 2019).

225 Ware, 'Towards a sociology of resentment', 6.1.

226 Gurminder K. Bhambra, 'Brexit, Trump, and "methodological whiteness": on the misrecognition of race and class', *The British Journal of Sociology* 68.1 (2017) 214–32 (emphasis in original), https://onlinelibrary.wiley.com/doi/full/10.1111/1468-4446.12317 (accessed 26 September 2019).

227 Danny Dorling, 'Brexit: the decision of a divided country' (2016), www.dannydorling.org/?p=5568 (accessed 26 September 2019), cited in Bhambra, 'Brexit, Trump, and "methodological whiteness"'.

228 El-Enany, 'The next British Empire'.

229 James McDougall and Kim Wagner, 'Don't mistake nostalgia about the British Empire for scholarship', *Times Higher Education*, April 2018, www.timeshighereducation.com/blog/do nt-mistake-nostalgia-about-british-empire-scholarship (accessed 26 September 2019)

230 Dorling and Tomlinson, *Rule Britannia*, 72.

231 Ibid.

232 Mukherjee, 'Empire', 76. See also Bhambra and Holmwood, 'Colonialism, postcolonialism and the liberal welfare state'.

233 See El-Enany 'Empire en vogue'.

234 Rowena Mason, 'Nigel Farage: Indian and Australian immigrants better than eastern Europeans', *The Guardian*, 22 April 2015, www.theguardian.com/politics/2015/apr/22/nigel-farage-immigr ants-india-australia-better-than-eastern-europeans (accessed 26 September 2019)

235 Theresa May, 'The government's negotiating objectives for exiting the EU: PM speech', 17 January 2017, Lancaster House, London, www.gov.uk/government/speeches/the-governments-negotiating-objectives-for-exiting-the-eu-pm-speech (accessed 26 September 2019).

236 Kojo Koram, 'Britain's blindness: how did "national liberation"

become a rallying cry in what was once the world's largest empire?', *Dissent Magazine*, 6 February 2019, www.dissentmagazine.org/online_articles/britains-brexit-blindness (accessed 26 September 2019)

237 See El-Enany, 'The next British Empire', for a discussion of recent initiatives which suggest an appetite for attempts to rehabilitate colonialism as a political project.

238 Boris Johnson, 'Beyond Brexit: a global Britain', Chatham House, 2 December 2016, www.gov.uk/government/speeches/beyond-brexit-a-global-britain (accessed 26 September 2019).

239 Ibid.

240 Ibid.

241 Ibid.

242 Ben Quinn, 'Hate Crimes Double in Five Years in England and Wales' *The Guardian*, 15 October 2019, www.theguardian.com/society/2019/oct/15/hate-crimes-double-england-wales (accessed 1 December 2019).

243 Sivamohan Valluvan, *The Clamour of Nationalism: Race and the Nation in twenty-first century Britain* (Manchester: Manchester University Press, 2019).

Conclusion

1 TextaQueen, *The Australian*, artwork image, www.jura.org.au/images/texta-queen-image (accessed 6 February 2019).

2 See Hannah Jones, Yasmin Gunaratnam, Gargi Bhattacharyya, William Davies, Sukhwant Dhaliwal, Kirsten Forkert, Emma Jackson and Roiyah Saltus, *Go Home? The Politics of Immigration Controversies* (Manchester: Manchester University Press, 2017).

3 See Bhattacharyya, *Rethinking Racial Capitalism*.

4 See *Mabo* v. *Queensland* (No. 2) ('Mabo case') [1992] HCA 23; (1992) 175 CLR 1 (3 June 1992).

5 See Watson, 'Buried alive'; Verily Kerruish and Jeannine Purdy, 'He "look" honest – big white thief', *Law Text Culture* 4 (1998), 146–71; Coulthard, 'Subjects of empire', 456.

6 Coulthard, 'Subjects of empire', 456.

7 Freeman-Powell, 'Windrush row over criminal deportation flight to Jamaica'.

8 Leah Wise and Gerald Lenoir, 'Black voices call for new approaches to immigration reform', Black Alliance for Just Immigration and Southeast Regional Economic Justice Network, 1, https://baji.org/wp-content/uploads/2017/11/REJN-BAJI-Reframing-doc-2.pdf (accessed 26 September 2019).

9 Stuart Hall, 'When was the "postcolonial"? Thinking at the limit', in Iain Chambers and Lidia Curti (eds), *The Postcolonial Question* (London: Routledge, 1996), 250, cited in Doreen Massey, *For Space* (London: Sage, 2005), 62.

10 Massey, *For Space*, 63.

11 Ibid.

12 Ibid.

13 For such a proposal, see Achiume, 'Re-imagining international law for global migration: migration as decolonization?'

14 bell hooks, *Yearning: Race, Gender and Cultural Politics* (New York: South End Press, 1990), 22, cited in Coulthard, *Red Skin, White Masks*, 3.

15 See El-Enany, 'Asylum in the context of immigration control'.

16 See, for example, Anna Lundberg and Mikael Spång, 'Deportability status as basis for human rights claims: irregularised migrants' right to health care in Sweden', *Nordic Journal of Human Rights* 35.1 (2017), 35–54.

17 George Orwell, 'Not counting n*****s', *The Adelphi*, July 1939.

18 Ibid.

19 Mukherjee, 'Empire', 74.

20 Ibid., 76.

21 Irfan Habib, 'Colonisation of the Indian economy', in *Essays in Indian History: Towards a Marxist Perception* (New Delhi: Tulika, 1995), 304–46, cited in Mukherjee, 'Empire', 76.

22 Utsa Patnaik, 'New estimates of eighteenth-century British trade and their relation to transfers from tropical colonies', and Shireen Moosvi, 'The Indian economic experience, 1600–1900: a quantitative study', in K. N. Panikkar, Terence J. Byres and Utsa Patnaik (eds), *The Making of History: Essays Presented to Irfan Habib* (London: Anthem Press, 2000), cited in Mukherjee, 'Empire', 76.

23 Ibid., 77.

24 Habib, 'Colonisation of the Indian economy 1757–1900', cited in Mukherjee, 'Empire', 77.

25 See Patnaik, 'New estimates of eighteenth-century British trade'.

26 See 'David Cameron rules out slavery reparation during Jamaica visit', BBC, 30 September 2015, www.bbc.co.uk/news/uk-34401412 (accessed 26 September 2019).

27 Ibid.

28 Ibid.

29 Peter Stubley, 'UK to spend £700,000 building new wing on notorious Nigerian prison to house foreign criminals', *The Independent*, 8 March 2014, www.independent.co.uk/news/world/africa/uk-

build-nigeria-prison-foreign-criminals-deport-jail-space-boris-john son-a8245756.html (accessed 26 September 2019)

30 Keenan, *Subversive Property*, 16.

31 Massey, *For Space*, 68.

32 Ibid.

33 Ibid.

34 Ibid., 70, drawing on Johannes Fabian, *Time and the Other: How Anthropology Makes its Object* (New York: Columbia University Press, 1983).

35 Massey, *For Space*, 69–70.

36 See Dorling and Tomlinson, *Rule Britannia*.

37 Liam Fox MP on Twitter, 4 March 2016. See https://twitter.com/ LiamFox/status/705674061016387584 (accessed 26 September 2019).

38 Daniel Boffey, 'Brexit: visa-free travel plans spark Gibraltar "colony" row', *The Guardian*, 1 February 2019, www.theguard ian.com/world/2019/feb/01/gibraltar-colony-row-flares-as-eu-mak es-travel-visa-free-for-britons (accessed 26 September 2019).

39 See Daniel Fernández Pascual and Alon Schwabe (Cooking Sections), *The Empire Remains Shop* (New York: Columbia University Press, 2018).

Acknowledgements

I hope readers of this book could not glean from its pages that I derived little pleasure from writing it. British politics is mired in a right-wing, populist surge and life for racialised people in and trying to reach Britain is becoming increasingly dangerous. Acknowledging thanks becomes ever more important when hope is snatched away, when cynicism and depression threaten to set in, when we need to rely more heavily for survival and sustenance on those around us.

Even in the absence of crushing political defeats, the process of writing is difficult. It requires being still for lengthy periods of time, something which I find difficult. Had I found someone willing to chain me to my laptop and lock the door, this person would be first in any order of thanks and this book would have appeared sooner. That said, Sarah Keenan taught me how to trick myself into sitting still for long periods of time, a tip that might be useful for readers struggling with writing projects. Dedicate yourself to 20 minutes of writing a day, no less, and you will find those minutes become hours, and hours become a book.

Writing also requires believing that what one has to say might be of interest to others. In this regard, there are many people to thank for their tireless encouragement, whether in the form of reading, re-reading and commenting on chapters, or lengthy sessions of unremunerated counselling. Patricia Tutt and Sarah Keenan read the manuscript a number of times. Without their insight and help I could not have completed the book. Sherene Razack, Bridget Anderson and Marie-Bénédicte Dembour also generously gave their time to reading and commenting on a draft. Their feedback allowed me to significantly improve the text. Bruno de Witte, Colin Yeo and David Shulman provided me with detailed comments on significant parts of the book. I am extremely grateful to them. Priyamvada Gopal, Luke de Noronha, Sita Balani and Bernard Keenan deserve special thanks for dropping everything to read sections at short notice. Nicolette Busuttil and Liam Thornton were so kind as to provide me with pointers and signposts to references when I needed them.

Joining the editorial board of *Feminist Legal Studies* midway through the project made writing much less lonely. Fellow *FLS*-ers, Diamond Ashiagbor, Nicola Barker, Katie Cruz, Ruth Fletcher, Nikki Godden-Rasul, Emily Grabham, Sarah Keenan, Julie McCandless, Sheelagh McGuinness, Yvette Russell, Harriet Samuels and Dania Thomas were an endless and invaluable source of feminist care, advice, humour and TV recommendations. I owe the book's title to Emily Grabham, who was a constant source of enthusiasm and encouragement. She went so far as to draw me a set of cartoons on how to submit the book when I needed a final push into production.

Adil Essajee pushed me to write the book in the first place. He told me to get on with it when I needed to hear that the most. I have counted on his friendship, care, endless patience and legal expertise in more ways than I can begin to count.

Vipasha Bansal, Emma Brännlund, Nisha Kapoor, Craig Reeves and Sivamohan Valluvan have counselled and encouraged me, sometimes at ungodly hours, with no effort spared, until the end.

It is impossible to compile an exhaustive list of the friends, colleagues and students at many institutions, including the London School of Economics, the European University Institute, Brunel University and Birkbeck College, in the Law School and at the Centre for Research on Race and Law who have shown me support along the way: Sita Balani, Gurminder Bhambra, Gargi Bhattacharyya, Bill Bowring, Eddie Bruce-Jones, Damian Chalmers, Mariana Chaves, Marise Cremona, Luke de Noronha, Gareth Dale, Bruno de Witte, Adam Elliott-Cooper, Başak Ertür, Denise Ferreira da Silva, Nadia Fadil, Katjana Gatterman, Dalia Gebrial, Narine Ghazarayan, Eve Haque, Christelle Heidelberg, Marta Jimenez, Alison Johnson, Terese Jonsson, Kojo Koram, Sarah Lamble, Gail Lewis, Jess Mac, Radhika Mongia, Carmela Murdocca, Stu Marvel, Kerem Nisancioglu, Debra Parkes, Gabriela Popa, Costanza Rodriguez d'Acri, Anton Schutz, Tanya Serisier, Janine Silga, Lisa Tilley, Waqas Tufail, Paul Turnbull, Sarah Turnbull, Tine van Criekinge, Karen Wells and Alexandra Xanthaki.

Friends I have counted on for support, laughter and good food along the way are Nathasha Aly, Zohra Ali, Megha Amrith, Umar Azmeh, Rothna Begum, Szu Ping Chan, Laura-Jane Channing, Emma Coates, Sara El Sheekh, Hannah Elsisi, Rouben Freeman, Ramues Gallois, Suzuka Gallois, Satdeep Grewal, Rachel Harger, Karen Lee-Samuels, Len Lukowski, Marwa Nasser, Magali Pierucci, Teresa Querios, Saeher Qureshi, Lubna Rahman, Zoe Stewart, Elina Valkonen and Zora Zekina.

I owe a special debt of gratitude to Tom Dark for his

editorial enthusiasm and commitment to this book. His belief in its importance meant I got my wish, that it be relatively accessible, no small feat in academic publishing. His guidance, support and generosity made the process of publishing a very enjoyable one. I am also very grateful to Richard Hart, Sinead Moloney, Andrew Kirk, Humairaa Dudhwala, Chris Hart and to the external reviewers and readers for their invaluable comments and attention to the text.

My family, near and far, have been an endless source of encouragement, joy and distraction: Zeinab, Uncle Taher, Amitou Shou Shou, Tant Hayam, Tant Fifi, Salwa, Nuha, Lubna, Mona, Mai, Mohamed, Hala, Ashraf, Auntie Nadia and Yaseen. Sami, I am grateful every day that you share my political and intellectual passions. Our conversations and your creations inspire and comfort me in myriad ways. Sonia, thank you for always being by my side, my confidante and my aide. I am so fortunate to have never known life without you. I am especially grateful to you and Aled Jones for the absolute legendary joy that is Maya El-Enany-Jones. Maya, at 10 months you managed to type 'pub' on a page of the draft manuscript, proving what a force to be reckoned with you are. Sarah Keenan, I have so heavily relied on your time, creative input, encouragement and praise that it is difficult to see this project as anything other than ours. Your love, friendship, care, kindness and faith in me are the conditions which make the work of writing and political struggle possible. Finally, to my parents, Wafa Iskander and Rasheed El-Enany, you taught me everything I know. Thank you for always showing me the way.

Index